WRITING THE BREAKOUT NOVEL

Donald Maass
foreword by Anne Perry

WRITER'S DIGEST BOOKS
Cincinnati, Ohio
http://www.writersdigest.com

Visit our Web site at http://www.writersdigest.com for information on more resources for writers.

To receive a free weekly e-mail newsletter delivering tips and updates about writing and about Writer's Digest products, register directly at our Web site at http://www.newsletters.fwpublications.com.

05 04 03 02 01   5 4 3 2 1

Library of Congress Cataloging-in-Publication Data

Maass, Donald
    Writing the breakout novel / Donald Maass; foreword by Anne Perry.—1st ed.
      p. cm.
    Includes index.
    ISBN 0-89879-995-3 (alk. paper)
     1. Fiction—Authorship. 2. Fiction—Technique. 3. Fiction—Authorship—Marketing.
  I. Title.

PN3365.M245   2001
808.3—dc21   2001022036
                                                      CIP

Edited by Donya Dickerson and Jack Heffron
Designed by Angela Wilcox
Cover by Matthew Gaynor
Production coordinated by Sara Dumford

for Anne Perry
Great author, great friend

ACKNOWLEDGMENTS

Thanks to my clients and the many novelists who have discussed their work with me over the years, helping me to refine the ideas in this book.

Thanks to my staff, who held the fort: Michelle Brummer, Jennifer Jackson, Beth Lincks, Ben Sahl and Andrea Somberg.

Thanks to my editor, Jack Heffron, who helped me brainstorm the premise of this book then left me alone to write it; and to Donya Dickerson, whose suggestions and line editing were invaluable.

Thanks, forever, to my wife, Beth, breakout playwright; and to Samantha and Annabelle, who helped.

ABOUT THE AUTHOR

Donald Maass is president of the Donald Maass Literary Agency in New York, which he founded in 1980. He represents more than one hundred fiction writers and sells more than one hundred novels per year to top publishers in the U.S. and overseas. Recently he has obtained six- and seven-figure advances from publishers such as Warner Books, Ballantine Books, Penguin Putnam Inc. and others for authors like mystery writer Anne Perry, fantasy author David Zindell, and science fiction writers David Feintuch and Todd McCaffrey. He is the author of fourteen pseudonymous novels and of the book *The Career Novelist* (Heinemann, 1996). He is currently president of the Association of Authors' Representatives, Inc. (AAR).

TABLE OF CONTENTS

Foreword

by ANNE PERRY

If anyone asks me, "Should I be a writer?" I always have the same answer: "If anything I can say will make any difference to you, then, no, you shouldn't because to stay through the disappointments and the failures, the financial hardships and the dents to the self-esteem, you have to not just want to write but to need to. Then you will ignore all the warnings and the negative advice in the world, and proceed to prove them all wrong."

This book is advice for those of us who are charging ahead regardless, whether we are just beginning or well on our way but would like to do even better—and which of us would not? Most of us could cope very nicely with making more money with our writing. If you are that highly unusual person who cannot think of something urgent to do with the extra money, the tax man will always think of something for you. (I like to imagine mine all goes to help the poor, the old and the sick, but I'm probably kidding no one but myself.)

But seriously, writing is more than a job. We are all entertainers in possibly the oldest form known to man and certainly one of the best. Is there any age or society that doesn't respond to "Tell me a story"? We create a world, fill it with people and then have them do what we wish. Whether we mean to or not, we are preachers of our own particular philosophy. Are there any writers who would not like to reach as wide an audience as possible and to move them as deeply? A little wider audience with each successive book? Or even a lot wider!

Writing the Breakout Novel will help you identify the roadblocks to that kind of achievement and then offer ways of removing them. This book will not tell you what to say, only how to say it more effectively. Each chapter deals with a different area, and I suggest you even read about those areas where you feel you have no problems. There still might be something you can improve. At the least, you can perceive your strengths and make sure that in altering other things, you don't unintentionally lose your strong points.

At the end of each chapter is a "Breakout Checklist" to fix the chapter's key ideas in your mind, guidelines to pin up somewhere clearly in sight.

I remember attending a lecture given by Don a year or two ago where he asked his audience of writers why they bought books. Almost all of us admitted it was either because we already knew the author's work or because someone had recommended it. In other words, it had nothing to do with publisher, jacket, promotion, reviews or any of the other things outside the content of the book itself. Considerable discussion was distilled to a single fact: You are in control of your success or failure. If you write a book people want to read—a story that grips; characters that people care about, identify with, are interested in—your book will sell. Your destiny is in your own hands.

That's good news.

This book will break down the constituent parts of each element of a novel, and tell you what often goes wrong and how to fix it.

Think about what you enjoy reading most. Why is it so often not what we write? That is one of the most painful questions ever asked me—incidentally in the same lecture. I must admit the thought had not occurred to me before. I began to consider the possibility that what I believed was "good" or "clever" writing, or what others would admire, is quite honestly the part I tend to skip through when reading. Now shouldn't that tell one something? It did!

Now I am a good deal more honest in my thinking—not perfect yet, still self-indulgent here and there I expect but definitely improved. Let's be frank: If you don't enjoy reading your own work, probably not many other people will either. That was one of my big steps forward.

Conflict is essential to a story. Nothing to fight against, nothing to win, nothing to lose . . . why bother reading it? In the end, who cares? You don't; you have a better book to read or write or both.

Sometimes I am asked, "Is it true you should write what you know about?" I say, "No, write what you care about. If you don't know, you'll find out. But if you don't care, why should anyone else?"

Most of the chapters in this book will help you to channel your care into an order with a purpose and a drive that will impel your story forward so not a page can be missed. They will tell you about multilayering, so your writing has depth and texture; varying your characters; and at times, telescoping two or three characters into one so they become more complex and memorable. I can remember both Don and my London agent Meg Davis telling me to do that—and it hurts! I was very reluctant, but years of experience have taught me that my agents do actually know what they are talking about. I tried. I succeded. It worked! I ended with fewer and far stronger characters, which resulted in a more compelling story.

The chapter on telescoping characters will also remind you of the difference between "ordinary people," such as you encounter every day in life, and those in literature who are beyond the ordinary, and who seem more interesting and more exciting, yet remain people with whom you can identify. After all, if you don't care about the protagonist, we will not read the book.

This is not as simple as it sounds! Being likeable and being compelling are not necessarily the same thing. Chapter five will explain in more detail. If the characters fail to engage us, all else is a waste of time, no matter how evocative the place, how original or witty the dialogue, how daring the plot or, above all, how lyrical the prose. If the average reader is not involved in the life of the characters, he will stop after a chapter or two at the best.

And we want the average reader! We want as many readers as possible! We want all sorts: average and extraordinary, omnivorous and selective, casual and diligent, devoted fans and those who are trying our work for the first time. The trick is to make absolutely certain it is not the last!

There are still original ways of telling stories, creating new and exciting characters, taking people to fascinating times and places. It requires skill and hard work, willingness to plan and rewrite, the ability to listen to advice and consider it. Use what you believe in, and go on learning all the time. I have just finished a fifth writing of a story I care about passionately, after having parts of it ripped to shreds by Don and Meg. It hurt like flesh being cut, but now I know how much better it is. I feel satisfied that it is as deeply powerful and complex as I can make anything, and as compulsive. And yet, after all their suggestions, it is still *My Story*, not different at heart, just better told.

Put yourself on the page and all that you think and feel about life, but do it with discipline; do it with skill. Then the good agents and the good publishers will get your work into the hands of the good readers, who will tell their friends, "You've got to read this; you'll love it!"

Good luck. There's room for us all. They'll just build bigger bookshops!

—Anne Perry
Portmahomack, Scotland
August 2000

Introduction

Book publishing is full of surprises, not the least of which is an unexpected leap in an author's sales. When novelists whose previous work merely has been admired suddenly have books vault onto the best-seller lists or even achieve a large jump in sales, publishing people say they have "broken out." The book in question is a "breakout novel."

Breakout novels can be planned or at any rate encouraged, and a few of them are simply the payoff of a slow and steady growth in an author's readership. More often, though, breakouts take publishers by surprise. All at once the author's publicist must scramble. Extra printings are hastily scheduled. Salespeople get into high gear. The author's editor, meanwhile, smiles wisely and pretends he knew the breakout would happen all along.

No doubt about it, a breakout is an exciting and welcome event in an author's career. Even when *The New York Times* best-seller list is not involved, a sharp, upward jump is likely to bring an author significantly larger advances and a previously unfelt degree of respect. Throughout my twenty-three years in book publishing—especially in my twenty years as an independent literary agent—I have kept a constant watch for signs that a client is breaking out.

As for authors, their reactions to this lightning strike are remarkably consistent. For most, a sudden elevation into the ranks of literary stardom feels very natural. Such authors begin to call their editorial director by his first name, toss around wholesale numbers like baseball stats, and generally display the ease and confidence of someone who has made it big through long and dedicated effort.

The truth, though, is that underneath these assured exteriors, agents, editors, publicists, salespeople and even authors themselves generally do not have the foggiest idea why this sudden leap in popularity has happened. Ask publishers and they will probably comment, "Oh, we've been building him for years. It was his time."

Bull. Most novelists are launched with no support at all. Advertising budgets for first novels are nil. Author tours are reserved for celebrities and experts in baby care or cancer prevention. The situation is little better for most second, third and fourth novels. Any boost that a developing novelist gets is likely to come from outside sources: good reviews, award nominations, hand-selling in independent bookstores. Publishers do at times contribute to a promising career—those front-of-store displays in chain bookstores do not come cheap—but by and large the fortunes of fiction writers depend upon a certain kind of magic.

What is that magic? In the business, it is called "word of mouth." In the real world, it is what happens when your friend who reads too much grabs you by the arm, drags you across the bookstore aisle, snatches a novel from the shelf and thrusts it into your hands, urging, "You have *got* to read this. It's fantastic." You sample the first page and, persuaded, get in line to pay.

Word of mouth. When a bookstore clerk who reads too much does it, it is termed "hand-selling." Whatever the label, it is the power of personal recommendation, the persuasiveness of everyday salesmanship. Word of mouth is the secret grease of publishing. It is the engine that drives breakouts. It must be. What else can explain why breakouts frequently catch publishers by surprise?

Do you believe in magic? I do not. At times I am caught by surprise of course, but fundamentally I believe that word of mouth does not happen by accident. It happens because ordinary consumers read an extraordinary book. They delight. They talk. Word spreads faster through the population than any mathematical model can explain. Soon, a hot title is going out of stock in places as far removed from each other as Anchorage and Atlanta.

It's as if there is a telepathic link among readers, though of course there is not.

The link is the author, or rather, the story he has told. Something about it has gripped his readers' imaginations in a way that his previous novels did not. His characters are in some way more memorable, his themes more profound. For some reason or other, this new novel sings. It matters more. His readers project themselves into the world of the novel and think about it days after its final page has been turned. What is going on? What are the elements that make this new novel so much bigger and better?

The answer to that question is the subject of this book. I believe it is possible for a writer to understand, at least in part, the mechanics of the breakout novel and to apply these devices to his writing.

Now, there is such a thing as inspiration. No formula can predict the sudden plot twist that leaps from an author's unconscious mind to his fingertips to the computer screen, causing him to whistle and exclaim, "Where did *that* come from?" Is that true magic? In a way. But it is dangerous to hope that random flashes of lightning will make one's fortune as a writer.

A sounder plan is to learn the techniques of the breakout novel and commit to them. Great novels—ones in which lightning seems to strike on every page—result from their authors' refusal to settle for being "good." Great novelists have fine-tuned critical eyes. Perhaps without being aware of it, they are dissatisfied with sentences that are adequate, scenes that merely do the job. They push themselves to find original turns of phrase, extra levels of feeling, unusual depths of character, plots that veer in unexpected directions. They are driven to work on a breakout level all the time. Is that magic?

Not at all. It is aiming high. It is learning the methods and developing a feel for the breakout-level story. It is settling for nothing less.

Can anyone become a great novelist, an author of a body of enduring classics? Perhaps not. Anyway, few do. However, I do know this: Any author who can write a salable novel can also improve, and virtually all writers can write a breakout novel. How do I know? Because it happens all the time. I have seen it happen. So have you.

I first came to my conviction that the techniques of breakout storytelling can be learned around the moment that I first met one of my best clients, historical mystery writer Anne Perry. Her British agent was looking for an American agent to handle her fantasy novel. I was interested in Perry for a couple of reasons.

First, Perry's Victorian mystery novels featuring Inspector Thomas Pitt and his highborn wife, Charlotte, were not only something, at that time, relatively new—mysteries set in the past—they are also an open window into the Victorian world. Perry captures the social inequalities of Victorian times, especially with respect to women, without being in any way untrue to the period.

Second, Perry's novels have a compelling moral dimension, and her detection team has built into it an irresistible conflict: Charlotte has married beneath her, while her husband can never rise to the social level of his wife's family. Despite this gulf between them, they are drawn together with a common passion for social justice, puzzling crimes and each other. They are a powerful combination.

I offered to work with the fantasy novel, but I also asked my British colleague if I might assist with Perry's mysteries. She agreed. A new negotiation with Perry's U.S. publisher was underway. I read her contracts and reviewed royalty statements for clues to what might be a fair deal for this author at her stage of career. I could see that she was being underpaid and somewhat underpublished, especially in hardcover. I offered, oh so casually, to step in and help her out.

There was something else behind my probably too-apparent eagerness: Perry's latest book at the time *Silence in Hanover Close* (1988), the ninth in the series, was extraordinarily strong. Whereas before I had enjoyed the deft mixture of private drama and public crime in her stories, this one offered something extra, something deeper.

In this book, Pitt is asked to reopen a three-year-old case involving the murder of a diplomat. In doing so, he stirs up not only a hornet's nest of suspects but also whispers of treason. He picks up the trail of a mystery woman connected to the case but winds up in jail accused of her murder. Only with the resourceful help of his wife can he hope to clear his name, uncover the truth and lay aside a grave threat to the nation.

The stakes in this story are higher than in any of her previous novels. The outcome would affect more than just the characters' lives or the administration of justice. All of society would be different, perhaps all of history. Suddenly, the action of the story mattered in a larger sense. Its subject matter was one of real and lasting common concern. Perry had raised the stakes.

I realized that Anne Perry's writing had just made a leap. This novel was bigger. It had the potential to break out, and eventually the novel's paperback numbers did show a large rise over her previous sales.

I told my British counterpart that it was imperative that her publisher recognize what was going on, and pay and promote her accordingly. It was too late for me to step into the negotiation underway; I tried, but the publisher balked, and in any event, the deal in question was for three novels in a then new and untested series. In the next negotiation for Pitt mysteries, however, I quadrupled her previous advances.

More importantly, I spoke with Perry and explained to her why I felt her fiction had grown larger. She nodded and said, "Right. That's worth keeping, then." In the next Inspector Pitt novel, Pitt is removed from routine homicide cases and given the assignment of handling cases of special sensitivity and political import. He has been doing just that ever since, and his ten subsequent adventures have involved him in the issues of Irish independence, anti-Semitism and the Church of England's crisis over Darwin's theory of evolution, among others.

Anne Perry's sales have continued to grow, and I have quadrupled her advances twice again. Perry's publisher has given her exceptional support, with twice-a-year tours and ad campaigns that most authors only dream about. Overseas publishers have discovered her, too, and she has appeared on best-seller lists not only in America but also in France. *Sacrebleu!* Perry's fantasy novel, too, has been published (*Tathea*, 1999). What has caused all this success?

Much as I would like to take credit or to share it with her publisher, the garlands belong to Anne Perry. Her storytelling has achieved new depth and power, even in the context of an ongoing mystery series. She has many imitators today, but so far no other period mystery writer has equaled her breadth of research, depth of character, fiendishness of plot and gravity of theme. She is truly a breakout author: one who has enlarged her fiction and reaped the rewards.

Writing at breakout level can bring those rewards in advance of publication, too. More recently, science fiction author David Zindell came to me with his career in crisis. His first novel, *Neverness*, had come out in hardcover in 1988 to great acclaim, winning him an Arthur C. Clarke Award nomination. Ten years later his fourth novel was published as an original paperback that shipped less than ten thousand units, a level that today is a certain kiss of death.

However, Zindell was at work on a large-scale fantasy novel, *The Lightstone*, the first in a quartet. His proposal was salable, but with more work I felt that it could be very big indeed. We talked over dinner in New York. I recommended that he use several of the techniques discussed in this book, among them inner conflict, a subplot for the love interest, and unification of the story's inner and outer climaxes. Zindell not only used my suggestions, but he embraced their spirit and went far beyond them, lifting his proposal to a higher plane.

When I read the revised proposal, I knew I had a winner. I phoned an editor friend, described the project and named the high six-figure sum that it would cost her to acquire it. Two weeks later she not only met my price but threw an ad and promo budget of $100,000 into the bargain. A week after that, I was at the Frankfurt Book Fair. A German editor dropped into a chair at my table in the "Agents Centre" and offered me $75,000 for the project, sight unseen. I demurred, then quickly started an auction that continued for two weeks after the fair. With British and Dutch deals thrown in, in the span of just a few months, Zindell was guaranteed advances worth just a few dollars less than one million dollars.

Did I mention that those guarantees were given on the basis of fifty-four pages and a detailed outline? That is the power of breakout storytelling.

You Have the Power to Break Out

If Perry and Zindell can do it, so can you. Novels are written one word at a time, and the choices made along the way can as easily produce a mildly engaging midlist novel as a highly memorable breakout. I believe that the difference lies in the author's commitment to great storytelling. But that commitment cannot be realized without the necessary tools. Giving you the necessary tools is my purpose in writing this book. Over the last twenty years, I have learned a lot about what lifts a novel out of the ranks of the ordinary and into the realm of the breakout.

Reading thousands of unpublished novels will do that to you. At my offices on West Fifty-seventh Street in New York City, each year we receive about 7,500 query letters, partial manuscripts and completed novels. This material disappoints 99.9 percent of the time but not because its authors are incompetent (very few of them are). Rather, the material disappoints because its authors have failed to muster the techniques available to them in service of great stories. Their vision is small. Their themes are weak or overly familiar. Their characters run to stereotypes. Their plots mirror recent newspaper headlines, hit movies and established best-sellers.

Writing the breakout novel is as much about cultivating an outlook as anything. It is the habit of avoiding the obvious or of covering familiar ground, and instead reinforcing the conviction that one's views, experience, observation of character and passion for chosen story premises can be magnified and pushed so one's novels achieve new levels of impact and new degrees of originality.

To write a breakout novel is to run free of the pack. It is to delve deeper, think harder, revise more, and commit to creating characters and plot that surpass one's previous accomplishments. It is to say "no" to merely being good enough to be published.

It is a commitment to quality.

Can any one set of tricks or techniques vault you onto the best-seller lists? Not really. Far too many other people are involved in such a massive publishing effort: your agent, your editor, your publicist, your bookstore friends and many others. Still, while I do devote a chapter at the end of this book to the mechanics of breakout publishing, you yourself will do the primary work of making a breakout happen at your word processor (or with your quill and parchment, or whatever works for you).

Best-seller status is never guaranteed, either by adopting the techniques described in this book or even by getting a six-figure advance. The best plan for most, and the plan that I recommend for you, is to work toward elevating your fiction to the next level. Big rewards accrue to big books, but more to the point, a large-scale story is one that is likely to please a larger number of readers.

And readers are the ultimate customers in this business, right? If you believe otherwise, I'm afraid there is no book that can help you.

You will also find in this volume no single formula for the breakout novel. A truly *big* book is a perfect blend of inspired premise, larger-than-life characters, high-stakes story, deeply felt themes, vivid setting and much more. It is a kind of literary gestalt, a welling up of inspired material, enriched by close observation, or at least detailed research. It flows together in ways that seem destined to be.

Formulas also achieve predictable effects. I am not interested in punching out cookie-cutter best-sellers, so-called "blockbuster novels." Rather, it is my mission to help every author elevate his own unique style of storytelling to its highest form. Indeed, I believe that adhering to best-seller "rules" is antithetical to breaking out. A true breakout is not an imitation but a breakthrough to a more profound individual expression. It demands that an author reach deep inside to find what is truthful, original, important and inspiring in his own world view.

It requires that the author be true to his own "voice."

How to Use This Book

Breakout novels can be written in any genre, just as any nongenre novel can fail to catch fire. Authors also bring natural strengths to their fiction. Some are brilliant with characters but terrible with plot. Others have the gift of description but write characters with flat inner lives. Hence, in this book I will discuss many aspects of breakout novel technique: stakes, settings, characters, plot, subplots, theme and more.

Needless to say, this book is not for those who wish to get rich quick. There is nothing quick about the fiction game. Instead, it is a book for dedicated craftspeople: The kind of folk whose work is so fine and apparently effortless that onlookers call it art.

What if you are a first-time novelist? Can you hope to achieve breakout level right away? Some authors do, of course, but the truth is that most first manuscripts do not sell, let alone break out. That is not due to lack of talent. It is not due to lack of effort. I have written fourteen novels myself, so I know that writing hundreds of pages of fiction is not an activity for the lazy! Rather, the high failure rate of first manuscripts happens simply because a novel is a large, complex, fluid and difficult-to-manage undertaking. It is a tough art form to get right, one tougher still to master. This book can show you not only how to manage the various aspects of your first novel but also how to give them more power.

Over the years I have also noticed that first novels tend to feel small. The scope of the action is often limited. The horizons of the author's world are limited to a couple of characters. There is nothing wrong with that. It is natural. Strong first novels do get published and can even win critical acclaim. However, it is difficult for one to make a lasting impact—that is, to grow an audience—by continuing to write at that contained level. Absent a breakout novel, midlist authors tend to get stuck. And frustrated. Today, they also tend quickly to wash out.

I do not expect that this book will instantly turn every first-time novelist into a breakout writer. A lot of years and a lot of pages may be needed for that. However, what this book will do is accelerate the process. Even if you absorb and use only a few of the techniques discussed herein, you will already be ahead of the game.

Are you ready to take your writing to the next level? I am eager to help you get it there. As an agent, I find it relatively easy to turn up novels that are competent, salable and safe. It is far more difficult to find the novel that takes me on an unexpected journey; one that is, if not long, at least deeply absorbing, always gripping, constantly surprising, and ultimately memorable.

I believe in all of the work I sell to publishers. It is somewhat more rare for me to love it. Rarest of all are those novels that I can say have truly transported me, indeed, that have changed my life.

Are you ready to change your readers' lives? And your own? Good. Then let's get started.

CHAPTER ONE

Why Write the Breakout Novel?

When you are a first-time novelist, the world looks bright and promising, does it not? You enjoy the writing process. The world of your novel comes vividly alive in your mind. You steadily rack up pages. It is only a matter of months before you finish, find an agent and make that first sale, right?

Published novelists can quit chuckling now. You might be due for a reality check, too, even if your career is already underway. Perhaps you have two, four, eight or more novels under your belt. Your next one is under contract. Your publisher could do more to promote you, heaven knows, but there are many positive signs. You have fans. You have been through several editors, perhaps, but while your latest is alarmingly young, it does not seem that he will be bolting to a dot com anytime soon. Life is good, right?

Of course, there are disturbing signs. Your agent does not seem as excited about you as he once was. Sales on your most recent novel declined, but, hey, that was not your fault. That jacket was not exactly a work of art. A few overseas publishers have dropped you, but that is a minor concern. They were not paying much to begin with. Speaking of advances, your U.S. publisher *could* be a little more lavish. With each new contract, getting them to go up a few thousand dollars is like getting a hamster to jump through a flaming hoop. They cite "the numbers." It is irritating. They know your work. They understand that an outline is just an outline. They ought to know by now how reliable a writer you are.

Despite all that, things are OK. You are certainly not in the position of *some* novelists you know. Like the one whose mystery series was dropped after four titles: It is a year later and no other publisher has picked up his fifth book, poor bastard. There is also a romance writer living in your town. She cannot seem to break out of the category lines. Her publisher has even forced her to write "house" series novels—novels linked thematically or otherwise by the publisher. It sounds humiliating, but what the heck . . . she is not a great writer. Those romance writers rarely are, right?

Yup, all-in-all things feel solid. You are in, part of the club. You have made the grade. You have proven that you are not only good enough to get published but good enough to keep winning contracts. *So tell me, Mr. Agent Man, where is the problem?*

As a New York agent coming up on twenty-five years of experience in the fiction game, it can be alarming to meet certain novelists at writers conferences. I feel a bit like a cardiologist shaking hands with someone who is dangerously overweight. *Sure, I think, you may have been on the tennis court this morning, but I can predict, give or take a few months, when you are going to have the* Big One: *your first heart attack. And looking at you, I am concerned that it might be fatal.*

It is not only midlist authors who worry me. Another high-risk group are authors who have gotten blue-sky advances: those mid-six-figure, envy-producing, out-of-nowhere lightning bolts of good fortune that produce feelings of smug security. Have you met this type? Their serenity can be annoying to those who perceive themselves as lower on a ladder. Being on a higher rung, though, means there also can be farther to fall. And fall these types do—far more often than anyone will admit, least of all their high-octane agents.

Sadly, too many novelists phone me, the fiction-career cardiologist, only after the Big One has landed them in the emergency room. The warning signs were all there: declining sales, poor covers, no promotion, indifferent publishers and agents. It was only a matter of time. But still they did not see it coming.

Worst of all, the plainest indications of illness were right there in their novels. After a "promising" debut book, a weak second novel sold through poorly; meaning the unsold copies came back to the publisher by the truckload. Reviews of the next few novels were "mixed." The fifth book never caught fire, and having been let down by the last few, I did not even buy it. These are novelists who are slipping off my radar screen, and if that is how *I* feel, it is a sure bet that their publishers, bookstore chains and, most especially, their readers already feel exactly the same way.

So one day, without apparent warning, it hits: An option book is not picked up. A confident novelist hits the pavement looking for a new publisher. But none is to be found. "The numbers" are a problem, the agent one day admits to the worried author. Time drags on. Desperation sets in. Out of the closet come unsold outlines, anthology ideas, screenplays, proposals for sequels to out-of-print novels . . . *anything* that has a chance of selling. But there is no magic medicine to salvage the author's pride. A horrible prospect looms: return to the dreaded day job. Admit to failure.

It is about this time that I (and presumably a few of my colleagues) get a 911 call. A chronology of the author's complaints is aired. Causes and villains are identified: an agent who "lost interest," an editor who left, poor covers, publishing mistakes by the dozen. By far the most common complaint I hear in these crisis calls is, "My publisher did not get behind my books."

What is going on here? What happened to the golden promise that made that first sale so sweet? How can this be happening? Isn't it good enough, after all, to get published?

First-timers, take note: The world of professional fiction writing is not as simple, clear and easy as it may first appear.

The Truth About Book Publishing

Today, fiction careers are biting the dust all over the place. In the free and easy 1980s, it was a cinch to start up. In the brutally competitive economy of the new millennium, it is a struggle just to survive. I know. I get the 911 calls.

What am I hearing? Mystery series cancelled after two titles. Romance writers being pushed around. Even big names on the literary scene are struggling. On the day I am writing this paragraph (June 8, 2000), the book industry columnist for *The New York Times*, Martin Arnold, reports that although major novels have been published this year by three of America's preeminent novelists—Saul Bellow, Philip Roth and John Updike—only one made *The New York Times* best-seller list (Bellow's *Ravelstein*) and only for one week.

Looked at historically, even commercial best-sellers do not have much to be smug about. When I began in publishing in the late 1970s, a top paperback could net over ten million units. Today, two million is good. Big commercial fiction is getting blown off the adult best-seller lists by, of all things a book for children, *Harry Potter*. Good grief! What is happening? Have the muggles gone mad?

There are many macroscopic reasons for our current situation: consolidation of publishing houses, bottom-line business thinking, changes in bookselling and in the way people use their leisure time. Book prices are up; sales are down. (Doesn't anybody get that?) There is also the decline of editing—fiercely denied by publishers but widely reported by authors—and the much-remarked dearth of promotional dollars. All of the above have contributed to the much-discussed "death of the midlist."

Now, the midlist has been in crisis since I was a green editorial assistant in 1977. Its demise has been pronounced many times. I never believed it . . . until now. At the turn of the millennium, even I must admit that our five major publishers—HarperCollins, Penguin Putnam Inc., Random House, Simon & Schuster and Time Warner—are no longer willing to support authors with middling sales for more than a couple of books.

Getting published today is as tough as ever. Staying published is an enormous challenge.

The Truth About Authors

It would seem that novelists have plenty of reasons to gripe. The cards are stacked against them. Publishers, it seems, have become giant unfeeling conglomerates with little concern for the very engines of their profits: the authors.

All of that may be true, but to my way of thinking, those factors are not sufficient to explain all individual career failures. In addition, struggling novelists must face up to a couple of hard facts: (1) Despite the unhelpful conditions in our industry, a number of authors not only continue to grow but become best-sellers. (2) Even more surprising, many of them begin their climb with no support whatsoever from their publishers.

The best-seller lists are dominated by familiar names, it is true. But along with those names, there are novels by unknowns that hit the lists long after their release: *The Bridges of Madison County* (1992), *Cold Mountain* (1997), *Memoirs of a Geisha* (1997). We are not talking blockbusters with a highly commercial profile here but literary novels with decidedly *un*-commercial subject matter.

Why does that happen? As we shall see, there is a reason, but for now it is important only to understand that success does happen despite publishers' inadequacies and not only at best-seller level. Even below best-seller status, novelists are finding and growing audiences all on their own.

When I get a 911 call from a novelist in crisis, the first thing I hear are the author's bragging points. Then come tales of the negligence, errors and disappointments suffered at the hands of his agent and publisher. Through all that I murmur sympathetically. Finally, a new manuscript is offered. That is when I get interested. *At last, I think, a chance to diagnose what really has gone wrong: the author's own writing.* With that comes a chance to steer the author in the direction of new respect and rising sales.

I have seen it happen. I have been part of the story. That story begins with a return to the first fundamental of the fiction business: storytelling.

Storytelling matters above all other considerations, as becomes clear when the promised manuscripts arrive in my office. Ten times out of ten, what I read is moderately flawed. Three times out of ten, it is seriously flawed. The lazy habits of some authors have gone uncorrected. Others have blind spots or a poor grasp of plot structure. These are published novelists in midcareer?

All have strong points too, I must add, but their weak points are killing them. Aren't there editors to take care of flawed books? And really, how much does good craft have to do with success anyway? The work of certain best-sellers is riddled with flaws! Isn't it really about promotion? Don't publishers, after all, pick which authors to support and make them a success?

That is dangerous thinking. Before going further, let me take a few pages to debunk some of the harmful myths about success in the business of fiction.

The Myths of Success
A Big Advance Equals Instant Fame

Once upon a time, book publishing worked in a simple, mechanical way: The bigger the author's advance, the more promotion that author received and, consequently, the better he sold. Getting a high advance was like getting an insurance policy. Many authors and agents still cleave to that principle, but it is outdated. Nowadays, with the shots increasingly called by a few giant bookstore chains, advances do not always have a strong relationship to a book's performance.

Big advances are written off all the time. That is common with second novels in pricey two-book deals. If the first title did not sell through strongly, no amount of spending is going to convince the chains to "support" (i.e., order) large numbers of the second title. It happens all too often. Just this week I got a call from a thriller writer whose last deal, negotiated by one of the top agents in the business, was for $1.3 million. The second of his three novels has been shelved indefinitely, and the third is coming out under a pseudonym. Some insurance policy! (At least he keeps the money.)

Even more interesting to me is what went wrong with novel number one. Was it only publishing mistakes? The author believes so. I am not so sure. His latest manuscript (sent to me overnight) shows considerable skill but also has some problems— a situation, as I said, I find all too familiar.

In case you still believe that advances immunize authors against disaster, let me ask you this: Have you ever read the work of Marti Leimbach, Charles Stella, Layne Heath, Naomi Ragen, Kristen McCloy or John Lucas? No? In 1988 these authors got advances ranging from $100,000 to $600,000 for their first novels. Dollars alone do not a brand name make.

An Editor Will Make Your Novel Shine

The second myth of book publishing is that editors will catch and fix all of a novel's problems. Now, do not get me wrong. Publishing is full of smart, dedicated, hardworking editors. I know hundreds, and not one does *not* seem to care a great deal about his authors and the books they publish. And yet . . . have you recently read a novel you would swear never received a blue pencil mark? When I ask this question at writers conferences, large numbers of hands go up.

Best-selling authors are not immune; indeed, they may be especially prone to this problem. Why do publishers let this happen? Are they just too big to notice or care? I do not think so. As I said, the editors that I know uniformly take pride in their books. On the other hand, they work a lot harder than they did twenty years ago. A typical editor at a hardcover imprint may be responsible for twenty-four titles a year. Paperback editors can be given much heavier loads; three a month is not uncommon.

One editor I know is responsible for one hundred titles annually!

Soft editing results from more than the pressure to get books "into production" at the end of every month. Today's workloads mean that editors tend to be oriented toward the completed manuscript. Few are heavily involved with the author at early stages of development, such as in the outline stage. None that I know of critiques first drafts. (Not knowingly, anyway.) At late stages, fundamental problems with plot design, point of view or cast composition can be difficult to address.

It is not that editors cannot see these flaws; they can. Frequently, there is just not enough time available to pull a book from its "slot," send the author back to work and subsequently critique several additional drafts. In particular, I have noticed that second novels suffer from inattention. So do third novels in trilogies and novels in series that are on a once-a-year schedule.

Some authors have turned to outside editors for help. There are good ones, but they are expensive. Few authors starting out can afford that luxury. Critique groups are free, but not all novelists belong to them. A group also is only as strong as its keenest editorial eye. And who keeps an eye on the author's long-term development; sensing, for instance, his work has grown repetitive, or he is straining at the confines of his genre and needs to power up?

That role has become the province of agents, but here again not all agents are created equal. One top genre agent whom I know does not, as a matter of practice, ever comment on his authors' work. (His commission is lower than mine, however.) Another high-powered agent pushes his clients to follow his formula for stories at the best-seller scale, whether or not that type of novel matches their style and natural inclinations.

Some old-school authors do not feel it is their agents' place to guide them editorially. They want their agents to be advocates, possibly even sharks. They believe that when careers go wrong, it is their agents' job to fix them with a phone call. Clout is everything in this philosophy. The 911 calls have shown me, however, that clout only goes so far. At some point attention must be paid to the writing.

Given all that, is it any wonder that some novelists crash and burn?

Promotion Is the Key to Stardom

Even acknowledging all of the above, most novelists continue to believe in the third myth of publishing success: The biggest factor in making an author a brand name is promotion.

So holy is this belief that a fervent self-promotion movement has swept the community of authors in recent decades. The booklet *Shameless Promotion for Brazen Hussies*, made available to members of Sisters in Crime, is perhaps the bible of this religion. It is full of valuable advice and has indeed helped some authors widen their readerships.

Others pay professional publicists. One new client confessed to me that she had paid all of her advances and royalty earnings from her first five novels to her publicist. The publicist was smart and supportive but was serving as little more than a speakers' bureau. (To be fair, there is a reason for that: It is difficult to get media attention for fiction. Reviews, easy; TV, hard.) My client's resources had not been wasted, just not perfectly allocated.

Most authors feel, properly, that it is the publisher's job to promote. Jealous eyes are cast upon fellow writers who get signing tours and drive-time satellite linkups. "How can I get that treatment?" is a question frequently asked of me. The short answer "Write a novel that commands it" rarely satisfies. Most imagine that it is caprice or the relative influence of their editors that are the magic factors in winning promotional dollars.

In truth, all this angst over promotion is misplaced. Advertising certainly does not sell books. Ask an editorial director in a candid moment, and he will tell you: Ads in *The New York Times Book Review* are placed there mostly to make the author feel good. Media also has a limited effect on fiction sales. TV addicts are not high-volume novel readers, Oprah's Book Club members being the big exception to that rule. In general, radio is better at selling books, especially National Public Radio, but that special audience does not embrace all types of fiction.

You do not need to commission a marketing study to understand the limitations of promotion. Use common sense. What is your dream tour? Ten cities? Twenty? You will do some media and appear at perhaps two or three bookstores in each city? Let us suppose your readings and signings are fabulously well attended, say by one hundred people at each store. (I can hear my publicist pals howling with laughter in the background, but pay them no heed. This is your dream tour.)

OK, do the math. How many people, maximum, can you personally meet on a book tour? Six thousand? That is unlikely for all but Stephen King and his ilk. Let's be more realistic: two thousand? Suppose that every one of those people bought your novel. That is two thousand sales. Not bad, but that is just a fraction of what you will need to sell in order to thrive.

What about media? As we have seen, when we are talking about fiction, media does little to move units off bookstore shelves. So, all you can really count on are two thousand units. Where, then, are the rest of your ten, fifty or one hundred thousand unit sales to come from? Good question. The answer goes to the heart of how the fiction business really works.

And how is that?

The fact is that roughly two-thirds of all fiction purchases are made because the consumer is already familiar with the author. In other words, readers are buying brand-name authors whose work they already have read and enjoyed. The next biggest reason folks buy fiction is that it has been personally recommended to them by a friend, family member or bookstore employee. That process is called word of mouth. Savvy publishers understand its power and try to facilitate its effect with advance reading copies (ARCs), samplers, first chapters circulated by e-mail, Web sites and the like.

In most cases, though, word of mouth happens on its own.

Someone reads a novel, gets excited about it and tells a friend. Sound simple? It is. Seem powerful? It may not, but it is the only thing that can explain why some novels sell large numbers in an industry that introduces fifty-five thousand new products every year, with promotion given only to a few.

Did you spot the key phrase in the paragraph above? *Gets excited about it.* What causes consumers to get excited about a work of fiction? Reviews? Few see them. Awards or nominations? Most folks are oblivious to them. Covers? Good ones can cause a consumer to lift a book from its shelf, but covers are only wrapping. Classy imprints? When was the last time you purchased a novel because of the logo on the spine? Big advances? Does the public know, let alone care? Agents with clout? Sad to say, that is not a cause of consumer excitement.

In reality there is one reason, and one reason only, that readers get excited about a novel: great storytelling. That is it. End of story.

The E-Revolution

Hold on! It cannot be that simple! There must be a trick! Sorry, there is not. There is only craft—that and inspiration, sustained effort, luck and timing. But mostly craft. Sound scary? It should not. It means the most important component of success is in your own hands. You control your fiction career.

It is amazing how mightily some novelists resist that truth. They would rather put their faith in formulas, gossip, connections, contract language—*anything* but their own novels. Ironically, it is often this same group that gets excited about electronic publishing. Its promise to tear down the existing structures of book publishing and put control into the hands of authors seems to them a welcome certainty. Are they correct? Is e-publishing going to bring an end to paper books within five years, as some predict? Will it put the means of production and distribution into the hands of writers?

Many novelists think so. They believe that e-publishing is

a revolutionary force, even though some e-publishers' business models are little different than those of vanity presses.

Let us look at this final myth of publishing success: What is likely to happen and what is just hype? Once again, common sense can tell us a lot. New technologies do come along in publishing. Audio books were an innovation that I witnessed early in my career. That business has not matched the extravagant claims at first made for it, but books on tape have found a place in bookstores, libraries and in consumers' lives.

Or, rather, in their cars, for that is where audio cassettes fill a genuine need. If you spend long hours in your car, as many Americans do, books on tape make it possible to "read" a novel while driving. Lost time can be filled with fiction. Audio sales closely mirror book sales. Needless to say, best-sellers in paper are also top sellers in audio.

What need is filled by electronic book readers such as the SoftBook and the Rocket eBook? Paper books are portable, plentiful, convenient and (relatively) cheap. Electronic book readers are battery dependent, not widely adopted, cumbersome to load and expensive. Those last three points will change, boosters promise, but my original question remains: What genuine need do electronic book readers fill?

Well, they do lie flat. They hold multiple volumes, too, which is good news for vacationers and students with backpacks (but bad news for collectors). Plus, their screens glow softly. You can read in bed without keeping your spouse or partner awake. That is good, but how many people are seriously inconvenienced by such things? Enough to fire a revolution?

Manufacturers probably would highlight the high-tech features of their products (instant large print, word definitions on demand) as well as the way in which young people relate to technology. If you have grown up on the Web, they say, as an adult you will demand your information in electronic form.

That may be true, though I have my doubts where fiction is concerned. However, common sense tells us that even if electronic readers drop in price, become easier to use and have a wider selection of titles available, they still stand little chance of replacing traditional paper books—at least not in numbers that will soon shift the paradigms of our business.

So, will e-books save us from the harsh realities of traditional trade book publishing? No. I'm afraid that is just another myth.

Far greater change is underway in the realm of bookselling. Book printing is also undergoing significant innovation. Print-on-demand technology allows small pressruns, even as small as a single copy. We are a long way from the demise of warehouses and the rise of printing kiosks in bookstores, but the promise is clear: Even now, no book need go out of print. Hundreds of start-ups are at work bringing out-of-print backlist titles to the public. Here, at last, a genuine (if small) need is being met. Everyone benefits.

But back to the revolution . . . is there no hope that the heartless hegemony of the publishing conglomerates can be broken? Will e-publishing ride to the rescue of the midlist?

Speaking for myself, I am keeping a close eye on developments on the electronic front. My colleagues and I have won new contract language, such as definitions of when a book is "in print." (Think about it: If a book never goes out of print, at what point do your rights revert?) I also am experimenting with a few of the electronic start-ups. Why not? Their deluge of solicitations is a nuisance, but the future must start somewhere.

But revolution? Sorry to say, it is unlikely to happen. No doubt novels will be downloadable for my portable computing devices, and that's fine. I look forward to it. But books are not going away. Neither are publishing conglomerates. Not soon. Small presses are enjoying a surge of submissions right now, but few are well enough capitalized and staffed to publish authors on a breakout level. In ten years, success in the fiction game will still happen largely as it does now.

Certainly one thing is not going to change: the wide enjoyment of great storytelling. Novels may not be eternal; indeed, they are a recent development in our cultural history. But for the foreseeable future, they will continue to be popular. Not everyone will prosper in the fiction game, however. All the trends are toward fewer titles, faster sales and higher expectations.

What this means for you (and for me) is that success, if not survival, depends on writing breakout-level fiction. Whether you write genre novels or gigantic sagas, the principles of breakout fiction will serve you well. Indeed, they may be the only things that save you when others are drowning.

Where to Go From Here

In the following pages you will find a guide to writing deeper, stronger and more memorable novels. The principles and techniques I describe I have learned from years of analyzing breakout fiction. My teachers have been our era's greatest authors. Applying these techniques has yielded dynamic and profitable results for me and for my clients.

They will work for you, too. As you go forward, you will notice some overlap between topics. That is because no element of fiction lives in isolation. Deepening character will affect plot. Adding layers to plot will intensify your themes.

In enhancing your work, you may notice it growing lengthier. Within limits, that is not bad. Breakout novels are highly detailed and generally complex. Their authors do not stint if adding material will deepen the impact of their stories. Many breakout novels are long. Do not be afraid of that. This is not to say that length is a virtue all by itself. It is not. But if you attend to all the techniques explained in this book, such as conflict on every page, you will be grounded in breakout methodology. You will not go too far wrong; indeed, you and your readers quickly should see an improvement in your work.

When should you start using the techniques in this book? Right away. If you have a finished manuscript, you probably will find things about it that you can improve. If you are at the earliest planning stages of your next novel, you can begin developing plot layers and fully dimensional characters immediately. There is no wrong time to write a breakout novel.

A word about terms: There is no agreement in the book business about what exactly constitutes a "breakout," let alone what is a breakout novel. It is, and should be, many things. Breakouts can happen on many sales levels. The first novel that soars to a top five spot on *The New York Times* best-seller list is the dream breakout scenario. For me, however, any sharp upward movement in sales and in attention paid to a novelist by publishers, bookstores, the press and the public is a breakout. Some may be minibreakouts, but all growth is good.

In citing examples throughout this book, I have tried to use acknowledged breakout novels wherever possible. Not all novels cited are the actual works that first broke their authors upward. Some are later works. I have also skewed my examples toward recent titles and away from classics. Citing classic novels makes authors resistant. "Oh, well," they say, "of course that worked for Jane Austen! We can't write that way now." The preponderance of novels from the last few years to which I refer is designed to leave you with no excuses. Authors are breaking out all the time, including right now. The techniques they use are available to all writers.

Quotes from authors on technique are not included here, either. Neither are author interviews. I do not learn much from most novelists' discussions of their working method. I have found everything that I, and you, need right at the source: on the pages of breakout novels. They are our textbooks.

The object of writing breakout fiction is not only to bring oneself greater success; it is also to write better fiction, whatever the type of fiction you write. Breakout novels can be breakneck thrillers or quiet coming-of-age stories. It does not matter. What matters is that your characters, your story and your fictional world live for you intensely.

And for your readers. Breakout novels are novels that leave a lasting impression. While turning their final pages, your readers ought to mutter aloud the words "Now, *that* was a great story!"

What if you find this book overwhelming? What if the complexity of a breakout-level novel is too much for you? That is OK. Most first novels are small scale mostly because their authors are still getting a handle on the many forces that must be balanced in a novel. Experienced writers can also feel that their projects are spinning out of control.

Complexity will do that to you. Do not panic. Trust the structure of your outline; or if you are an organic writer who works in successive drafts, trust your unconscious mind. The story is there inside you, in all its complexity. Patience certainly is needed to bring it out. So is time.

Speaking of that, perhaps the most daunting aspect of writing the breakout novel is the commitment of time it involves. If you are used to turning out an 80,000-word mystery every year or a 60,000-word category romance every few months, spending a couple of years writing one novel may feel uncomfortable.

It may not seem financially feasible, either. If so, I recommend a hard look at your career: Are you getting ahead writing the same old way, or are you noticing the warning signs of a career meltdown? If change is called for, find a way to do it. Do not be afraid. Remember that in the past, authors have had to grow their careers in the face of economic depression, war, paper shortages and censorship. In some parts of the world today, novelists risk their lives to write.

If they can write deeply memorable fiction under such conditions, so can you. Anyway, why did you choose novel writing to begin with? Because it is easy? Because of the quick validation? I imagine not. I suspect you chose this business because you are a born storyteller, because you love putting words together. Your most treasured time is the time that you spend working at your word processor, am I right?

I thought so. Well then, what is a little more time spent doing the thing you love best when it means the novel you ultimately produce might be a breakout? I think the investment is worth it. Once you have made it, I believe that you will, too.

BREAKOUT Checklist: Why Write the Breakout Novel?

✓ To survive in today's book publishing industry, it is not good enough just to get published.

✓ The midlist is in trouble, and this time it is real.

✓ Even so, authors are breaking out.

✓ The root cause of most midcareer meltdowns is the author's own writing.

✓ Success does not come from agents, advances, editors or promotion. . . . It comes from word of mouth.

✓ The e-revolution may not save us; indeed, it may not happen.

✓ Breakout-level fiction is the key to survival and to getting ahead.

CHAPTER TWO

Premise

So, now that we know an author can break out thanks to nothing more than the support of readers, what is next? How to generate that enthusiasm? Can you plan your breakout novel, or are breakout novels always unexpected gifts of the unconscious that take everyone, including the author, by surprise?

It sure sounds like the latter. Listen to authors try to explain their breakout novels, and it usually sounds something like this: "One day I was fascinated by a drop of bright red blood on a pure white rose, and I just started writing. The next thing I knew, I had four hundred pages. I had no idea that it would be so popular! Heck, I just wrote what I felt."

Helpful, isn't it? If we are to believe those self-effacing storytellers, a breakout novel is nothing more than the end product of an inspired idea, a story that writes itself. Do you really believe that? As you know by now, neither do I.

A ton of craft goes into any novel, much more so, I suspect, with a work that can grip the imaginations of millions of readers. At a certain point in the process, even the process of organic writers, choices are made: Story paths are selected, scenes are tossed out, new layers are added. Those choices can make a story larger, deeper, more memorable, or not. You may experience that process as outlining or revision, but whatever you call it, it is planning your story.

So, time to make some choices. Assuming you are beginning

from scratch, writing the breakout novel starts with something small doesn't it? An image? A moment? A springboard from which the tale leaps into the air? A point from which all the action flows and to which all the narrative threads return? A wellspring? A source?

In short, an idea. Not just any idea, though, but one with soil rich enough to grow a highly memorable novel; one that will both feed the author's imagination and, finally, nourish millions of readers. What I am talking about is a breakout premise.

That is not to say the breakout premise arrives all at once or that the plot for which it is the bedrock is built in a day. Far from it. For some writers the breakout premise is shaped gradually in the course of a first draft, a revision or perhaps after putting the novel in a drawer for a time. For others it finds its focus not in the writing of their manuscripts but only later (sadly) in the composition of their query letters.

Some authors have their premise in place, fully formed, before a single keystroke, but do not envy those folks. A premise that is not yet backed up by all the details of setting, character, conflict and theme can prove difficult to sustain. Many a brilliant premise dies young. It can be a sad thing lying dead on the page. Believe me, I know. I've received many a dynamite-sounding query letter only to be disappointed by the tinny cap-gun pop of a weak manuscript.

There's a lot of mystery surrounding this breakout premise business. It sounds like magic. It is not. Notions for stories come to everyone, all over the place, all the time. The trick is not in having a flash of inspiration but in knowing how to develop that scrap into a solid story premise; and, as important, in recognizing when to discard a weak premise that will not support the mighty structure of a breakout novel. Breakout premises can be built. It is a matter of having the right tools and knowing how to use them.

A breakout premise need not be narrative; that is, a mini outline. It can be something smaller, but if so, it must have the energy of a uranium isotope. It could be the cold bright light of a November afternoon, the feel of a black-edged telegram in a mother's hand, the putrid smell of a week-old corpse in the trunk of a BMW, the ricochet of wedding bells through a canyon of skyscrapers, a woman's sworn oath before God that she will never go hungry again. In short, a premise is any single image, moment, feeling or belief that has enough power and personal meaning for the author to set her story on fire, propel it like a rocket for hundreds of pages, or perhaps serve as a finish line: an ending so necessary that every step of the journey burns to be taken.

Most authors commit to story premises instinctively. Their gut tells them *this is the one*. There is nothing wrong with that, except the gut can sometimes be mistaken. It cannot hurt to subject your breakout premise to a little scrutiny.

Not too much, of course. It is as possible to talk yourself out of a great story as it is to be fooled by a weak premise in a moment of need. How can you tell the difference between a good premise and a bad one? That is what this chapter is about. Read it through. If your premise measures up, great. If not, you will have new tools with which to work.

The Stories That You Love

Here's where to start: What are your top three favorite novels of all time? You know, the books you have reread so many times that they are falling apart? The ones whose best lines you have memorized, whose characters seem to you real people, whose low moments are as vivid in your memory as your own senior prom?

No doubt you have far more than three, but choose three for starters. Write down their titles right now, or pull them off your shelves and stack them in front of you. Yes, for real. No kidding. Right now. I'll play a game of Freecell while I'm waiting. . . .

OK, got them in front of you? Makes you smile just to look at them, doesn't it? A great novel is like a great love affair. Even when short, the experience is intense. A great novel can live in memory more vividly than real life. The bond of affection that you feel for your favorites is impossible to erase. Unlike people, your top stories of all time will not age, move away, get divorced or stab you in the back. They are forever a part of you, the truest of friends.

Are any of your choices children's stories? If so, that is not surprising. Formative reading experiences stay with us indelibly, like comfort foods. One of the favorites I pulled off my shelves while writing this chapter is *The Wolves of Willoughby Chase* (1962) by Joan Aiken. Without opening it, I can still vividly picture two Victorian cousins, a poor city girl and her rich country cousin, bundled in a sleigh beneath fur blankets, racing through a winter forest; the coachman whipping the horses to keep them ahead of the starving wolves that are giving chase; a servant on the sleigh's rear platform discharging a blunderbuss into the snarling pack behind them.

Are there classics among your selections? That is natural enough. I happened to pull down from my shelves the grand Russian epic *Dr. Zhivago*. (More snow. Hmm.) Perhaps you chose *Tess of the d'Urbervilles*, *The Europeans*, *Jane Eyre* or *Huckleberry Finn*. I would also be very surprised if *Gone With the Wind* or *Rebecca* were not in many stacks.

What about contemporary epics? *From Here to Eternity*. *Hawaii*. *Shōgun*. *Lonesome Dove*. The best of the twentieth century? Hemingway. Fitzgerald. Faulkner. What about others from the southern contingent: Robert Penn Warren, Walker Percy, Flannery O'Connor, Ernest J. Gaines, Lee Smith . . . oh my god, someone stop me!

What about genre novels? For me it was a tough choice between J.R.R. Tolkien's *The Lord of the Rings* and Frank Herbert's *Dune*. *Dune* won out, possibly because I read it first. On the other hand, it would be hard to beat Sir Arthur Conan Doyle, Agatha Christie, Raymond Chandler, John D. MacDonald or Erle Stanley Gardner (though I must confess I have read Gardner in bulk rather than in depth). Are you blown away by John Le Carré? Frederick Forsyth? Ken Follett? Ira Levin? Stephen King? The heavens of romantic fiction have too many stars to count, though Phyllis A. Whitney, Georgette Heyer and Danielle Steel are favorites that are frequently mentioned to me.

Is there in front of you a novel first published within the last ten years? If so, I am impressed, but how do you know it is one of your top three of all time? Can you have reread it often enough to be sure? Well, OK. I'll take your word for it.

Four Facets of Three Great Novels

Now, stop rhapsodizing and start thinking. What do your three novels have in common? On the surface, perhaps little. But consider less the genre, setting or style of each novel, and consider more the experience it gives you as a reader.

Probably all of your favorites are novels that swept you away, whisked you into their worlds, transported you to other times or places, and held you captive there. That is significant. Being taken somewhere else is a quality of great fiction. I am not talking about writing mere escapism or about sticking to historical settings. The quality I mean is the one of creating a fictional world that exists convincingly, wholly and compellingly apart and unto itself.

For your breakout novel, it may be a world you know intimately, just as Mark Twain knew the Mississippi River of his boyhood. Or you may have to research it. The point is it is different from the usual, an experience that most people do not have, or, if they do, one that they do not experience intimately. For example, we have all been in airports, but how many of us have smelled the stale coffee smell in the control tower? The world of Washington politics is familiar from television news, but how many of us know the color of the carpet in the West Wing? A great fictional world is the sum of details that to most readers are unknown.

Your top three selections probably also involve characters whom you cannot forget. Ask most people to name a memorable hero or heroine and Sherlock Holmes or Scarlett O'Hara will probably be among the first that are mentioned, followed closely by Hannibal Lecter, who technically was a villain.

Take your pick. What is certainly true of all great characters is they are larger-than-life. I do not mean that they are unrealistic. Quite the contrary. What I mean is they act, speak and think in ways you or I most of the time cannot, or at any rate do not. They say the things we wished we had said. They do things we dream about doing. They grow and change in ways we wish that we could. They feel feelings authentically and without turning away. That is as true of Judy Blume's sixth grader Margaret Simon who talks to God while waiting to get her period as it is of Clive Cussler's Dirk Pitt while he is raising the Titanic.

Again, I do not mean great fictional creations provide only shallow fantasy fulfillment; rather, I mean they express for us our greatest purposes and our deepest desires. They are us. That is the reason we identify with them.

Almost inextricable from that is another quality your favorite novels probably have in common: What happens to the characters in the course of the story is unusual, dramatic and meaningful. A great story involves great events. Not wars or wonderments, necessarily, but certainly events with impact.

Consider Virginia Woolf's 1927 masterpiece *To the Lighthouse*. In a plot sense, how much actually happens? Not much. The Ramsay family vacations on the Isle of Skye between 1910 and 1920, talks about sailing to a nearby lighthouse but never does. That is hardly the premise for a suspenseful page-tuner. Even so, *To the Lighthouse* has thrilled generations of readers. It has even changed lives. Why? Because the action—or in this case, the inaction—matters to the novel's characters, particularly to Mrs. Ramsay, whose need to understand her family and the people around her is so detailed and deeply felt that it becomes a universal struggle to reconcile that which would seem irreconcilable in human nature. Do the nonevents of *To the Lighthouse* have impact? Yes. That impact is still being felt today.

Are there novels that have changed your life? Of course there are. Why did they change it? Here is the last quality I suspect all your selections may have in common: Above and beyond the setting, characters and plot, these are probably novels that altered your way of seeing the world. If they did not actually change your opinions or beliefs, they at least showed you something about humanity (possibly divinity) you had not previously realized. They are about something. They present an outlook. They have a message.

Breakout novels are written from an author's passionate need to make you understand, to expose you to someone special or to drag you somewhere that it is important for you to see. No breakout novel leaves us feeling neutral. A breakout novel rattles, confronts and illuminates. It is detailed because it is real. Its people live because they spring from life, or at least from the urge to say something about life. Their stories challenge our hopes, plumb our fears, test our faiths and enact our human wills.

These novels change us because their authors are willing to draw upon their deepest selves without flinching. They hold nothing back, making their novels the deepest possible expression of their own experience and beliefs. There is purpose to their prose.

Is there as strong a purpose to yours? If not, how are you going to develop it? It starts with a premise, the very earliest form of the novel-to-be. Like building the novel itself, constructing a premise is a task that is best undertaken by breaking the job into smaller parts.

The Little Components of Big Ideas
How, exactly, do you know whether you are constructing a premise that will work? For most first-time novelists, there comes a point early in the creation process when it feels like their story has the stuff of greatness. Few do, as my slush pile attests.

What is it that fools beginners about their fiction? I believe it is living in a fictional world for the first time. It is so alive! So real! So vital! What the inexperienced novelist has not yet learned is how to make all that vivid stuff as vivid to the reader as it is in the writer's mind.

Even much-published novelists can have a tough time telling whether they are in the grip of a breakout premise or whether they are fooling themselves. One dangerous trap can be "the novel I have always wanted to write." Breakout fiction like 1999's *The Poisonwood Bible* by Barbara Kingsolver and *Cryptonomicon* by Neal Stephenson have successfully capitalized on a lifetime's passion, but for the most part, dream novels disappoint. The most common reason they do, I believe, is that their premises are not adequately developed. In most cases a germ is there. It must be. If it were missing, the idea would not have nagged away for years.

But the germ of a premise is not enough. The key ingredients that I look for in a fully formed breakout premise are (1) plausibility, (2) inherent conflict, (3) originality and (4) gut emotional appeal. How do I measure and think about those things?

Plausibility

When an author pitches a great story premise, almost always the first question that springs to my mind (and I will bet to yours, too) is this: *Could that really happen?* It is an odd question. Fiction is not life. And yet for some reason most readers, me included, need to feel that the story we are being presented has some basis in reality.

Why? The answer to that question lies in part in the psychology of storytelling, or rather story receiving. A work of fiction grips our imaginations because we care, both about the characters in the tale *and about ourselves.* To put it another way, we are concerned about the outcome of the story because what is happening to the characters could happen to us.

Looked at that way, the requirement that a premise be plausible is not so strange. If it could not really happen, then why should we bother with it?

It is probably because natural storytellers innately understand this principle that so many breakout premises are inspired by a family memory, a newspaper clipping, a tantalizing fact found in the course of research and so on. Like the best lies, the real whoppers, a breakout premise has a grain of truth. It is that truth that persuades us to care and convinces us that this story contains the stuff of life. A breakout premise comes from someplace real.

While a story idea can be too far-fetched, it can also be too obvious. A starting point that is ordinary, expected, common knowledge or common sense has little power to excite us. On the other hand, we wonder at a fact that is strange, off-center, unexpected, intriguing, little known or in some other way unusual. It provokes questions, draws us deeper. It piques our imaginations and sends them roaming. It causes us to ask ourselves that supremely rich question, "What if . . . ?"

Have you ever had a writing buddy spin a story idea, only to hear yourself say doubtfully, "I suppose that *could* work. . . ." Often such ideas are too predictable or too improbable. A premise that is surprising yet credible is one that is far more likely to make us exclaim, "I wish I had thought of that."

Inherent Conflict

The next question to ask yourself is this: Does the world of my story have conflict built into it? Opposing forces, both strong, perhaps both in the right? If the milieu of the story is not only multifaceted but also involves opposing factions or points of view, then you have a basis for strong, difficult-to-resolve conflict. To put it another way, if problems already exist in your "place," that is a good thing.

Indeed, that may be why it is difficult to write a great novel about the suburbs. The suburbs are safe. Their purpose is to create comfort, not conflict. In contrast, many great novels have been set on the battlefield, in courtrooms, jails, cities, schools, in the wild, in the Catholic Church, in outer space . . . in short, anywhere that is *not* safe. It does not matter whether it is man against nature, man against himself or reason against faith. Where there is conflict, there is rich soil in which to plant a story.

But suppose you *do* want to write about the suburbs? What if that is the world you know and the place to which you want to bring your readers? That need has been felt by John Cheever, John Updike and Anna Quindlen, to name a few. All three successfully have set stories in suburbia. For them, paradise abounds with problems. A requirement of safe and comfortable places as settings for a breakout novel, in my experience, is that they have in them hidden dangers.

Inherent conflict can be a facet of more than just your novel's setting. Mother-daughter relationships are full of conflict. So are father-son relationships. So are most groups. Generations have gaps. Armies have divisions. Our government . . . well, need I follow that thought any further? Institutions are full of opposing factions. Think of police stations, hospitals, art museums, corporate boards, circus tents, PTAs. . . . All these are plagued by power struggles and ideological opposition. Even the Boy Scouts of America cannot agree on basic membership criteria. The Boy Scouts! If they cannot get it together, then what hope has anyone else?

Anywhere that there are people, there is inherent conflict: the cockpit, the kitchen, the battlefield, the backyard. . . . If your place is lacking trouble, dig deeper. It is there. Your job is to bring it out. Drilling into deep wells of conflict is a fundamental step in constructing a breakout premise.

Originality

Let's stick with the suburbs for a moment. They will help me illustrate the next factor that can make a story idea a breakout premise.

Assuming you want to set your breakout novel in the suburbs, ask yourself this: Is the threat you've found in the suburbs, the dark side you want to show people, genuinely new? It is? I have a hard time believing that. I suspect that if the darkest doings of Greenwich, Connecticut, were exposed on page one of tomorrow's *The New York Times*, most people would merely nod their heads and remark, "Uh-huh. Doesn't surprise me." Even so, over the next few years, there are bound to be breakout novels set in the suburbs.

Why? Although human nature may never change, our ways of looking at it will. To break out with familiar subject matter—and, really, it has all been written about before—it is essential to find a fresh angle. There certainly are no new plots. Not a one. There are also no settings that have not been used, and no professions that have not been given to protagonists.

That is disheartening, but it is also a challenge. Working out an original approach can be highly rewarding. Take World War I: You would not think that there is anything new to say about the horrors of that war, but that is what one novelist recently has done. In *The Ghost Road* by Pat Barker, which won the 1995 Booker Prize, war is horrible (no surprise), but through psychologist Dr. William Rivers and soldier Billy Prior, we learn how even a shell-shocked wreck of a man can be drawn back to the trenches by a real desire to experience the triumph of the final victory.

Now that is a different story! Barker's perspective is unusual, and that is what originality is often about: a previously unexplored angle on a familiar subject. Every week I receive at least one query letter, usually from a doctor, offering me a novel that exposes the evil nature of HMOs. Did you know our health insurance companies are, in effect, "killing" people for profit? Well, of course you knew. Everyone knows that. These authors err not in their choice of subject matter but in their attempts to fashion a surprise.

That said, fresh angles can be found for all kinds of familiar material. The number of breakout novels based on vampire lore, fairy tales and Arthurian mythologies is, at this point, somewhere up in the hundreds (think *Interview With the Vampire* [1976] by Anne Rice, or *The Mists of Avalon* [1982] by Marion Zimmer Bradley). Sherlock Holmes novels appear with regularity. Few have broken out, but *The Seven-Per-Cent Solution* (1974) by

Nicholas Meyer, *The Whitechapel Horrors* (1993) by Edward B. Hanna and *The Beekeepers's Apprentice* (1994) by Laurie R. King all gave significant boosts to their author's careers.

Are sequels to classic novels original? Can they break out? Most editors agree, I find, that literary sequels have been wildly overdone in recent years. When commercially motivated, they frequently have disappointed. Susan Hill is a superb novelist. Her ghost story *The Woman in Black* (1986) is a favorite of mine, one of the best to emerge in Britain's current revival of the gothic novel. However, her sequel to Du Maurier's *Rebecca*, *Mrs. de-Winter* (1993), was largely dismissed by critics. *Scarlett* (1991), Alexandra Ripley's sequel to *Gone With the Wind*, hit *The New York Times* best-seller list but was roundly disliked by critics and readers alike. Success is difficult to borrow.

When derivative novels *are* successful, they are often not direct sequels but rather riffs on some aspect or other of the original work. In *Wide Sargasso Sea* (1966) Jean Rhys imagined a backstory to *Jane Eyre*, the tale of Rochester's "mad" Caribbean wife, and in so doing created a classic work of feminist fiction. In a more lighthearted vein, Gregory Maguire's *Wicked: The Life and Times of the Wicked Witch of the West* (1995) is an alternative point of view on L. Frank Baum's *The Wonderful Wizard of Oz*. The most intriguing story is often not a wholly new fiction but rather a fresh angle on a tale that is already well known.

Two other ways to be original are (1) by doing the opposite of what we expect and (2) by combining two discrete story elements. For instance, coming-of-age stories are very familiar. So are Hollywood novels. A combination of the two, however, would be very original—and was for Diane Leslie in her 1999 debut novel *Fleur de Leigh's Life of Crime*, the story of the daughter of a B-movie actress and a TV game show producer, and the girl's upbringing by a series of bizarre nannies.

At a writers conference a few years ago, I heard Warner Books executive editor Rick Horgan explain "high concept" premises in a similar way. He cited the example of a story idea about a woman's recovery from cancer. Nothing special in that. But take another story idea—a woman's dream of climbing Mount Rainier, say—and put them together. Now you have a high concept premise: a woman's recovery, physical and spiritual, as she struggles up a snowcapped peak in the Pacific Northwest.

Unusual combinations are particularly beloved of so-called crossover novelists, who like to mix genres. Time travel romances and fantasy detectives are two common examples. However, crossover novelists are wrong if they imagine that a combination of story forms will by itself draw readers from more than one section of the bookstore. That is not so. Crossover novels are mostly one thing or another, and appeal mostly to one type of reader or another.

To transcend even one genre, let alone two, a novel needs to be built on a breakout scale as is, say, Diana Gabaldon's 1991 novel *Outlander*, the story of a married nurse who after World War II travels back in time to 1743 Scotland and finds herself married, a second time, to a Scottish renegade from English justice. This is not your typical historical romance. Nor, it must be said, is it really science fiction. Gabaldon borrows a little from each genre but only as much as she needs to tell her own unique large-scale story. *Outlander* has plot layers, high stakes and depth of character. It has violence, torture and rape. Gabaldon has plenty to say about fidelity and desire, Scottish history, herbal healing and more. That is why *Outlander* broke out, not because it happened to "cross," or mix, two genres.

Unexpected directions? Literary novelist Ron Hansen began his career with two western historicals (*Desperadoes*, [1979] and *The Assassination of Jesse James by the Coward Robert Ford* [1987]), then caught critical attention in 1991 with a psychological mystery about a young nun who displays stigmata in an upstate New York convent in 1906, *Mariette in Ecstasy*. Afterward, I wondered whether Hansen would ever again come up with a concept so fresh. His 1996 National Book Award finalist *Atticus* was an emotionally intense father-son story but for me lacked the dazzling originality of *Mariette in Ecstasy*.

Then in 1999 Hansen published a romance, but not just any romance, one that is strikingly original because it delivers the opposite of what we expect. The novel, *Hitler's Niece*, is about love, sure, but its hero and heroine are an unlikely pair: Adolph Hitler and his much younger niece Geli Raubal. A romance about Hitler? I will admit that this premise does not sound terribly romantic, but you have to admit that it is highly original.

A couple of years ago, a client of mine, mystery writer Parnell Hall, used a reversal of the expected to build the premise for a wildly successful new series. Hall's prior series, hilarious novels about a reluctant PI named Stanley Hastings, was dropped by his publisher. No other publisher could be found to take up the series. After some months of angst and grieving, I told Hall it was time to come up with something new and suggested to him an idea: Since puzzle plots are a strength of his, and since the puzzle plot is in relative decline, why not buck the trend and write the ultimate puzzle series . . . mysteries featuring a little old lady who is a crossword puzzle constructor? In fact, why not include actual crossword puzzles in the books?

Two months later Hall walked into my office with a manuscript titled *A Clue for the Puzzle Lady*. Included in it was a crossword puzzle that could be worked to learn the solution to the crime. The premise was already commercial, but Hall had given it an original twist. *A Clue for the Puzzle Lady* introduces Cora Felton, putative author of a nationally syndicated crossword puzzle column. She looks like a sweet little old lady, but in fact she is anything but sweet: She is a lush, a gambler, a smoker and a sharp-tongued pain in the ass.

Worse, Cora Felton knows nothing about crossword puzzles. The puzzles actually are written by her young and beautiful niece Sherri, a puzzle genius who had trouble breaking into the stuffy puzzle business precisely because she is young and beautiful. No one took her seriously—that is, until she hit upon the idea of having her Aunt Cora front for her.

All would be well except that Aunt Cora fancies herself an amateur sleuth. When a murder happens in their sleepy Connecticut town and a scrap of paper in the pocket of a murdered teenage runaway seems to have written on it a crossword puzzle clue, Cora dives in. In an alcoholic haze, she tries to solve the crime. Disaster ensues. Sherri must juggle the police, a nosy local reporter and her rogue aunt in order to keep her aunt alive and keep the secret of The Puzzle Lady.

Twist follows upon twist, and in the end Aunt Cora actually does uncover the identity of the murderer. In a double reversal, Hall has Cora prove herself to be a puzzle genius, too, but only with respect to puzzles that involve actual death.

A test round of submissions suggested that the points of view in A Clue for the Puzzle Lady were improperly weighted. Hall revised, and the second round hit the jackpot. Within twenty-four hours, I had negotiated a six-figure floor bid. I auctioned the book a few weeks later. It was published in hardcover in December 1999 by Bantam and required two extra printings. Hall's career is back on track and trending upward.

What about your premise? Is it truly a fresh look at your subject, a perspective that no one else but you can bring to it? Is it the opposite of what we expect or a mix of elements such as we've never seen before? If not, you have some work to do.

If so, you may have something there.

Gut Emotional Appeal

One final question: Does your breakout premise make people shiver? Does it get them in the gut? No? Better work on it. One of the qualities I notice again and again in breakout novels is they have a strong emotional appeal. Something about the very premise of such stories grabs me, hollows my stomach and makes me look hard at my life.

If a premise has gut emotional appeal, the novel will start to write itself in my mind. The very idea invites me to imagine characters, complications and dramatic climaxes. It gets me. It feels personal. That, I believe, is because it touches emotions that are deep, real and common to us all.

Love stories are an interesting area in which to hunt for gut emotional appeal. I mean, how many ways can you tell a basic boy-meets-girl tale? Despite its familiarity, authors are nevertheless forever coming up with new takes on a tired old formula.

Male authors in particular—with their pseudoliterary, semi-tragic novels about sensitive men who find their one true love, only to lose her—never cease to amaze me. I would have thought that Erich Segal's *Love Story* (1970) made all other novels in the genre merely derivative. Not so. *The Bridges of Madison County* (1992) by Robert James Waller is one recent example of the male romance that broke out big time.

A more recent example is Nicholas Sparks's *The Notebook* (1996), which contains an instructive example of how to turn a stale formula into a breakout premise using gut emotional appeal.

In the framing opening of the novel the hero, Noah Calhoun, is in his eighties and living in a nursing home. He is in a reflective mood:

> My life? It isn't easy to explain. It has not been the rip-roaring spectacular I fancied it would be, but neither have I burrowed with the gophers. I suppose it has most resembled a blue-chip stock: fairly stable, more ups than downs, and gradually trending upward over time. A good buy, a lucky buy, and I've learned that not everyone can say this about his life. But do not be misled. I am nothing special; of this I am sure.

Golly gee, have you ever met a more self-effacing guy? Immediately we get the impression that this is a good man, a humble man, an honest man. Having won our sympathy for Noah, Sparks then sends him shuffling down the hallway of the nursing home with a worn notebook under his arm; a daily trek, we learn. He enters the room of a woman who cannot care for herself. He waits for the nurses to leave. He is a stranger to the woman, but nevertheless he puts on his glasses and begins to read her the story that is written in the notebook.

Can you guess what is going on here? It is obvious: This is the woman he has loved for a lifetime. She has Alzheimer's. What he is reading to her is the story of their relationship, in the faint-but-loving hope that she will remember, just for an instant, a piece of the tale that has given his life its meaning.

Grabs you in the gut, doesn't it? It is a good starting point for a story. The author's bio in the back of the book relates that Sparks based the story on his wife's beloved grandparents. I am not surprised. This has the feel of a story driven by an author's passion to tell a tale that springs from life. Sparks believes in his bones in the healing power of love.

Having sunk his emotional hook, Sparks is then able to flash back for a lengthy and, to my eye, low-tension account of Noah and Allie's courtship. The middle of *The Notebook* holds few surprises, but the emotional appeal of the story frame easily carries us through. In the end, Sparks returns to the nursing home for this climactic exchange between Noah and his wife of, now, forty-nine years:

> "I think I know who Allie went with at the end of the story," she says.
> "You do?"
> "Yes."
> "Who?"
> "She went with Noah."
> "You're sure?"
> "Absolutely."
> I smile and nod. "Yes, she did," I say softly, and she smiles back. Her face is radiant . . .
> "I've always loved you, Noah."

You have probably noticed from these excerpts that the prose and dialogue in *The Notebook* is rudimentary. However, for all that the writing is plain, it is also sincere and heartfelt. The situation of boy and girl at the end of their lives together, catching one last flicker of a love that ignited decades of happiness, tugs at our hearts. No matter that it is sentimental, it is a gut grabber and thus makes a breakout premise. Since *The Notebook* sat near the top of most best-seller lists for more than a year, many readers obviously agreed.

Where is the gut emotional appeal of your story? It is there somewhere, waiting for you to draw it out. How? Let us look a bit deeper at how your premise can be developed.

Build It and the Breakout Premise Will Come

So, how does your current premise measure up? Does it have plausibility, inherent conflict, originality and gut emotional appeal? Not quite as much as you'd like? Do not panic. With development, many an unpromising story idea can be turned into a breakout premise.

Let's look at some examples: Suppose that you want to write a novel about the problem of race in America? Already you are unoriginal. Now choose a boring profession for your protagonist, in a milieu completely lacking in inherent conflict: How about "elevator inspector"? What a bad story premise!

However, those are the very starting points chosen by Colson Whitehead in his much-praised 1999 debut novel *The Intuitionist*. His fully developed premise meets all of my breakout criteria. Inherent conflict exists because his department of elevator inspectors is divided into two sharply opposing camps: "Intuitionists" and "Empiricists." Emotional appeal arrives with the plot's main event: An elevator crashes on the watch of Whitehead's protagonist, Lila Mae Watson, an Intuitionist. Although she is not wholly responsible for the crash, she nevertheless takes considerable blame. Who cannot identify with that? Lila's situation has gut emotional appeal.

Is Whitehead's plot plausible? Elevator plunges are quite rare, but we all fear them. Originality? Race is not a new subject, but Whitehead's angle on it, as seen through the lives of elevator inspectors, is fresh and unexpected. You see? From a dismal idea grows a breakout premise. It is a matter of development.

Let's try another example: Does a novel about the life of a dwarf sound emotionally appealing? How about Nazi Germany as a setting? Has that been done before? Clearly, this idea already has two originality strikes against it. However, when the dwarf is Trudi Montag, who harbors Jews in her cellar in the Nazi era, then you have hit upon Ursula Hegi's 1994 novel *Stones from the River*, a wildly successful literary novel, an Oprah Book Club pick, and a story with tremendous gut emotional appeal and originality.

Here is another: Have you ever found yourself alone in an airport, thinking, *You know, I could get on any one of those flights right now, not tell anyone where I am going and start a new life?* Or have you ever stayed in a hotel and fantasized about not checking out? Getting away from it all is an eternal and highly appealing fantasy. We all have felt that urge, I will bet, and airports and hotels are two common portals for escape.

Rutgers writing teacher and poet Lisa Zeidner used this highly plausible scenario in her 1999 breakout novel *Layover*. Her three prior novels had won acclaim but suffered anemic sales. Zeidner told *Publishers Weekly*, "I was aware that I wasn't going to have many more shots in today's publishing climate." She spent five years working on *Layover*, stretching herself to write about, as she put it, "a smart, middle-aged woman, a grownup," traveling saleswoman Claire Newbold, who falls into the kind of dislocating grief anyone might experience: Her young son has died and her husband has been unfaithful. Claire refuses to check out of her hotel room and embarks upon a series of sexual adventures that, while driving her toward madness, also illuminate her conflicting need for lust and control.

Zeidner dug deep, and as a result Claire Newbold achieves a

kind of Everywoman depth and power. Emotional appeal, a rare-but-credible decision to drop out and the conflict inherent in a married woman plunging into a mind-numbing, soul-freeing bout of sex all combine to make a breakout premise. Poetic and honest writing then turn that premise into a breakout novel. *Layover* got help from its eye-catching cover (an out-of-focus naked woman in a hotel room; in the foreground, a telephone receiver off its hook), great reviews and a modest promotional effort from Random House. But those commercial gimmicks are not what sent the book back to press and won it a mid-five-figure floor bid for paperback reprint rights.

That was purely what readers found between the sheets . . . er, covers. As Zeidner's editor Daniel Menaker said shortly after publication, "This is becoming a great example of being able to still 'make' a book the old-fashioned way, through good reviews and word of mouth."

Brainstorming the Breakout Premise

Let's try one more example, this one of our own making. Let us start with the most horribly trite story idea we can think of . . . oh, say, a story about a boy who dreams of batting in the winning run in the big baseball game. No, that is too dramatic. Let us make his sport track and field, running.

Wait, even that is not commonplace enough. Let us cripple that bland premise even more. Let's say the boy is . . . um . . . in a wheelchair. *Oh, barf!* you say. *That is the stuff of TV movies. Sentimental slop.* Good. Let's apply the principles of building a breakout premise and see what we can do. As we develop our premise, notice that we will steer away from obvious choices for setting, character and plot in order to build originality. Credibility we have got, I think, but we will hunt for inherent conflict and emotional appeal wherever we can.

Notice, too, our frequent application of the question "What if?" This time-tested development tool is a way of escalating stakes, adding layers to plot and character, and opening new thematic dimensions.

Where is our story set? A ghetto elementary school? Too obvious. Let us do the opposite: give our protagonist advantages that do not, unfortunately, help him toward his goal. Let's make him white and send him to an exclusive prep school where he has high-minded teachers, supportive friends and an athletic staff that is dedicated to helping him reach his highest potential. But it is not enough. He lacks—what?

No one knows, least of all himself. All he knows is while he does well in wheelchair races, he rarely wins. Good. Here we have a more subtle and interesting central conflict. Instead of a simple goal-and-obstacle, we have a psychological mystery.

So, what next? Complicate the problem. How? What if our hero has a hero of his own? An older brother? Too easy. Let us go in the opposite direction and make his hero someone distant and unreachable: a marathon runner. An adult.

A Nigerian! A black man. Yes, that is credible. Now, what kind of character is this Nigerian? Highly trained? Sure. Confident? No, let us go the opposite way: Our Nigerian runs like an antelope, but when competing anyone can see on his face that he is frightened. Maybe that is why our hero is fascinated with him. Watching him on TV, our wheelchair athlete sees on his idol's face a fear he cannot understand.

So far, so good. Now the American and the Nigerian must meet, don't you agree? How? Let us locate our hero's prep school in Massachusetts. Let us also bring the Nigerian to the Boston Marathon. Our hero is selected to present the winner's trophy. So they meet on the winner's platform—?

Too predictable. Let's have the Nigerian place second in the marathon. Our hero locates the Nigerian after the ceremony, wrapped in a silvery Kevlar blanket, looking into the distance.

Unseen our hero wheels up. He blurts out, "Why are you afraid? When you run?"

Again, let us steer away from the obvious course. The Nigerian cannot answer that question; better still, he does not want to answer it, is offended by it. They get off on entirely the wrong foot.

And yet . . . what if at a Special Olympics preliminary race the following week, the Nigerian approaches our hero in the parking lot. They talk. Our boy asks technical questions, but the Nigerian says that he thinks too much. They begin to form a bond. From there, a relationship grows. A simple one?

Let us make it complex. Hero and worshiper would not have a one-dimensional association. A hero likes to be worshiped, I will bet, but might hate it, too. Expectations of others are hard to bear. The worshiper, too, may feel resentment. In fact, what if our hero envies the fear that makes the Nigerian run so fast? Our hero does not have that driving him. Our hero is normal, well-adjusted and only half successful. His advantages cripple him more thoroughly than his useless legs.

Is this premise getting better? Maybe, but it still needs more dimensions, extra levels, to lift it out of the ordinary.

What do we have to work with? Two friends of different races, pun intended. Each is unequal to the other in important ways: inherent conflict. Yet they also have a kinship as runners. Plus, they need each other. We know why our hero needs his Nigerian idol—he holds the key to our hero's underperformance—but why does the Nigerian need our prep school boy?

The answer to that question could send our novel in some interesting directions. Certainly the Nigerian ought to visit our hero's privileged home in . . . oh, let's say Greenwich, Connecticut, since suburbia is on our minds. Should our hero visit the Nigerian's home village in Africa? Possibly. That would be very different. Plunging our two main characters into cultures so unlike their own is bound to produce more conflict.

Now we are cooking.

We have the inner story working, but what about the outer conflicts and opposition? Build a secondary cast of characters of your choice: parents, coaches, a girlfriend, race organizers, a journalist. . . . What strikes your fancy? All might bring interesting outside forces to bear upon this odd hero/worshiper match. Cultural differences, racism and reverse racism, sports psychology . . . all could complicate the unfolding friendship that is the key not only to our prep school boy's dreams but that might also prove liberating for our marathoner.

For me, a central question in our story is what our marathoner is afraid of. Go ahead and make a choice. I might go for a gut-wrenching reason: The Nigerian's father is dying; he runs fast so his father will have a reason to stay alive. You might prefer a political reason, or perhaps one that is darker and more deeply psychological.

At this point it may not matter. Our cheesy premise is taking on dimensions it did not at first deserve. It is turning into a story about hero worship, running, racism, and perhaps not overcoming an inner fear but instead embracing it. We have layers. The principles of building the breakout premise have helped us begin to lift our story from its humble origins.

Starting premise: A schoolboy dreams of winning a race. The problem? He is in a wheelchair.

Breakout premise: A prep school boy, wheelchair bound, enjoys all the advantages in his quest to be the best in track and field. But he cannot seem to win. His advantages cripple him as surely as his useless legs. His life changes, though, when he meets his idol: a world-class Nigerian marathoner. The fear that drives the Nigerian to run proves to be the key to breaking the prep school boy's mental block, but first the two must overcome barriers of culture, race and their very different ways of running toward a dream.

Do we have credibility? Yes, this story could happen. Do we have originality? Yes. At any rate, I do not remember reading this story before. Do we have inherent conflict? Yes, and we are working on building it even more. Finally, gut emotional appeal? The basis for it is now built into the premise.

Turning that premise into an actual breakout novel will obviously require a great deal of technique. Still, we now have a solid foundation. Once you have laid a solid foundation for your own novel then you are ready to move forward with confidence. You have built yourself a breakout premise.

BREAKOUT Checklist: Premise

✓ A breakout premise can be built.

✓ Your favorite novels sweep you away, have characters you cannot forget, and involve dramatic and meaningful events.

✓ A breakout premise has plausibility, inherent conflict, originality and gut emotional appeal.

✓ Plausibility means that the story could happen to any of us.

✓ Inherent conflict means problems in your "place."

✓ Originality can be new angles on old stories, the opposite of what we expect or story elements in unexpected combinations.

✓ Gut emotional appeal springs from the emotional situations that grab us in life.

✓ Even an unlikely starting point can be built into a breakout premise.

✓ To brainstorm a breakout premise, steer away from the obvious, seek inherent conflict, find gut emotional appeal and ask, "What if . . . ?"

CHAPTER THREE

Stakes

If there is one single principle that is central to making any story more powerful, it is simply this: Raise the stakes.

Sure, you think. Like all the best advice, this chestnut is so familiar your mind glazes over when you read it, doesn't it? Mine does. Everyone knows that high stakes are important. It is as fundamental as putting a period at the end of a sentence. Why, then, do so few fiction writers put this principle into effective practice?

You are not guilty of that lapse, right? Of course not. But let me ask you this: If you are a first-timer, is your manuscript bringing a flood of calls from agents offering to represent you? If you are published, was your last novel a breakout? Did it go back to press five times? Did the review clippings come in thick batches from your publicist? Did your editor phone your agent with suspicious haste to offer an option deal? No? Excuse me for mentioning it, but I have a point to make: High stakes yield high success.

Think hard. Be honest with yourself. Are the stakes in your current manuscript as high as they possibly can be? Can you define the stakes right now? Can you point to the exact pages in which the stakes escalate, locking your protagonist into his course of action with less hope of success than before?

Low stakes are easy to diagnose in the work of beginning novelists. In one-on-one meetings at writers conferences, I can usually stop a story pitch dead in its tracks by interjecting the following: "Hold on, your protagonist wants to [insert goal here], but let me ask you this, if he is not successful, so what?" What follows that question is generally a stare of disbelief or, if I am lucky, choked stammering. "So what? Well, if he didn't then . . . then . . ."

Then what? That is the essence of defining what is at stake. What would be lost? A day? A job? A love? A life? Beginning thriller writers love to put their protagonists' lives in jeopardy. One inexperienced novelist once asked me, "What higher stakes can there be?" The truth is that running for one's life has become commonplace in mass entertainment. With people sprinting for survival several dozen times a day on television, life-and-death stakes are nearly soporific.

Even so, there are plenty of novels in which the main characters run for their lives, and we are on the edge of our seats. Why? The reason we care about a character in mortal danger is that we care about that character, period. His life has meaning, purpose or value. Life-and-death stakes are empty unless they are tied to underlying human worth.

To put it another way, building high human worth is the first step in building high stakes, whether or not your protagonist's physical survival is in doubt.

Creating High Human Worth

Let us construct an example: Who is running for his life? A cop? Commonplace. A soldier? Normal. An accountant? Hmm. A lawyer? Better. Lawyers are educated, competent, in control, sometimes aggressive. For someone ordinarily so much in command, to be forced to run merely to survive has a contradiction built into it. It is intriguing. Still, the idea does not yet grip.

Why? Because there is not yet high human value attached to our lawyer. Some would say we have a job ahead of us, but let us keep working. Suppose our lawyer needs to stay alive not because he has a case to win. Nothing special in that. Let us say instead he needs to survive because he is a single dad with a daughter to raise. Or he is a bone marrow match. Or his passion for justice is the only thing standing between an innocent man and execution.

None of those is very original, but they illustrate my point: For anyone's life to be worth saving (in fiction), it needs added value. And in the scale of values, nothing is more compelling than high principles and codes of personal conduct. We admire principled people. We try to emulate them. They are the model citizens without which our society would not be civilized.

To put a principled person at risk is to raise the stakes in your story to a high degree. Better still is to test that individual's principles to the utmost. There is something gripping about the inner struggle to remain loyal to a passionately held belief. We may cheer at the moment when a hero defeats a villain, but we are moved far more deeply when that hero eschews an easy choice and honors his code.

Honesty, integrity, loyalty, kindness, bravery, respect, trust and love of one's fellow men are all measures of high human worth. They also are the keys to making life-and-death stakes count, or any lesser stakes, for that matter.

One of the two best-selling novelists of the twentieth century was Erle Stanley Gardner, creator of the trial lawyer Perry Mason. At the height of Gardner's career in the mid-1960s, some seven thousand copies of his books were sold *every hour*. The *Perry Mason* TV series certainly boosted their sales, but Gardner's indomitable lawyer was popular long before that.

Why was he so beloved? Certainly Mason was smart, but his appeal has a deeper reason: At the beginning of each case, Mason meets a client who is charged with murder (or is shortly to be accused). Mason's detective pal, Paul Drake, usually warns him off the case. It is a loser. The client looks "guilty as hell." But Mason is not put off. A gut instinct tells him that the client is innocent, and he holds to that conviction through every complication. In fact, Gardner often makes the client herself (they are mostly women) the biggest problem. She digs herself deeper into trouble, handing the district attorney more and more damning evidence. Mason, however, sticks to his guns. Nothing shakes his faith.

It is his loyalty to his clients in the face of extreme opposition that makes Perry Mason heroic, and that gives Erle Stanley Gardner's novels their high-stakes gravity. Gardner did not need to put Mason's life at risk, although he sometimes did. Most of the time, it was enough for Mason's high principles and code of personal conduct to be tested to the limit.

Having understood the basics of stakes, let us now be more discerning. In every novel stakes work on two levels, public and private. How can you elevate the stakes on each level regardless of the type of story you are spinning?

Good question. In answering it we shall see that a combination of high public stakes and deep personal stakes is the most powerful engine a breakout novel can have.

Public Stakes

When discussing stakes, most writers start at the top: with what society as a whole might lose should the outcome of the story prove unfavorable. *The fate of the free world hangs in the balance!* Or perhaps . . . *everyone in the city will perish if they are not evacuated by the time the hurricane hits!* It is easy to invent stakes like that, far harder to make them credible.

However, making such stakes believable is exactly what thriller writers must do. Face it: The grand-scale disasters that pose a threat in most thrillers are not likely to occur in real life. I mean, how many times in human history has civilization been wiped out in a day? Historians may correct me here, but I believe it has almost never happened. Still, without enormous stakes most thrillers would not thrill.

How do you make such enormous public stakes seem real? As we have seen, it starts with a grain of truth in the premise. It grows with detailing that lends the threat high plausibility. A fuller discussion on this topic is given in chapter two, but I think it is no accident that top legal thrillers are written by lawyers, popular medical chillers are crafted by doctors and top espionage stories are spun by former spies. These experts know the inside stuff, the details that can make an essentially ridiculous scenario seem utterly real.

Needless to say not all threats need be global or galactic in scale. Plenty of novels with far less at stake have broken out. Moving down the scale of how-much-is-on-the-line, we find serial killer stories and pure mystery novels. These make good case studies. Here the stakes are necessarily lower. A serial killer can only murder so many people, and while in a murder mystery it is important to bring an unknown killer to justice, there is generally less pressure to do so.

Why is it, then, that some serial killer and mystery novels soar to the top of best-seller lists while others languish on genre shelves? Here is where lower-stakes wagering achieves the status of art.

Take, for example, Thomas Harris's massive best-seller *The Silence of the Lambs* (1988). At its most basic level, Harris's novel is no different than the hundreds of other serial killer stories that followed it: A homicidal psychopath is on the loose. He is holding a young woman prisoner in a pit while preparing to slaughter her. The FBI knows his "cycle," so they are aware there is only so much time left before he begins to cut. Ho hum. Another day, another serial killer at work.

Except that the writer at work is Thomas Harris. The essentials of his plot may now be familiar, but Harris deepens its complications relentlessly and thoroughly. By broadening the impact of the novel's events, its public stakes rise. How? First of all the killer, Jame "Buffalo Bill" Gumb, has a particularly gruesome MO: He skins his victims, saving a different portion of their epidermis each time. Harris knows what every good crime writer knows: A shocking, visceral and easily visualized means of death rivets public attention.

Next, Harris takes Buffalo Bill national. Bill has killed multiple times before the novel opens, dumping his victims' bodies in several states. The national press is in a lather. Then a new victim is captured; this time, not just any girl but a senator's daughter.

The stakes are already quite high, but Harris does not stop there. He gives the FBI a tool to crack open the case: a psychiatrist who has enough insight to lead them to Buffalo Bill. Unfortunately, this man is himself a pure sociopath, the imprisoned and infamous Hannibal Lecter. Getting information from Lecter certainly will prove tricky, the more so if the press gets hold of the story (which they do).

The chief of the FBI's Behavioral Psychology section, Jack Crawford, sends a smart but pliable trainee, Clarice Starling, on a pretext to talk with Lecter. Her chances of success are exceedingly thin. As time ticks away and Lecter amuses himself playing mind games with Starling, tension mounts.

The stakes in *The Silence of the Lambs*, however, rise due to more than mere plot mechanics. Harris deepens them by deepening his principle characters' personal stakes, taking us far inside the minds of both his investigators and his killers. All are trapped in inescapable fates; all suffer inner pain that seeks relief. With Lecter, a bit of this driving agony begins to surface when Starling asks Lecter about his cell:

> "Did you do the drawings on your walls, Doctor?"
>
> "Do you think I called in a decorator?"
>
> "The one over the sink is a European city?"
>
> "It's Florence. That's the Palazzo Vecchio and the Duomo, seen from the Belvedere."
>
> "Did you do it from memory, all the detail?"
>
> "Memory, Officer Starling, is what I have instead of a view."

Later, having proved his credentials by sending Starling to a previously undiscovered victim who is linked to Buffalo Bill,

Lecter offers to give Starling information to help the FBI, and he reveals his reason:

> ". . . I want something Crawford can give me and I want to trade him for it. But he won't come to see me. He won't ask for my help with Buffalo Bill, even though he knows it means more young women will die."
>
> "I can't believe that, Dr. Lecter."
>
> "I only want something very simple, and he could get it." Lecter turned up the rheostat slowly in his cell. His books and drawings were gone. His toilet seat was gone. Chilton had stipped the cell to punish him for Miggs.
>
> "I've been in this room eight years, Clarice. I know that they will never, ever let me out while I'm alive. What I want is a view. I want a window where I can see a tree, or even water."

For a moment, just a moment, Harris gives us a window into the private hell of the infamous Lecter. His simple desire for a view (although it turns out later that his desire is more ambitious) tweaks our sympathy for the monster in the tower. Lecter's personal stakes rise, and thus, so do the novel's stakes overall.

What finally brings the novel's stakes to their highest level, however, is Clarice Starling's powerful need to investigate, to understand, to stop Buffalo Bill. So powerful is this need, she is willing to pay a high price, willing even to exchange pieces of her life, intimate memories, with Dr. Lecter for scraps of information.

Her reasons seem altruistic, but they have a deeper source as Dr. Lecter discovers when drawing her out about a key childhood incident, in which as a ten-year-old, she rescued a blind horse from a slaughter farm:

> "What triggered you then? What set you off on that particular day?"

"I don't know."

"I think you do."

"I had worried about it all the time."

"What set you off, Clarice? You started what time?"

"Early. Still dark."

"Then something woke you. What woke you up? Did you dream? What was it?"

"I woke up and heard the lambs screaming. I woke up in the dark and the lambs were screaming."

"They were slaughtering the spring lambs?"

"Yes."

* * *

"Do you think if you caught Buffalo Bill yourself and if you made Catherine all right, you could make the lambs stop screaming, do you think they'd be all right too and you wouldn't wake up again in the dark and hear the lambs screaming? Clarice?"

"Yes. I don't know. Maybe."

Through this exchange we know Clarice is driven by an inner need too powerful to be talked away. Harris accomplishes this feat by opening dimensions in her, in all his characters, and pushing them to extremes far beyond what most authors would attempt. He does not stop until the stakes in his story, both public and personal, are as high as possible.

By doing so, Harris finds the universal in the particular. Every author probably feels he does that in his fiction, but Harris shows how strong a commitment to high stakes is necessary to pull it off. Clarice Starling is Everywoman. Harris makes her so not by wishing it but by setting her a task that is truly impossible, one akin to the tasks set for the gods of mythology, then pushing her to extremes of effort. Her role becomes truly heroic.

A similar dynamic can be seen in some recent breakout mystery novels. Most folks think of David Guterson's best-selling 1994 novel *Snow Falling on Cedars* as literary fiction; after all, it won the PEN/Faulkner Award. In plot terms, though, it is a romance wrapped inside a courtroom mystery. How does Guterson transcend genre? Through a detailed portrait of a remote island in Puget Sound in the 1950s, yes, but also through elevation of his novel's public and personal stakes.

In 1954, journalist Ishmael Chambers is covering the trial of a high school classmate, Kabuo Miyamoto, who is accused of the murder of a local fisherman. Uncovering the truth of the case would provide enough in the way of stakes to justify the story, but Guterson adds more. Miyamoto, a Japanese American, was imprisoned during World War II along with the rest of his community, an event which has left traces of guilt running through the island of San Piedro. After the war, Miyamoto was cheated out of land for which he had previously paid, giving him a motive for the murder but also stirring up issues of prejudice against Japanese Americans.

The public stakes are quite high, but there is more. Miyamoto's wife, Hatsue, was Chambers's teenage love. Thus while as a reporter he seeks the truth of the case, as a man he must struggle with complex feelings about a passion he has not fully left behind. His personal stakes are high, as is made clear in the flashback sequences that recount his forbidden love affair with Hatsue:

> Sometimes at night he would squeeze his eyes shut and imagine how it might be to marry her. It did not seem so far-fetched to him that they might move to some other place in the world where this would be possible. He liked to think about being with Hatsue in some place like Switzerland or Italy or France. He gave his whole soul to love; he allowed himself to believe that his feelings for Hatsue had been somehow preordained. He had been meant to

meet her on the beach as a child and then to pass his life
with her. There was no other way it could be.

Clearly, this is the love of a lifetime but history intervenes.
Hatsue is imprisoned during the war, during which time she mar-
ries Miyamoto. Chambers, meanwhile, is drafted into the ma-
rines. When he loses his left arm in a beachhead assault in the
Pacific, he is embittered about the Japanese and about life.

Later, his mixed feelings clash powerfully when he uncovers
the evidence that will exonerate the husband of the woman whom
he loves. His stakes soar. Will he play his hand so as to make Hatsue
indebted to him, or can he find a way, finally, to let her go?

> The truth now lay in Ishmael's own pocket and he
> did not know what to do with it. He did not know how
> to conduct himself and the recklessness he felt about ev-
> erything was as foreign to him as the sea foam breaking
> over the snowy boats and over the pilings of the Amity
> Harbor docks, now swamped and under water. There was
> no answer in any of it—not in the boats lying on their
> sides, not in the white fir defeated by the snow or in the
> downed branches of the cedars. What he felt was the chilly
> recklessness that had come to waylay his heart.

The jury goes out. Miyamoto's conviction looks probable.
Chambers's moment of decision comes that night when he re-
reads a good-bye letter that Hatsue sent him from the internment
camp. Here Chambers's inner heart is tested to the utmost. What
sort of man, finally, is he to become? Can he live without the
love that has given his life its meaning; a love that thanks to
culture, history, prejudice and the unknowable human heart cannot ever be his?

> He read the letter a second time, gravitating now to-
> wards its final words: *"I wish you the very best, Ishmael.*

*Your heart is large and you are gentle and kind, and I know
you will do great things in this world, but now I must say good-
bye to you. I am going to move on with my life as best I can,
and I hope you will too.''*

But the war, his arm, the course of things—it had all
made his heart much smaller. He had not moved on at
all. He had not done anything great in the world but
had instead reported on road-paving projects, garden club
meetings, school athletes. He had coasted along for years
now. . . . He read her letter another time and understood
that she had once admired him, there was something in
him she was grateful for even if she could not love him.
That was a part of himself he'd lost over the years, that
was the part that was gone.

He put the letter away in its box and went down the
stairs again.

* * *

And finally he was on the Imadas' porch and then in
the Imadas' living room, sitting with Hatsue and her
mother and father where he had never been before. Hatsue sat beside him, just beside him, close, wearing a night-
gown and her father's old bathrobe, her hair awash in light
along her back, falling in cascades around her hips, and
he reached into his pocket and unfolded the notes Philip
Milholland had written on September 16, and Ishmael
explained what the shorthand meant and why he had
come at ten-thirty in the night to speak to her after all
these years.

Miyamoto is released and so, in another way, is Ishmael
Chambers.

A larger significance can be attached to the outcome of just
about any story. It is a matter of drawing deeper from the wells

at hand, particularly the story's milieu. For instance, every setting has a history—and what is history if not a chronicle of conflicting interests? Every protagonist has a profession—and what profession lacks ethical dilemmas?

Even criminal life has codes of conduct. Patricia Highsmith in her *Ripley* series and Mario Puzo in his *Godfather* saga used those principles to build classics. You may not think of Tom Ripley or the Corleone family as highly ethical, but by attending to notions of right and wrong in their worlds, however twisted, those authors lent their stories high public stakes.

Is there a strong combination of personal and public stakes in your current novel? If not, work on that one-two punch. It will strengthen your story. Admittedly, not every novel lends itself to easy development of both its personal and public aspects. Even so, it always can be done. Always. How? Let us see.

Public Stakes in Nongenre Stories

So far we have been discussing stories with underlying genre structures. Genre plots necessarily impose stakes upon a story. Those stakes may be big or small, elaborately developed or malnourished, but nevertheless, whatever their level, the outcomes of crime and suspense tales, say, have built-in consequences.

What about nongenre stories? Can one construct meaningful public stakes in a literary or mainstream novel? Yes, obviously. But what is required? Must one fall back on plot tricks, on hanging the fate of the free world in the balance?

The vague advice to "up the ante" is heard almost universally at writers workshops. That is easy to do in a novel set in a public realm or in terms of a protagonist's own life, his personal stakes. Making the outcome of a story feel relevant to all of us is somewhat harder to do, though, when the scale of a story is small, say, when it is about a family, a small town, a solo journey or a character transformation.

Suppose your story is about a car salesman whose marriage is falling apart? What is so special about that? How can you make the end result matter to the rest of us? If you are John Updike writing *Rabbit, Run* (1960), you do it by reaching deep into your protagonist's life to grasp hold of that which makes him emblematic of us all. Harry "Rabbit" Angstrom is a quintessential man of his times, the 1950s. He buys into the American Dream only to have it betray him. So thorough and compelling is Updike's examination of this betrayal that hundreds of books, papers, essays and reviews have explored his themes, not the least of which are the roles of adultery and religion in American life. Updike does not think small.

Of course, exposing the American Dream has long been the sport of novelists: F. Scott Fitzgerald's *The Great Gatsby*; Theodore Dreiser's *An American Tragedy*; Irwin Shaw's *Rich Man, Poor Man*; Jane Smiley's *A Thousand Acres* and Steven Millhauser's *Martin Dressler* are a few examples that come to mind. What makes them different from other treatments of American disaffection?

It is two things:

First, these authors detail their protagonists' worlds—a family farm, a business empire, high society—with such thoroughness that they come to represent all of America. Pause on that point: Do you see the irony? For a setting to feel broadly representative, it must be highly specific. You would think generic settings would be the most universally appealing since anyone ought to be able to project himself into them. That is not so. As we saw in the last chapter, one of the qualities of a highly memorable novel is that it takes us *somewhere else*. That somewhere else may be here and now, but the breakout novel nevertheless creates its own complete, detailed, logical and unique world. Here and now, yes, but here and now as seen by the author.

Second, these authors grant their protagonists the American Dream. Thanks to bootlegging, Jay Gatsby has grown rich. Shaw's and Millhauser's heroes build business empires. The three Cook daughters in Smiley's novel are given the family's one-thousand-acre farm. There are no half measures here. The protagonists go all the way to the top. They get everything they want (that *we* want) and more. Because they fly so high, their fall is also correspondingly low. It is their steep climbs and sharp drops that make these novels so resonant.

To put it another way, these authors are able to tackle the American Dream because they set their personal stakes at such a high level that they become public property. The characters' fortunes—that is, what they have to lose—are of such magnitude that they stand in for all our fortunes. Setting high public stakes, then, can be more than just making a looming disaster seem convincing or testing a protagonist's principles. It can reach down into the heart of us. By risking what we most desire, a novelist can show us who we are.

And just who are we? What constitutes our collective self? The answer to that question can be found by looking inside. What matters to *you*? What gift, treasure or right would it most devastate you to lose? What disaster would leave you feeling the most bereft, insecure, alone, shaken, fearful and lost?

Can you say? Good. Build your novel around that disaster. Play for personal stakes so high that they become public stakes.

Public Stakes Past and Present

One final point: Public stakes change with the times. Once, preserving American freedom was our nation's highest goal. Today, with our public institutions held in low esteem, the public good is perceived differently. Personal liberty and family bonds are many people's most precious possessions. Is it surprising, then, that our top thrillers today are set in police stations and courtrooms? I think not. The realms of politics, international security and espionage simply do not matter as much to most of us as they once did.

To take another example, in the world of women's fiction Judith Krantz ruled the best-seller lists of the 1980s with glitzy fantasies that set female protagonists squarely in positions of wealth and power. Nowadays women do not feel as empowered.

The have-it-all lifestyle has become overwhelming. The gains won by the feminist movement today can seem somewhat hollow.

So who now is on top of the best-seller lists? Mary Higgins Clark. Her portrayals of women as prey (though not, it must be said, as helpless victims) clearly strike women readers as resonant. Clark has caught the mood of our times.

Romance novels and mysteries have had many distinct periods. Historical novels frequently reflect their own times more accurately than the past. Even science fiction has fashions: The Age of Wonder, Dystopian Science Fiction, the New Wave, Cyberpunk . . . such trends are markers of their times. In our own computer- and technology-driven era, science fiction has, interestingly, lost ground to fantasy. It is an odd reversal in some ways, but, if you think about it, with its magical thinking and hierarchical societies, fantasy fiction gives readers a safe haven from their fast-changing and insecure workaday world.

How can you catch the mood of our times? How can you be sure your breakout novel will speak to contemporary readers? By being awake to life as it is around us. By living in our times. That might seem to contradict the breakout imperative to make one's fictional world a place apart. Indeed, to historical novelists my advice may sound ridiculous.

I do not think it is. Writing the breakout novel demands a commitment to life. How can you engage readers in your fictional world if you, the author, are not engaged by your own world? To write about life, you must live it. You cannot make readers cry or feel joy until you have wept and exulted yourself.

Plot problems and the yearnings of your characters do not come from nowhere; they come from you. Whether your story is set deep in the past or far in the future, that is also true of your story's stakes. If they matter to you, they will matter to your readers. Take your stakes from life, and they will resonate like a temple gong. The public stakes in the breakout novel are born of what exists around us: Our society's tragedies and triumphs, our world's pains and promises.

Use them. They are the stuff of life, and of breakout fiction.

Personal Stakes

Near the beginning of this chapter, I mentioned a devastating question that can be posed about any novel: So what? If you have an answer for that question, you have established your novel's stakes. Now, here's a second, and tougher, question: If your stakes are X or Y or Z . . . *why should I care?* This one, too, can reduce most beginning novelists to a choked sputter.

Fortunately, there is help.

Let us take a closer look at the personal stakes of any novel's protagonist. It is easy to create a need, a yearning or a goal that matters to your hero. What is more difficult is to make that need, yearning or goal matter as much to the reader.

Look at it in real life: What matters most in the world to, say, your best friend? Got it? OK, now why does that thing, whatever it is, matter to *you*? It is obvious. Because you love your friend. You have a history together. You empathize.

The wishes, needs and objectives of strangers are, to most of us, of little concern. The same is true in a reader's relationship to a character in a story: That character's stakes will seem strong only to the extent that the character is sympathetic. If the character feels cold, distant or veiled, it is impossible to care. The personal stakes in the story feel low. Reader interest is weak. On the other hand, when characters are strong and appealing, and better still are portrayed warmly and with intimate candor, the stakes feel high and reader interest runs high, as well.

Take the case of the bastard son of a private school nurse. Is there any reason we should care about such a character? Not really. However, in *The World According to Garp* (1978), John Irving's portrait of his protagonist is so warm, compassionate and detailed, we not only care, we care greatly.

What about dolts and idiots? Same thing. By putting their

low characters into situations of high drama and significance, Jerzy Kosinski in *Being There* (1970) and Winston Groom in *Forrest Gump* (1986) make their protagonists' stories matter in a public sense. However, the real reason we care so deeply about Chauncy "Chance" Gardiner and Forrest Gump is that they are highly endearing. Both have in abundance the wisdom of fools.

"Bein an idiot is no box of chocolates," says Forrest Gump in his story's first line, and already we are on his side. Chance Gardiner is illiterate. He compensates for his disability with vague aphorisms that strike the rest of the world as profound and visionary. Chance rises to become a counselor to the powerful and rich, even to the president. It is a satiric rise, meant to look ridiculous, and yet Chance's warm and humble humanity has us cheering for him all the way.

There are other reasons these biographical novels work (discussed in chapter nine), but the high stakes in these stories originate in the extreme warmth and depth of their characterizations.

How can you generate in the reader the same warmth, concern and love you feel for your protagonist? By allowing the reader to know the protagonist as intimately as you do. I mean, you do know your main character, don't you? You know where he went wrong in high school? You know his proudest moment? You know his deepest shame? You know whom he loves more than anyone in the world, and why? Great. Those things are essential to facilitating care in your reader.

That principle works even when characters are offbeat, odd, goofy, misfits, rogues, cheats, cutthroat competitors or bums. The fact is, we cannot help but like people that we know very well, whatever their faults. Understanding leads to sympathy. Sympathy in turn gives power to stakes. That is one reason why a well-written villain will always be sympathetic.

Go back to my second devastating diagnostic question: Why should I care? There is another possible answer that is useful to examine: One cares because the protagonist cares. In other words, to the degree that your main character feels passionately invested in his own life, the reader will feel invested, too.

What is your favorite political issue? You know, the one you can really get worked up about if given half an opportunity? Campaign finance reform? Universal health care? Home schooling? Saving the whales? Abortion? Limiting nuclear arms? Victims' rights? The Confederate flag? Am I pushing any hot buttons? How did this get to be your pet issue? When did you first get fired up about it? Watching the news? Reading the papers? Talking to a friend? It doesn't matter. Somewhere along the line, you found out about it and discovered that you care. But hold on . . . *you first found out about it.* You did not come up with the idea of victims' rights in a vacuum, right? Passionate concern comes from somewhere concrete. Experience comes before advocacy.

Now, personal and life issues: Which relationship has been the most profound, or possibly difficult, for you? Your father? Your first love? Have you struggled with ego or feelings of inadequacy? Do you have a smart mouth that gets you into trouble? (Ah, hidden hostility!) Is there a struggle in your life you cannot seem to get over? With others? With yourself? With God? Uh-huh. I thought so. How did you come to understand that personal issue? Pure introspection? Psychotherapy? An insight given to you by a mentor? Through hard experience, possibly repeated failure? Life has its inner struggles, and the moments when they hit, when they come into sharp focus and sting . . . ah, those slaps, turns and realizations are the defining moments of life, don't you think?

Now back to your novel: What does your protagonist need? What is his goal? For what does he yearn? What must he at all costs avoid? What drives him or freezes him in a state of paralysis? More to the point, how do you, the author, know that? Because your character tells you. Now you tell the reader or, alternately, have someone in the story do it.

Dramatize the inner struggle. Bring its changes home in key moments of high drama. Every protagonist needs a torturous need, a consuming fear, an aching regret, a visible dream, a passionate longing, an inescapable ambition, an exquisite lust, an inner lack, a fatal weakness, an unavoidable obligation, an iron instinct, an irresistible plan, a noble ideal, an undying hope . . . whatever it is that in the end propels him beyond the boundaries that confine the rest of us and brings about fulfilling change.

If establishing personal stakes is a matter of defining what matters to your character, then raising personal stakes can be accomplished by asking of your story, "How can what is happening matter more?" Make that inner whatever-it-is palpable in your prose and active in the action of your story, and you will banish the question, *Why should I care?*

Escalating Stakes

If you have identified the stakes in your story and made them plain to the reader, there is a further technique you can employ in your novel to give it the expansive feel of a breakout book: escalate the stakes. Put more at risk. Much more.

This often means not making the basic danger deeper, that is, worse in the same way. Rather, it means adding different types of danger, those unanticipated extra losses that compound misery. To put it another way, if a gigantic meteor from space is going to wipe out Earth in three days, there is no way to make that imminent calamity worse. Heck, we are all going to die! However, you certainly can make the intervening three days more hellish. War could break out. *What? With only three days of human life left to live?* Sure. Why not?

One sort of novel in which it is common to see stakes fail to escalate is the category romance. In a typical romance, the heroine and hero meet early on. It is obvious from the beginning they are meant to be together, but something about their circumstances or they themselves keep them apart. That's fine as far as it goes, and often that *is* as far as it goes. Unskilled romance writers recycle the main conflict chapter after chapter, deadening its effect with repetition. If you have ever felt impatient with a romance (*Oh, come on! Kiss the guy already!*), then you know what I am talking about.

Skilled romance writers know how to grow the passion between heroine and hero over the course of their stories, to escalate it, or perhaps to restrain it at first so its full power emerges later. That heightened love is, in effect, higher stakes. As the story goes on, there is more to lose.

An essential question to aid the construction of rising stakes is this: How could things get worse? A related question is the following: When would be the worst moment for them to get worse? Escalation of stakes is enhanced by sharp timing.

A final point to consider: How can the stakes become not just a possible loss but one that has palpable, dread-producing immediacy? Here is where the close call, the minidisaster, the preliminary loss can prove useful. It is one thing to warn of danger. It is another to let it take a bite out of the people in your story early on, or perhaps at a later moment as a reminder of just how devastating the ultimate disaster could be.

Achieving that effect demands that you, the author, be willing to make your characters suffer. That can be tough to do, but consider this: Being nice does not engender great drama.

Trials and tests are the stuff of character building, of conflict. Ask yourself, who is the one ally your protagonist cannot afford to lose? Kill that character. What is your protagonist's greatest physical asset? Take it away. What is the one article of faith that for your protagonist is sacred? Undermine it. How much time does your protagonist have to solve his main problem? Shorten it.

Push your characters to the edge, and you will pull your readers close. In short, escalate the stakes and bring them home with a practical demonstration of how they might hurt, and you will add dimensions to your novel that will lift it above the crowd.

Your Own Stakes

Making your reader care is first and foremost a matter of ensuring that you, the author, care. A key question to ask yourself is this: *Why am I writing this novel?* A second necessary question is the following: *If I stopped writing this novel, why would that matter?*

If the answer to that second question is *I won't get published,* or *I will have wasted my time,* or (worst of all) *I will miss my deadline and forfeit my delivery advance,* then you are writing your novel for the wrong reasons. It likely lacks fire. Some essential driving force is missing. Your convictions are weak. Building them up is a matter of building up your beliefs. Some say success as an author requires a big ego; I say that it requires a big heart.

What do you passionately believe about human conduct? How should we live? What are the principles that ought to guide us? What are the tests, trials and tortures that make us better people? What must we understand in order to grow? The moral underpinning of a story is one source of its thematic power, but it does not come from your readers. It comes from you.

Perhaps you are not a moralist but rather are a realist. Maybe you are awed by the ambiguity of it all. Life does not seem to you cut and dried but instead a many-hued experience of joy and pain, deep meaning and high absurdity. If your purpose is to portray life in all its variety, painting the world with the rich textures of an artist's eyes, that is great. Dig deep. Look hard. Show me life the way that it really is. Make it a rich experience, though, or I will not care.

So, why are you writing your current novel? No, really, why? I hope you can say. High stakes ultimately come from your own high commitment, either to moral truth or to truth in the telling of your tale. In writing the breakout novel, it does not matter which purpose motivates you. It matters only that you have a purpose. Without it, your novel has little chance of breaking out. Its stakes will be too low.

BREAKOUT Checklist: Stakes

✓ High stakes yield high success.

✓ Stakes say what could be lost.

✓ To test stakes ask, "So what?"

✓ High stakes start with high human worth.

✓ Making public stakes real means starting with a grain of truth.

✓ Breakout novels combine high public stakes with high personal stakes.

✓ Deep personal stakes dig down so far that they show us who we are.

✓ Public stakes change with the times.

✓ To raise personal stakes ask, "How can this matter more?"

✓ To raise overall stakes ask, "How could things get worse?"

✓ Keep danger immediate. Make your characters suffer.

✓ High stakes come from your own stakes in writing your story.

CHAPTER FOUR

Time and Place

Many novelists seem to think of setting as something outside of their story. It is necessary, but it is a bother. It has to be included, yet ought to be dealt with as efficiently as possible. After all, who wants to read pages and pages of description?

Just as many novelists seem to feel that setting is one of their novel's most important elements. They open their works with establishing passages that set the mood and thereafter catalog the surroundings in every scene.

Which approach works best in the breakout novel?

In my experience there is no advantage in being either pro-setting or anti-setting; however, one is at a distinct disadvantage by feeling indifferent to the time and place in which one's story is set. Relegate setting to the backseat or make it the chassis on which everything else rides, but do not ignore it.

The truth is every story has a context. It is there whether you put it into words or not. Those novelists who eschew description are probably infusing other aspects of their story with a strong sense of time and place: their dialogue, for instance. A novel is a world unto itself. It is not the real world, though it may reflect it, but it is a world that lives and breathes, alternates between day and night, changes and grows, acts upon the characters or is indifferent to them.

In nineteenth century novel writing, it was usual to treat the landscape as a character in the story. In the twenty-first century, we may have less patience for scenery, but we certainly expect a novel to show us the world as a vital force in which the characters move. It may be hostile or seductive, sprawling or confined, gritty or charming, closely observed or wildly improvisational. Whatever the author's approach, we want to live in the world of the story.

Proof of this can be found in the highly popular fields of science fiction and fantasy. Here, scene setting is a high art. Because the worlds of science fiction and fantasy authors can be vastly different from our reality (they would say "reality"), they construct their settings in logical and exhaustive detail.

Their process is called *world building*. Simply put, it is a disciplined method for creating a convincing alternate time and place. The most elementary world building exercise goes like this: Take our history *and change one thing about it*. Now, project the implications for us today in as many ways as possible. Certain things about our life now will be different. The South won the Civil War? Well OK, today we could be driving six-wheeled automobiles. *Huh?* An expert world builder will not only spring surprises but will base them so thoroughly in logical extrapolation that they are utterly convincing.

One of the most dazzling pieces of world building in science fiction literature is William Gibson's 1984 novel *Neuromancer*. This prescient novel not only introduced the world to the term "cyberspace," it projected a near future in which hard-wired information wranglers plug into the web, a virtual reality, as a way of life, even as a way of crime. Sound familiar? In 1984 Gibson's ideas were utterly new; indeed, they were as farsighted, yet as chillingly believable, as George Orwell's Big Brother was upon *1984*'s first publication in 1949.

So logically extrapolated was Gibson's future that when I first read *Neuromancer* I was overwhelmed. I thought, *This is how the future will be.* Then, in 1995 a client of mine, British science fiction author Paul J. McAuley, delivered the manuscript of a novel called *Fairyland*. Later a winner of the Arthur C. Clarke

Award, Britain's "Hugo," McAuley's novel cast me forward to a near future in which bioengineering has radically transformed society. Designer drugs give the club crowd highly specific hallucinations: visions, say, of the Virgin Mary. Sentient humanoid pets called "dolls" have been created. They are harmless . . . that is, until a rogue designer meets a child genius named Milena whose goal is to make the dolls an autonomous race. McAuley's detailed and logical projections come fast and thick. When I read *Fairyland*, I was overwhelmed. I thought, *This is how the future is going to be*. And, of course, it is nothing like Gibson's future.

Science fiction and fantasy fans frequently say one of the chief reasons they enjoy that genre is it takes them to alternate times and places that are utterly convincing. They love the details. But what about the majority of fiction writers, we "mundanes" (in science fiction fan argot) who merely want to set our stories in the world as we know it?

As our colleagues in science fiction and fantasy have shown us, building breakout time and place starts with the principle that the world of the novel is composed of much more than description of landscape and rooms. It is milieu, period, fashion, ideas, human outlook, historical moment, spiritual mood and more. It is capturing not only place but people in an environment; not only history but humans changing in their era. Description is the least of it. Bringing people alive in a place and time that are alive is the essence of it.

Capturing a snapshot of place, moment, character or all three with clarity so vivid that it freezes indelibly in the reader's mind is the particular strength of literary novelists. For example, in Jane Hamilton's 1994 novel *A Map of the World*, her first-person heroine, Alice, begins to lose her bearings when her friend's daughter drowns in a pond. In chapter four, Alice goes with her husband, Howard, to a men's store to buy a suit for the funeral:

> At 6:15 the suit was finished. He paid a terrific sum, carefully writing the figures on Nellie's check, and then

he went into the dressing room to put on his finery. He emerged, silent, looking down, as if he couldn't believe that anything below his neck was still his own body. I stood back marveling at him, at the handyman, who didn't care how he looked, who had little use for daily personal hygiene, and there he was ravishing in his suit. It was only June and his face was tanned to a deep brown. His teeth were blindingly white, dangerous to look at, like an eclipse. It was impossible not to admire him, hard not to want to do something to contain that kind of beauty— drink him, ingest him, sneak into his shirt and hide for the rest of one's natural life. After six years of marriage he had the power to occasionally render me weak in the knees.

Freezing moments with snapshot clarity is valuable but is by itself only the start of creating a fictional world. Highly memorable settings have a palpable reality that is larger than the characters, larger than the story itself. Its boundaries stretch beyond the perimeter of each scene. It lives in the reader's mind after the plot is forgotten.

How does one establish a setting with such an expansive, living feel? How can you get some of that feeling into your own novel? Let us examine some of the techniques involved.

The Psychology of Place

Have you ever said to yourself, "This place gives me the creeps?"

If so, you have experienced the psychological influence of inert physical surroundings. We are affected by what is around us. Architecture, the art of enclosing spaces, is founded upon that fact. So is scenic design on stage and in film. Interior design has a vocabulary, rules and schools of thought. Why shouldn't novels use place as deliberately?

If written well, they do. What is less well understood is how they do it. The most common technique authors report using is making place a character in the story. But what does that mean? Reappearances? Changing moods? A story arc of its own?

Well certainly not that, but without a doubt a good setting has an impact upon the characters. If you have ever stood in a room designed by Frank Lloyd Wright, you know his interiors make you relax. The high-vaulting arches of Notre-Dame can lift you to a spiritual plane. A simple Shaker meeting room does both things simultaneously. It is inner peace and fervent piety captured in four walls.

How does your setting make people feel? That is the key, not how a place looks but its psychological effect on the characters in your novel.

Anne Rivers Siddons is good at evoking the world of the tidewater Carolinas. In her 1997 novel *Up Island*, however, she brings her heroine Molly Bell Redwine north to Martha's Vineyard to repair herself after a marital breakup. At the end of the summer season, Molly rents a small cottage on a remote up-island pond. The conjunction of house, landscape and shattered spirit is deftly detailed at the beginning of chapter seven:

> The house stood in full sun on the slope of the ridge that seemed to sweep directly up into the steel-blue sky. Below it, the lane I had just driven on wound through low, dense woodlands, where the Jeep had plunged in and out of dark shade. But up here there was nothing around the house except a sparse stand of wind-stunted oaks, several near-to-collapsing outbuildings, and two or three huge, freestanding boulders left, I knew, by the receding glacier that had formed this island. Above the house, the ridge beetled like a furrowed brow, matted with low-growing blueberry and huckleberry bushes. At the very top, no trees grew at all. I looked back down and caught my breath at the panorama of Chilmark Pond and the Atlantic Ocean. It was a day of strange, erratic winds and running cloud shadow, and the patch-

work vista below me seemed alive, pulsing with shadow and sun, trees and ocean moving restlessly in the wind. Somehow it disquieted me so that I had to turn and face the closed door of the big, old house. I had come here seeking the shelter of the up-island wood, but this tall, blind house, alone in its ocean of space and dazzle of hard, shifting light, offered me no place to hide.

It is the details, the nouns and verbs rather than any adjectives or adverbs, that visually fix the scene. But the power of this passage results from more than the objects that it describes. Molly is uniquely affected by the light and landscape around her. Another character might have seen it as bright and refreshing. Molly in her grief experiences it as harsh and comfortless.

You can deepen the psychology of place in your story by returning to a previously established setting and showing how your character's perception of it has changed. As a student I lived, wrote and starved (well, not literally) in London. I loved it beyond measure. To me it was all that was sophisticated, historic, romantic, artistic and free. It was the antithesis of where I was from, the suburbs. (Oh, you guessed that?) Some years later I went back on business. I was no longer starving. I had credit cards. I took taxis whenever I pleased. I was flush with a feeling of success. I had grown up, built a business and made a name for myself. I had appointments. People bought me meals I could never in the old days have imagined eating. I had made it.

For all the feelings of accomplishment that I had, however, for me London had changed. It remains a great city, but it was nevertheless just another city. I knew, for instance, the ins and outs of the publishing business I had come to discuss. I saw through its artifice, recognized its false promises and hidden problems. My old neighborhood had gentrified. In many ways it was not unlike the area from which I had come, New York's highly yuppified Upper West Side.

Had London itself changed? Somewhat, but in many ways

not at all. *I* had changed far more. The difference was inside, in the person observing the place. I would like to suggest that a useful principle for making place an active character is to give your characters an active relationship to place; which in turn means marking your characters' growth (or decline) through their relationships to their various surroundings.

That is not as easy as it may sound. It is an effort to chronicle that changing dynamic. Places do not speak dialogue. They do not take action. (Not too often, anyway.) To characterize them you must force a pause; or rather, go inside your characters and allow them a moment to discover their feelings about the place into which you have delivered them.

That in turn demands that you be writing in a strong point of view, regardless of whether your novel is first or third person. Place presented from an objective or omniscient point of view runs the risk of feeling like boring description. It can be a lump, an impediment to the flow of the narrative.

Point-of-view description, on the other hand, is essential to the narrative because it is integral to character, or, better still, a marker of character development. Do you have plain vanilla description in your current manuscript? Try evoking the description the way it is experienced by a character. Feel a difference? So will your readers.

Keeping Up With the Times

As important in a story as a sense of place is a sense of time, both the exact historical moment and the passing hours, days, years, decades, centuries or even millennia (if you are James A. Michener).

One of the appealing aspects of historical settings is not only discovering the charm or grittiness of a past era but finding that folks back then felt pretty much as we do now, even to the point of longing for their own "good old days." In contemporary stories of breakout caliber, a sense of the historical moment is also captured. What makes our time—this very moment in history—similar to or different from any other?

As I am sure you can anticipate, the answer once again lies in your characters' perceptions of these things. Our greatest contemporary satirist Tom Wolfe is a master of capturing our times. His 1998 novel *A Man in Full* is a dead-on accurate depiction of the South of the 1990s, Atlanta in particular. All the social aspirations and insecurities of its denizens are pinned, wriggling, to the novel's hilarious pages. His portrait of our era and its follies, though, does not have a dry, documentary quality. Its dynamic colors are delivered through strong points of view.

Early in *A Man in Full*, an upper middle-class black lawyer, Roger Too White, is on his way to an appointment when he finds himself stuck in a Spring Break traffic snarl. Gridlock sets in. Out of the passenger-side window of a Camaro in front of him slithers a young black woman who begins to dance in the street to a rap song thundering from the Camaro's stereo:

RAM YO' BOOTY! RAM YO' BOOTY!

* * *

The girl swung her hips in an exaggerated arc each time the fiends hit the *BOO* of *BOOTY*. She was gorgeous. Her jeans were down so low on her hips, and her tube top was up so high on her chest, he could see lots of her lovely light-caramel-colored flesh, punctuated by her belly button, which looked like an eager little eye. Her skin was the same light color as his, and he knew her type at a glance. Despite her funky clothes, she was a blueblood. She had Black Deb written all over her. Her parents were no doubt the classic Black Professional Couple of the 1990s, in Charlotte or Raleigh or Washington or Baltimore. Look at the gold bangles on her wrists; must have cost hundreds of dollars. Look at the soft waves in her relaxed hair, a 'do known as a *Bout en Train*; French, baby, for "life of the party"; cost a fortune; his own wife had the same thing done to her hair. Little cutie, shaking her booty, probably went to Howard or maybe Chapel Hill or the University of Virginia; belonged to Theta Psi. Oh, these black boys and girls came to Atlanta from colleges all over the place for Freaknic every April, at spring break, thousands of them, and there they were on Piedmont Avenue, in the heart of the northern third of Atlanta, the white third, flooding the streets, the parks, the malls, taking over Midtown and Downtown and the commercial strips of Buckhead, tying up traffic, even on Highways 75 and 85, baying at the moon, which turns chocolate during Freaknic, freaking out White Atlanta, scaring them indoors, where they cower for three days, giving them a snootful of the future.

* * *

—and then he took a look at his watch. Oh shit! It was 7:05, and he had to be at an address on Habersham Road in Buckhead, some street he had never laid eyes on, by 7:30.

* * *

. . . he couldn't stand the thought of being late for appointments—especially where important white people were concerned.

Wolfe is not afraid to spend an unusual number of words precisely detailing the fine degrees of distinction in black society; even between black generations. This is possible because such gradations matter to Roger Too White. His point of view demands that measurements be taken, and Wolfe takes them.

As with marking changing perceptions of place, it is also useful to chronicle characters' changing perceptions of their times.

M.M. Kaye's grand romantic epic of British Colonial India, *The Far Pavilions* (1978), is suffused throughout with details of the political and social shifts underway in that time and place. The novel tells the story of Ash, an English army officer raised as a Hindu, and of the Indian princess he loves, Anjuli, who eventually is married off to a wealthy Rana. When the Rana dies, Ash saves Juli from *suttee* (the immolation of living wives with their dead husbands) and proposes to marry her. They argue over this possibility. Even 659 pages deep into the novel, this minor moment is enriched with details that convey a sense of changing times:

> "They will never permit you to marry me," said Anjuli with tired conviction.
>
> "The Bhithoris? They won't dare open their mouths!"
>
> "No, your people; and mine also, who will be of the same mind."
>
> "You mean they will try to prevent it. But it's no business of theirs. This is our affair: yours and mine. Besides, didn't your own grandfather marry a princess of Hind, though he was a foreigner and not of her faith?"
>
> Anjuli sighed and shook her head again. "True. But that was in the days before your Raj had come to its full power. There was still a Mogul on the throne in Delhi and Ranjit-Singh held sway over the Punjab; and my grandfather was a great war-lord who took my grandmother as the spoils of war without asking any man's leave, having defeated the army of my grandmother's father in battle. I have been told that she went willingly, for they loved each other greatly. But the times have changed and that could not happen now."

This is not a historical romance bashed out in six months to meet a deadline. This is not a conversation happening between contemporary Americans dressed in saris. Kaye is intimate with the details of the Raj era and lavishes them on her splendid novel. So fine is her sense of that time and place, Kaye is able to vividly locate her characters in a particular moment in the long sweep of Indian history.

Her evocation of the changing times gives *The Far Pavilions* the expansiveness of setting that is so essential to breaking out. The vast sweep of history does not belong in every novel, but some sense of the times belongs in yours.

Your characters live in an era, but which one? And in what stage of its life? Find the moments in the story that delineate that distinction, detail them from a prevailing point of view, and you will be on your way to enhancing your novel with a sense of the times.

Working With Historical Forces and Social Trends

A breakout setting is even more than the psychology of physical surroundings and a sense of the times. Setting can also be social context. Social trends and political ideas influence our real actions and thinking, so why not those in our novels, too?

Conveying a sense of the larger human civilization around your story can help to enlarge it toward breakout level, but that technique is fraught with peril, as well. It is far too easy to slip into textbook mode. I am also rudely pushed out of the flow of a narrative when novelists drop gratuitous snippets of the outside world into their scenes: newspaper headlines, television or radio news in the background, sightings of movie marquees, pop tunes playing too obviously or, worst of all, famous historical figures who appear in the story for reasons that are slight or contrived.

On the other hand, I also find myself uninvolved in novels with historical settings in which there is too little sense of the period. Hairstyles, hemlines, product names, car models, slang, song styles and the like all can feel gratuitous, but made necessary in a strong point of view, they are clues and markers to their times. More convincing for me, and harder to convey, are historically contemporaneous attitudes.

Anne Perry's novel *Slaves of Obsession*, published in the fall of 2000, is an 1860s mystery featuring moody "agent of inquiry" William Monk and his wife, nurse Hester Latterly. In the novel's opening, conversation at a dinner party turns to the American Civil War, then just a few months old. A Union idealist, Breeland, wants the dinner's host, a British arms merchant named Alberton, to go back on his promise to sell a large quantity of state-of-the-art rifles to the South. Breeland's rigid morality is grating, but it has won over Alberton's passionately idealistic daughter, sixteen-year-old Merrit. It would be easy for Perry to give Monk and Hester moral positions (North good, South bad) that are familiar and comfortable to modern readers, but she does not:

> "But this is different!" Merrit's voice rose urgently. She leaned forward a little over the exquisite china and silver, the light from the chandeliers gleaming on her pale shoulders. "This is true nobility and sacrifice for a great ideal. It is a struggle to preserve those liberties for which America was founded. If you really understood it all, Mrs. Monk, you would be as passionate in its defense as the Union supporters are . . . unless, of course, you believe in slavery?"
>
> "No, I don't believe in slavery!" Hester said fiercely. She looked neither to the right nor left to see what other people's feelings might be. "I find the whole idea abhorrent."
>
> Merrit relaxed and her face flooded with a beautiful smile. An instant warmth radiated from her. "Then you will understand completely. Don't you agree we should do all we can to help such a cause, when other men are willing to give their lives?" Again her eyes flickered momen-

tarily to Breeland, but he seemed barely aware of it. Perhaps it was modesty which restrained him.

Hester was more guarded. "I certainly agree we should fight against slavery, but I am not sure that this is the way to do it. I confess, I don't know sufficient about the issue to make a judgement."

Hester, who nursed on the battlefield of the Crimean War with Florence Nightingale, knows the horrors of war all too well, a memory which, for her, overrides all other considerations. Later, the story takes Monk and Hester to America in pursuit of Merrit, who was either abducted from, or fled, London on the night of her father's murder and the theft of the guns, which Alberton had sold to the South but which have been diverted to the Union. Upon their arrival, Hester observes New York:

Hester was fascinated. It was unlike any city she had previously seen: raw, teeming with life, a multitude of tongues spoken, laughter, shouting, and already the hand of war shadowing over it, a brittleness in the air. There were recruitment posters on the walls and soldiers in a wild array of uniforms in the streets.

Business seemed poor and the snatches of talk she overheard were of prize fights, food prices, local gossip and scandal, politics, and secession. She was startled to hear suggestion that even New York itself might secede from the Union, or New Jersey.

There is also debate about whether the South has the right to secede and whether the North has the right to impose union. Later, in Washington, Monk and Hester meet up with an arms procurer for the South, Philo Trace, who wishes to help them find Merrit and Breeland. Trace's views on Northerners are those of a practical Southerner:

"Most of them have never even seen a plantation, let alone thought about how it worked. I haven't seen many myself." He gave a harsh little laugh, jerky, as if he had caught his breath. "Most of us in the south are small farmers, working our own land. You can go for dozens of miles and that's all you'll see. But it's the cotton and the tobacco that we live on. That's what we sell to the north and it's what they work in the factories and ship abroad."

He stopped suddenly, lowering his head and pushing his hand across his brow, forcing his hair back so hard it must have hurt. "I don't really know what this war is all about, why we have to be at each other's throats. Why can't they just leave us alone? Of course there are bad slave owners, men who beat their field slaves, and their house slaves, and nothing happens to them even if they kill them! But there's poverty in the north as well, and nobody fights about that! Some of the industrial cities are full of starving, shivering men and women—and children—with nobody to take them in or feed them. No one gives a damn! At least a plantation owner cares for his slaves, for economic reasons if not common decency."

By eschewing modern morality in her characterizations, Perry makes her people live with a realism that enlarges her fiction.

Another breakout novelist who captures period attitudes effectively in her work is Rebecca Wells. Her 1996 novel *Divine Secrets of the Ya-Ya Sisterhood* portrays the friendship of four women in the South in the mid-twentieth century. One of the novel's most vivid sequences is a trip three of the four friends take to Atlanta in 1939 to attend the world premier of the movie *Gone With the Wind*. The events are reported to the absent friend in letters:

Girl, there were already people on the streets of Atlanta out walking around in their Civil War finery and antebellum dresses! We had on the car radio and they were reporting everything like it was FDR himself coming to town. A whole bunch of stars were arriving at the train station, including Claudette Colbert, but we missed a lot of news because at 10:15 we were at the corner of White-hall and Alabama streets for the big lamp-lighting cere-mony. I never knew it before but that very lamppost man-aged to remain standing after Sherman's siege of Atlanta. And that very lamppost was relit to show that the Confed-erate spirit has not died. The three of us just cried and cried, thinking about the Confederacy. And then the Governor gave everyone the rest of the day off because Premier Day had been declared a state holiday.

Notice how deftly Wells deploys clues to the times such as FDR and Claudette Colbert. Those references do not feel gratu-itous because they are used by the letter writer, Viviane Walker, to convey a sense of the excitement of the day. Less deftly han-dled is the kindling of a Confederate heritage in these three girls of the "New South" of the mid-twentieth century; still, the sweep of social history registers and enriches the texture of the novel. Wells is not afraid to detail it.

Whatever the scope of your novel, it will benefit from a depiction of the social context in which it takes place. Your characters live in society, but in which strata? At what point is their social position most keenly felt? At what moment does it change? Does your heroine's status rise or fall? How can she tell? Are your cast of characters aware of the way in which society is evolving? No? Well, why not? A wide-angle view of the civiliza-tion around your story will magnify the story in exciting ways.

God at Work in the World

Fate or chance? Choice or predestination? What range of free-dom do you feel your characters have? Do they control their own destinies, or are their actions in part futile? Do unexpected events overtake them, or do they act according to a plan? You may not think of God as part of the setting of your novel, but the actions of the universe, if any, upon your characters are an important consideration in the novel's construction.

Whatever your religion, there is a shared sense that the universe is larger than us, wouldn't you agree? Do you not feel it on dark, clear winter nights when you stare at the array of stars in the Milky Way? Have you felt the flash of understanding that death is real, perhaps after just narrowly missing a fatal accident? Have you ever been moved to tears by the self-sacrifice of a genuine heroine? Does the love of your spouse sometimes reduce you to humble gratitude?

If you have experienced any of those feelings then you know what it is to be lifted out of yourself for a moment. To understand one's place in the universe is to feel small. Paradoxically, it is also to feel free and unburdened. We come away from those moments larger, unlocked, more capable of change, perhaps even resolved to take charge of our own destinies.

Where do such moments fit in a breakout novel? How are they part of the setting?

I would like to suggest if you do not have a moment of unexpected tragedy or grace in your novel, you consider where you might put it in. Shatter your protagonist with a tragedy, or give her an unexpected gift. These things happen in real life, and in a novel they lend an enlarged perspective, a sense that the universe is paying attention.

To put it another way, if God is at work in the world of your novel, then you have a chance at giving your readers an experience that is humbling, joyful and maybe even transforming. Is that not some of the effect you want your novel to have? Certainly it is a key characteristic of breakout novels.

How to weave a sense of destiny at work into the setting of your story? There are many ways to do that. The surrounding context of the novel's plot may provide an opportunity. Look for places, people and situations that are larger than your characters. Is the couple in your romance novel going to break up?

Where? In a car? OK, then why not place that car at a rise in a highway with a mile-long traffic jam stretching in both directions? Not only is the metaphor of being stuck now made visible, but you also have available to you a dramatic exit for one of your protagonists.

Are any of the scenes in your current novel set in a kitchen? Aha! Caught you! Kitchens, living rooms, offices and other commonplace settings are familiar and easy, but what resonance do they have? Usually very little. Think canyons, sports stadiums, airports, squad cars, life rafts, recovery rooms, whatever. Settings that are emptier or more crowded than usual, or that have change or inherent drama built into them can envelop your scenes with the unfolding of other destinies.

God works in little ways as well as big ones, so look for small moments of magic as well as large ones. Have you ever felt that something that happened to you was fated? Your first meeting with your future spouse, for instance? Many people share that experience. Paths intersect in ways that are not accidents. Small coincidences lead to large changes. People repeat those special stories for years, have you noticed?

Little miracles become our personal myths. What are the little miracles that bring your characters to their moments of grand destiny? Find them. Mark them. Revisit them in retrospect, and the hand of God will show in your story.

The Secret Ingredient

The great novelists of the past and the breakout novelists of today employ many approaches to setting, but all have one element in common: detail. A setting cannot live unless it is observed in its pieces and particulars. A place is the sum of its parts. The emotions that it evokes are most effective when they are specific, better still, when they are unique.

One of the great achievements in descriptiveness of recent decades can be found in the German novel *Perfume* (1987) by Patrick Süskind (stylishly translated into English by John E.

Woods). *Perfume* concerns an abominable perfumer's apprentice whose twisted pleasure is using the methods of his craft to capture the scent of young virgins at the moments of their deaths. He is a serial killer motivated by scent. The novel is set in eighteenth century France. All its description is olfactory. No sights, sounds, touch or taste are presented. Here is Süskind's opening description of this world:

> In the period of which we speak, there reigned in the cities a stench barely conceivable to us modern men and women. The streets stank of manure, the courtyards of urine, the stairwells stank of moldering wood and rat droppings, the kitchens of spoiled cabbage and mutton fat; the unaired parlors stank of stale dust, the bedrooms of greasy sheets, damp featherbeds, and the pungently sweet aroma of chamber pots. The stench of sulfur rose from the chimneys, the stench of caustic lyes from the tanneries, and from the slaughterhouses came the stench of congealed blood. People stank of sweat and unwashed clothes; from their mouths came the stench of rotting teeth, from their bellies that of onions, and from their bodies, if they were no longer very young, came the stench of rancid cheese and sour milk and tumorous disease. The rivers stank, the marketplaces stank, the churches stank, it stank beneath the bridges and in the palaces. . . . And of course the stench was foulest in Paris, for Paris was the largest city of France.

Phew! Some readers experience a heightened olfactory faculty while reading Süskind's novel. I did. My sense of smell is poor, but by the time I finished *Perfume*, I was smelling as keenly as a winegrower.

Notice how Süskind achieves this effect: with details. Manure, urine, cabbage, mutton fat, featherbeds, sulfur, lyes, unwashed clothes, rotting teeth, rancid cheese, sour milk . . . not once does he try to explain what those things smell *like*. Instead, he catalogs those awful odors, allowing his readers' memories to call up the necessary associations. It works, since unfortunately most of us can conjure many of those smells in our minds. If you have ever inhaled in a horse barn, I think you know what I am talking about.

Details can also convey a character's feelings about place. George R.R. Martin's 1982 novel *Fevre Dream* is not written in the first person, but nevertheless by writing from a strong point of view, Martin is able to let us know exactly how his characters feel. *Fevre Dream* is about steamboat captain Abner Marsh, who in 1857 dreams of setting a record for the journey down the Mississippi River to New Orleans. An icy winter has ruined his dilapidated fleet, but then a well-heeled stranger offers to build him his dream boat. Here is Marsh's first view of the finished vessel in a boatyard:

> The mists gave way for them, and there she stood, high and proud, dwarfing all the other boats around her. Her cabins and rails gleamed with fresh paint pale as snow, bright even in the gray shroud of fog. Way up on her texas roof, halfway to the stars, her pilot house seemed to glitter; a glass temple, its ornate cupola decorated all around with fancy woodwork as intricate as Irish lace. Her chimneys, twin pillars that stood just forward of the texas deck, rose up a hundred feet, black and straight and haughty. Their feathered tops bloomed like two dark metal flowers. Her hull was slender and seemed to go on forever, with her stern obscured by the fog. Like all the first-class boats, she was a side-wheeler. Set amidship, the huge curved wheelhouses loomed gigantic, hinting at the vast power of the paddle wheels concealed within them. They seemed all the larger for want of the name that would soon be emblazoned across them.

Notice how skillfully Martin uses his detailing to suggest the pride that Marsh feels in his new steamboat: *. . . gleamed . . . bright . . . fresh . . . halfway to the stars . . . seemed to glitter . . . a glass temple . . . black and straight and haughty . . . like all the first-class boats.* As it happens, Marsh's dream of setting a record on the Mississippi is thwarted by his new boat's owner, a vampire whose need is not to go fast but to drift slowly downstream in search of . . . well, you should read Martin's moody, atmospheric and entertaining novel, and find out for yourself.

Marshalling detail and learning the art of writing in nouns and verbs are essential to success in any type of writing. That is especially true in the breakout novel. An expansive setting is not vague. It is highly particular. But while a breakout setting is closely observed, it also has a wide focus.

The breakout novelist does not merely set a scene; she unveils a unique place, one resonant with a sense of time, woven through with social threads and full of the destinies the universe has in store for us all. She does not merely describe a setting, she builds a world. She then sets her characters free in that world to experience all it has to offer.

BREAKOUT Checklist: Time and Place

✓ Every story has a context, whether it is emphasized or not.

✓ Creating breakout time and place involves more than just describing setting.

✓ Using psychology of place means capturing how a place makes a point-of-view character feel.

✓ Convey a sense of the times.

✓ Portray historical forces and social trends through characters.

✓ Unexpected tragedy or grace adds a sense of destiny at work.

✓ Detail is the secret ingredient of breakout settings.

CHAPTER FIVE

Characters

What do folks remember most about a novel? I have asked this question many times, of all different kinds of people. Your answer is probably the same as that of most readers: the characters. Great characters are the key to great fiction. A high-octane plot is nothing without credible, larger-than-life, highly developed en-actors to make it meaningful.

Agents, editors and novelists alike often speak of character-driven stories. What do they mean by that term? Some are referring to stories in which the main events and narrative thrust are not generated by outside forces but by the inner drives of the main characters. To my way of thinking, though, all stories are character driven. Hot plot devices may propel a protagonist into action, even danger, but how involving is that when the action taken is what anybody would do?

Indeed, it is a common fault of beginning thriller writers to slam an Everyman, your average Joe, into the middle of something big and terrible. Such stories usually feel lackluster because the main character is lackluster. A plot is just a plot. It is the actions of a person that make it memorable or not. Great characters rise to the challenge of great events.

Real People vs. Larger-Than-Life Figures

When people in real life are colorful, outrageous, heroic, highly accomplished, great wits or otherwise memorable, they are said to be "like a character in a novel." When a fictional character exhibits qualities that are out of the ordinary, we say they are "larger-than-life."

Is it any wonder that as readers we are drawn to larger-than-life characters? The greatest characters in our literature are all larger-than-life. But how to construct them? Do you even want to? The whole concept can become a perplexing difficulty if a character with whom you are working is based upon an actual person, or if your purpose is to show your readers that people are the way you observe them to be.

There is nothing wrong with either intention, and in fact I believe it is possible to fashion breakout novels from the stuff of actual human experience. It just requires identifying what is extraordinary in people who are otherwise ordinary.

I am dismayed that some fiction writers bristle when I make that observation. It is as if deliberately constructing a character is a sin. Some authors feel that if characters are to be credible, then they must be exactly like real people. Others report their characters take on a life of their own: "They tell me what they are going to do! I just write it down!"

There is nothing wrong with these techniques, except that a naturalistic and *laissez-faire* approach may lead too easily to characters who are humdrum, inactive or uninteresting to read about. Even when they are based in part upon real people, characters always are reflections of the author's subconscious mind. And the mind can play tricks on the best of us.

For instance, authors who have hit a midcareer crisis are prone to create characters that are dark, depressed, unpleasant—sometimes even repellent. Usually, when I point out the drawbacks of such characters, the authors at first are indignant. "That is what I was going for," they say. "These are the best characters I have ever written! Believe me, there really are people like this out there!"

I am sure. But does anyone really want to read about them? Authors in crisis believe so. They write characters who they feel will win back for them the respect they lost. To bolster their positions, they point to artistic successes like Judith Guest's best-selling *Ordinary People* (1976) or Carolyn Chute's *The Beans of Egypt, Maine* (1985), a harshly detailed picture of rural poverty.

As we shall see later in this chapter, the Jarrett family in Guest's novel may seem ordinary, but their actions are not. The mean-spirited, white trash Beans in Chute's novel are anything but attractive, I will admit. So why did that novel break out?

Chute's characters *are* compelling, but the resistant author generally has not fully worked out how Chute accomplishes that feat. It certainly is not by making her people ugly inside and out. That cannot work. Most of us do not for very long tolerate people who make us feel frustrated, sad, hopeless or depressed—not in life, not in books. Chute does not try to change our feelings. She is subtle, but as we shall presently see, it does not fly against reader psychology.

Whatever your intentions, whatever the type of people whom you are drawn to write about, certain facts are fundamental to breaking out: The characters in your story will not engross readers unless they are out of the ordinary. How can it be otherwise? In life, ordinary folk do ordinary things every day. How much of that do we remember? Precious little.

In life and in fiction, when people act in ways that are unusual, unexpected, dramatic, decisive, full of consequence and are irreversible, we remember them and talk about them for years. Seemingly ordinary characters can stay with us, too, but usually only when their actions are "out of character."

What Makes a Character Larger-Than-Life?

What does it mean for a character to be larger-than-life? What qualities are we really talking about? Let us dig in and try to get a handle on the stuff of greatness.

Strength

If you look closely, I think you cannot avoid the recognition that what makes breakout characters broadly appealing is not their weaknesses but their strengths, not their defeats but their triumphs. Fiction is not life. It needs to reflect life if it is to be believable, but virtually all readers unconsciously seek out novels for an experience of human life that is admirable, amusing, hopeful, perseverant, positive, inspiring and that ultimately makes us feel whole.

OK, so what *does* "strength" mean to you? Cunning? Stamina? Insight? Intuition? Wisdom? Compassion? Courtesy? Discipline? Self-denial? Courage? Outspokenness? Cultural pride? Leadership? Knowledge? Open-mindedness? Reverence? Humor? Mercy? Hope? Evenhandedness? Thrift? Gambling for a good cause? Perseverance? Humility? Trust? Loyalty? Need I go on?

Even a plainly drawn, one-dimensional protagonist can grip the popular imagination if he is a character of strength. James Patterson's Washington, DC psychologist turned homicide detective Alex Cross is no one's idea of a character who is subtle, complex, ambiguous or deeply developed. He is a plain old hero: straightforward, honest, dedicated, hardworking and sensitive. He is portrayed with bold, simple strokes. At the beginning of Patterson's 1992 best-seller *Along Came a Spider*, Alex is in the kitchen of his home grabbing a quick bite of breakfast (served up by his rock-solid grandmother, Nana Mama) before rushing to a murder scene:

> "There's been another bad murder over in Langley Terrace. It looks like a thrill killer. I'm afraid that it is," I told her.
>
> "That's too bad," Nana Mama said to me. Her soft brown eyes grabbed mine and held. Her white hair looked like one of the doilies she puts on all our living room chairs. "That's such a bad part of what the politicians have let become a deplorable city. Sometimes I think we ought to move out of Washington, Alex."
>
> "Sometimes I think the same thing," I said, "but we'll probably tough it out."

"Yes, black people always do. We persevere. We always suffer in silence."

"Not always in silence," I said to her.

Did I mention Alex Cross is black? Cross knows what that costs but does not let it burden him. His priorities are in the right place. The murder turns out to be the mutilation and homicide of a woman and her fourteen-year-old daughter, both of whom worked as prostitutes. Also murdered is the woman's young son. This killing of an innocent is what gets to Alex. When he is yanked from that case to work on the abduction of two rich kids from a private school, Alex angrily confronts his boss, Chief of Detectives Pittman:

> "Cross, you just listen to what I have to say," he said as he came over to us. "There's been a kidnapping at this school. It's a major kidnapping—"
>
> "That's a real bad thing," I butted in immediately. "Unfortunately, a killer has also struck Condon Terrace and Langley neighborhoods. The killer's hit two times already. Six people are *dead* so far. Sampson [Cross's partner] and I are the senior people on that case. Basically, we're *it*."
>
> "I'm apprised of the situation in the Condon and Langley projects. I've already made contingencies. It's taken care of," Pittman said.
>
> "Two black women had their breasts sliced off this morning. Their pubic hair was shaved while they were tied up in bed. Were you apprised of that?" I asked him. "A three-year-old boy was murdered, in his pajamas." I was shouting again. I glanced at Sampson and saw him shaking his head.

Patterson's writing is not artful. If his novels offered us only their twisty plots, I am not sure they would hold us. Alex Cross, though, has moral conviction. His determination to do right is a strength that gives Patterson's novels a powerful appeal. Again and again they jump to the top of the best-seller lists. Some authors imagine that Patterson has been "made" by his publishers. Not so. No author can ride atop the lists for so many years without appealing to the public. What has "made" Patterson is Alex Cross.

Think about it: We read fiction not just to see ourselves but also to imagine ourselves as we might be. When we recognize ourselves in the characters of a novel, we are gratified. We identify with them. But that is just the beginning. If self-recognition was all we wanted from fiction, we would be as satisfied with letters, journals and statistical surveys of the population at large. But we are not satisfied with those things.

We crave stories, particularly the intensely intimate form of story called the novel. That is because a novel, uniquely among art forms, presents powerful points of view, strong conflicts and a helping of human life that affirms a higher truth. Characters in breakout fiction may seem realistic, even average, but they are bigger than their circumstances. They do not just suffer, but strive. They do not practice patience, but act. They do not merely survive, but endure.

Strength comes in many forms, and its power is evident in many types of novels. Mary Gordon's 1978 novel *Final Payments* was a highly praised literary debut about a young Queens woman, Isabel Moore, who from the ages of nineteen to thirty sacrificed her life in order to nurse her father. That fate would strike most of us as unfortunate, if not unhappy. And it is. Isabel Moore, however, has no regrets. The novel opens with her father's funeral. Isabel describes her sacrifice like this:

> I gave up my life for him; only if you understand my father will you understand that I make that statement not with self-pity but with extreme pride. He had a stroke when I was nineteen; I nursed him until he died eleven

years later. This strikes everyone in our decade as unusual, barbarous, cruel. To me, it was not only inevitable but natural. The Church exists and has endured for this, not only to preserve itself but to keep certain scenes intact: My father and me living by ourselves in a one-family house in Queens. My decision at nineteen to care for my father in his illness. We were rare in our situation but not unique. It could happen again.

Isabel's pride in her devotion anchors us firmly in sympathy with her. When she ventures forth at thirty to invent her life, we are behind her. She enacts for us a rebirth. Through her we are ourselves reborn. Strength in character has that power.

A great character is one that not only deepens our understanding of ourselves but that opens to us ranges of potential, a riot of passionate response to the problems of existence. Grim chronicles of human frailty are the job of sociology or, in literature, the business of minor genres like dialect novels, regional novels and docudramas. If you truly wish to write the breakout novel, commit yourself to characters that are larger-than-life. Your fiction will be bigger for it.

Inner Conflict

It is easy to catalog the qualities that we ordinarily associate with greatness: vision, insight, high intelligence, leadership, accomplishment, wisdom, to name a few. If you were to construct a character that embodied all of those qualities, however, you would wind up with someone about whom it is not very interesting to read. Why? Because there is nothing left to discover, nothing unresolved, about such a paragon.

Another way to look at it is this: Accomplishment already accomplished does not hold our attention. Striving to attain the impossible, though, is a struggle from which we cannot take our eyes. Do you watch the Olympics on TV? Who does not? Do you still care what happens to the bronze medal winners a month or two after the closing ceremony? No? Who does?

In a novel, struggle is far more compelling than satisfaction. Conflict is the first principle of plot construction, and it is also the underlying secret of great characters.

I am talking about inner conflicts, those seemingly contradictory sides of people that make them endlessly interesting to think about. Take Scarlett O'Hara: She longs for the solid comfort of Ashley Wilkes, but who is the great love of her life? The roguish Rhett Butler. It is a delicious contradiction; indeed, it has become a paradigm of women's views of men: Ashley or Rhett? Actually, I suspect the dichotomy originated in characters created by two sisters: Heathcliff in Emily Brontë's *Wuthering Heights* and Rochester in Charlotte Brontë's *Jane Eyre*, but never mind. My point is this: The unresolved conflict in Scarlett O'Hara is one of the primary qualities that makes her memorable.

In 1990, Anne Perry published *The Face of a Stranger*, the first in a series of Victorian mystery novels featuring Inspector William Monk. Monk is a police detective who after an accident has lost his memory. His current case remains active, but he knows nothing of it. Or himself. What he discovers disturbs him. He learns that he was a man for whom he does not much care. Why he was so feared by his colleagues on the force is a question that haunts him. The difference between who he was and who he would like to be is a powerful inner conflict. Eleven popular novels later, that conflict is driving Monk still.

Does the protagonist in your current manuscript have a strong inner conflict, or perhaps conflicting sides? If not, why not? Adding aspects of character that cannot easily be reconciled will ensure that your character cannot easily be dismissed. Inner conflict will keep your grip on your reader firm.

Self-Regard

A third marker of larger-than-life characters is they are self-conscious. I do not mean socially awkward, but that they have a sense of self-regard. Their emotions matter to them. They do not dismiss what they experience. They embrace life. They wonder about their responses to events and what such responses mean. They take themselves seriously—and by the way, a sense of humor about oneself is the flip side of the same coin.

Think about your favorite novels: How often does the main character experience a sharp turn of the plot only to remark, "Oh, it doesn't really matter"? A compelling hero does not deny his feelings but instead is immersed in them.

On the first page of Anita Shreve's 1998 novel *The Pilot's Wife*, Kathryn Lyons is awakened at 3:24 A.M. by a knocking on her front door. It would have been sufficient for Shreve simply to get her heroine out of bed, down the stairs and to the door to answer it, but Shreve instead details Kathryn's reactions upon waking:

> The lit room alarmed her, the wrongness of it, like an emergency room at midnight. She thought, in quick succession: Mattie. Then, Jack. Then, Neighbor. Then, car accident. But Mattie was in bed, wasn't she? Kathryn had seen her to bed, had watched her walk down the hall and through a door, the door shutting with a firmness that was just short of a slam, enough to make a statement but not provoke a reprimand. And Jack— where was Jack? She scratched the sides of her head, raking out her sleep-flattened hair. Jack was—where? She tried to remember the schedule: London. Due home around lunchtime. She was certain. Or did she have it wrong and had he forgotten his keys again?

Shreve brings us so deeply inside the pilot's wife's mind that when the knock on the door proves to be the tragic news such a woman dreads—her husband has died in an airplane explosion off the coast of Ireland—we are already intimate with her, involved in her world. Note that Shreve does not merely tell us that Kathryn feels alarm; she shows us Kathryn's thought process, her checklist of late-night worries. Through that we come to know what matters to her. We take her measure.

An even more effective application of this principle involves allowing your protagonist to measure himself over time. *How have I changed?* is a good question for your main character to pose. *What do I think has caused that change? Do I long to return to my old way of feeling, or am I determined never to return to that old frame of mind ever again?* The answers will give your readers a sense that your character has altered and grown—or perhaps that he pointedly has not.

Wit and Spontaneity

A fourth characteristic of larger-than-life characters is they do and say things that we ordinary folk would not. Have you ever spit in your father's face? Have you ever driven a car into a ditch just to scare the daylights out of your date? Have you ever slapped a man whom you later slept with? Have you ever told your boss that his ego is showing?

I do not do things like that, either, sad to say. I wish I did. Last summer a play that my wife wrote was presented at an international festival. The venue in which it played was busy. The actors shared a common green room. Preceding my wife's play was a self-indulgent one-woman show, the star of which annoyed one and all. Inexplicably, the woman was nominated for Best Actress at the festival. (So was the female lead of my wife's play.) The obnoxious actress won, and everyone was floored. On the last day of performances, an actor from another company approached her and said, "I just wanted to say congratulations on your award and that you are a total bitch."

Oooh, I wish I had said that!

Like me, I am sure that many times you have thought, too late, of the perfect insult or comeback. Well, guess what? Now is your chance. You are a breakout novelist, and you have characters with mouths to feed. Let loose with the snappy remarks and

New York attitude. You gobble that stuff up in other authors' novels, don't you? Your readers will eat it up in yours, too.

Romantic novelist Sandra Brown can be counted on for some good fun with larger-than-life actions and speech. In her 1993 best-seller *Where There's Smoke*, Dr. Lara Mallory sets up practice in Texas oil town Eden Pass, though not by choice. It is her only option. An affair with a Texas senator, Clark Thackett, whose family owns the local oil business and thus Eden Pass, erupted in a scandal that not only ruined the senator's presidential hopes but ultimately cost Lara the life of her husband and daughter. Her hopes of winning restitution from the Thackett family for all she has lost are pinned on the now-dead senator's wild and handsome younger brother, freelance helicopter pilot Key Thackett.

Unfortunately, Key does not see Lara as a victim but as the scarlet woman who ruined his brother. Lara learns that a gunshot wound for which she has treated Key was inflicted on him by a local wife whom he was bedding. (That larger-than-life incident happened when the woman's husband arrived home unexpectedly. The cheating wife had to find a way to make Key look like an intruder so, naturally, she shot him.) Sensing she has a moral advantage over Key, Lara confronts him. But Key deftly turns the tables on her:

> Not liking his train of thought he asked, "Picked out your next victim yet?"
>
> "Clark wasn't my victim!"
>
> "You're the only married woman he ever got mixed up with."
>
> "Which indicates that he was more discriminating than you."
>
> "Or less."

* * *

She shook back her hair. "Well?"

"You said that my accusations were unfair."

"That's right. They're grossly unfair. You don't know anything about my relationship with Clark, only what you've read in the tabloids or deduced in your own dirty mind."

He grinned. She had just placed her slender foot into the snare. "Well, you don't know doodle-dee-squat about my relationship with Darcy, or with anyone else for that matter. Yet you ambush me out here and start preaching sin like a fire-breathing Bible thumper. If it was wrong for me to jump to conclusions about you, shouldn't it be just as wrong for you to hang me without a trial?"

Before she had time to reply, he released her, slid into the front seat of the yellow Lincoln, and started the motor. Through the open window he added, "You're not only a whoring wife, you're a goddamn hypocrite."

Needless to say, these two are destined for each other. How eventually they get together makes for a roller coaster of a story.

That last barb in Sandra Brown's novel reminds me of another in Mary Gordon's *Final Payments*. Isabel Moore's friend Liz is married to a politician named John, whom Liz describes as "a six-foot walking penis with a social conscience." Do you see a pattern? Barbs are unexpected, possibly vulgar, shots from nowhere that cut through the polite fog of social niceties and tell it like it is. They shock. They sting with truth. Witticisms do not have to be vulgar, but like cold water, they are best when they snap your characters awake.

Actions speak louder than words, and that goes double in the breakout novel. What is the most outrageous thing your protagonist could do? Run naked through a wedding reception? March into the mayor's office and dump a pile of dead perch on his desk? Make love in a department store dressing room? Why is that stuff not in your novel? Put it in. See what happens. Are the other characters talking about it, about what it means? Good. Your readers will talk about it, too.

Elizabeth Peters, who also writes as Barbara Michaels, is one of the mystery and suspense field's most reliable storytellers. Her Amelia Peabody mysteries in particular, about an Edwardian-era Egyptologist, are textbooks for the study of larger-than-life character actions. *The Ape Who Guards the Balance*, first published in 1998, opens with Amelia Peabody in motion:

> "Pray do not detain me, my dear Emerson," I replied. "I am on my way to chain myself to the railings at Number Ten Downing Street, and I am already late."
>
> "Chain yourself," Emerson repeated. "May I ask why?"
>
> "It was my idea," I explained modestly. "During some earlier demonstrations, the lady suffragists have been picked up and carried away by large policemen, thus effectively ending the demonstration. This will not be easily accomplished if the ladies are firmly fastened to an immovable object such as an iron railing."
>
> "I see." Opening the door wider, he emerged. "Would you like me to accompany you, Peabody? I could drive you in the motorcar."
>
> It would have been difficult to say which suggestion horrified me more—that he should go with me, or that he should drive the motorcar.

Peabody's droll sangfroid is just the beginning. Peters's archaeologist-sleuth has often been compared to Indiana Jones. She seems a completely unrealistic woman for her times—that is, if you have not read the journals of the great Victorian women travelers such as Isabella Bird. Peters knows that interesting characters do interesting things; especially things that seem unlikely or "against" type.

While we're at it, let us apply some of these same principles to your antagonist. Is your villain sitting quietly-but-menacingly offstage, waiting to come on? Why? Bring him on! Get him busy. Bad guys do no good in the bull pen, only on the pitcher's mound. When you do put him to use, remember that employing inner conflict, self-regard, and bold speech and actions will make your villain, too, loom larger than usual.

Dark Protagonists

One of the most frequent faults I find in submissions, particularly from midcareer novelists in crisis, is that their main characters are unsympathetic. Ironically, this is often the truest of novelists in crisis who send me their latest manuscripts with the assurance, "This is the best thing I have ever written."

I have to admit when I hear that phrase my heart sinks and too often with good reason. The manuscript in question stands a good chance of being about characters who are dark, tortured, haunted (always by "demons"), angry, depressed, cynical or in some other way unbearable. When I just as inevitably point out this drawback, the response is usually, "But I like my characters flawed! That is what makes them interesting!"

I long to say, "You mean, *therapeutic?*" But I bite my tongue. Usually it is enough to mention that I grew so weary of the character's unrelenting misery that at some point I set the manuscript down. (If I need to make the point even more strongly, I mention the actual page number at which I stopped reading.)

Up to a point, those authors are correct: A perfect character is not engaging. Character transformation can be one of the most powerful effects in any story. In fact, it is a fundamental principle in the three-act screenplay form espoused by Robert McKee, whose seminars and book, *Story: Substance, Structure, Style and the Principles of Screenwriting*, are the sermons and bible of the screen writing business.

But there are tricks to working with dark and flawed characters; tricks that stuck, frustrated, impatient authors generally have not taken the time to master. Such authors sometimes mistakenly imagine that any character misbehavior is entrancing so long as at the end of the story that character is redeemed, changed, reformed, resolved or has grown.

Not so. The problem with redemption is that it happens only at the end. It ignores the hundreds of pages of wearisome middle in which the flawed protagonist may refuse to see the light. If you have ever found yourself thinking in the middle of a novel, "Oh, come *on!* Grow up! Get a life!" then you know what I mean. Dark protagonists are wearisome.

How can one forestall that reaction and keep readers engaged by a flawed character? In a nutshell, it is this: A character in trouble is engaging if he has sympathetic qualities; e.g., he is aware that he is in trouble and tries to change. We can forgive anyone who is trying to be good, even seventy-times-seven like the Bible says. What we cannot tolerate is willful self-destructiveness. There is little sympathy for that behavior.

Near the beginning of this chapter, I mentioned Judith Guest's *Ordinary People*. Have you read it? It is about the Jarretts, an "ordinary" family shattered by the tragic death of one of two teenage sons in a sailing accident. There are two principle points of view, father and son. The novel opens with the surviving son, Conrad, waking up one school morning and working hard to find the strength and a reason to get out of bed.

Can you imagine a drearier character and a more depressing choice of opening scene? Wait, it gets worse. . . . Guest raises the stakes and simultaneously makes the job of winning sympathy even more difficult by giving Con an even bigger handicap at that moment: He has been home only a month from a psychiatric hospital to which he was sent after a suicide attempt. Every morning he feels overwhelmed by the darkness inside of him. Whooboy! Guest has set Con, and herself, quite a task. How tough is it? Pretty tough:

> He rolls onto his stomach, pulling the pillow tight around his head, blocking out the sharp arrows of sun that pierce through the window. Morning is not a good time

for him. Too many details crowd his mind. Brush his teeth
first? Wash his face? What pants should he wear? What
shirt? The small seed of despair cracks open and sends
experimental tendrils upward to the fragile skin of calm
holding him together. *Are You on the Right Road?*

Crawford had tried to prepare him for this. "It's all
right, Con, to feel anxious. Allow yourself a couple of bad
days, now and then, will you?"

Sure. How bad? Razor-blade bad?

Yikes! Are you ready to turn your back on this kid? I do not
blame you. However, Guest is too generous to let us, and Con,
wallow for too long:

> His father calls to him from the other end of the
> house. He thrashes to a sitting position, connected at once
> to sanity and order, calling back: "Yeah! I'm up!" and,
> miraculously, he *is* up and in the bathroom, taking a leak,
> washing his hands and face, brushing his teeth. Keep mov-
> ing, keep busy, everything will fall into place, it always
> does.

Phew! Just in time! Con strives to break through his darkness, not always successfully but with a good deal of black humor
and a healthy dose of self-regard, which surfaces throughout the
novel, such as in this passing moment with his father, which is
shown from the father's point of view:

> [The father asks:] "How's it going?"
> "Fine. Great. He gave back the trig quiz today. I got
> an A on it."
> "Great. Terrific."
> "Well," he says and shrugs, "it was just a quiz."
> But a gift. To have it offered is to show that it must
> have value for the giver, also.

"That your first A this semester?"

He looks up from the paper. "Yeah. I'm getting back into the swing of things, huh?" He grins.

So truth is in a certain feeling of permanence that presses around the moment. They are ordinary people, after all.

In passages like these, Guest lets us know that Con is trying. That makes up for a lot. In fact, I don't know about you, but I found myself pulling hard for Con. I wanted things to come out OK for him. In the end they do, and his final self-acceptance, which comes in the epilogue as he contemplates the return of his mother from Europe, where she has gone, alone, to escape from her "perfect" life, could not be more moving:

> He will see her when she comes home, maybe drive over to his grandmother's house some morning, and say hello. Just hello, nothing important. No point in it anyway, because she knows it all, knows just as he does that it is love, imperfect and unordered, that keeps them apart, even as it holds them somehow together.

As you can see, character transformation can make the end of a story profoundly memorable; the trick is getting there. Flawed characters need hints of the qualities that make straight-ahead heroes feel larger-than-life. Readers need reasons to hope. To write the breakout novel, it is necessary to provide readers those reasons not just at the end but all the way through.

What if you just have to write about horrible human beings? What if the dark side is all that interests you? Can a breakout novel be built around a monstrous main character? Certainly it has been done. Vladimir Nabokov's darkly comic *Lolita* (1955) comes to mind. However, it is worth remembering two things about *Lolita*: (1) There is no one stronger than Humbert Humbert in the story; he wins our sympathy by default. (2) In the end

Humbert Humbert is destroyed by Lolita. Nabokov has a satiric and moral point to make.

Ian McEwan's Booker Prize-winning 1998 novel *Amsterdam* is touted by some as a breakout novel built around two utterly despicable protagonists. In bare outline, that would seem to be true; after all, while on a ramble in the Lake District, self-centered composer Clive Linley slinks away from a rape-in-progress because it is interrupting his train of thought on his symphony-in-progress. His friend Vernon Halliday, a newspaper editor, violates the life-embracing spirit of the lover (now dead) that they had in common by publishing scandalous pictures she took of yet another lover, the foreign secretary, in lurid drag. On top of that, the novel ends with them carrying out a mutual suicide pact in Amsterdam, where euthanasia is practiced (though not legal).

Clive and Vernon are loathsome yuppie scum. Yet a close reading shows that McEwan does not expect his readers to slog through a novel about two men whom nobody could like. They are cynical and self-absorbed, yes, but early in the novel, McEwan makes Clive and Vernon sympathetic. Before hurtling them to comic self-destruction, he shows us their human sides. Both were uplifted by the love of the woman they had in common, Molly Lane. When Vernon visits Molly's widower, memories of her return:

> In the semidarkness, during the seconds it took George to fumble for the light switch, Vernon experienced for the first time the proper impact of Molly's death—the plain fact of her absence. The recognition was brought on by familiar smells that he had already started to forget—her perfume, her cigarettes, the dried flowers she kept in the bedroom, coffee beans, the bakery warmth of laundered clothes. He had talked about her at length, and he had thought of her too, but only in snatches during his crowded working days, or while drifting into sleep, and until now he had never really missed her in his heart, or

felt the insult of knowing he would never see or hear her again. She was his friend, perhaps the best he had ever had, and she had gone.

It is difficult not to feel for Vernon at that moment or for Clive at similar points in the story. *Amsterdam* is a dark fable for our times, a morality tale, but McEwan is not heartless. He gives his heroes these and other moments of humanity so that we might have reasons to keep reading, to care.

Finally, let us examine the most unsympathetic family in recent fiction, Carolyn Chute's *The Beans of Egypt, Maine*. How bad are they? Pretty bad. Their yard is a mess, they eat anything they can shoot, their men are unemployed, their children are cretins, and their mentally retarded teenage daughter is perpetually pregnant. Trailer trash. The worst.

So why did this novel break out? The novel is not, at first, told from a Bean point of view. The narrator is a girl who lives across the road, Earlene Pomerleau, who is fascinated with the Beans. Earlene comes from a nicer family, sort of. Although her mother is in an institution, her father is a woodworker. He built their ranch house. His bedroom is pine paneled. He also warns Earlene away from the Beans, whom he calls uncivilized animals. It does no good. Earlene's fascination grows. She screams across the road, "HELLO BEANS!"

Such larger-than-life gestures make Earlene highly attractive. When later in the novel, as an older girl, she winds up pregnant herself and married to Beal Bean, we begin to see the Bean clan from the inside and to hope for them. Not much, I will admit. They are never heroic. But neither does Chute leave the reader without a sympathetic avenue into their world.

The Highest Character Qualities

Before we leave the subject of strength and sympathy, I would like to suggest that there are two character qualities that leave a deeper, more lasting and powerful impression of a character than any other: Forgiveness and self-sacrifice.

The biblical story of the prodigal son is the paradigm of forgiveness. If you recall, not only does the prodigal son leave home and spend all the money his father has given him on worthless pleasures, he stands in contrast to his dutiful brothers who stay home, work hard and obey their father. Yet when the prodigal son returns, broken and humble, the father loves and celebrates him above the brothers. It seems unfair, at first, but even so the story of the prodigal son's reception is deeply moving. (Hey, it has been told in churches for two thousand years. How many breakout novels will last that long?) The reason the story moves us is not that the son has repented but that the father has forgiven. Practice forgiveness in your fiction (and in your life!). It is a powerful source of character strength.

As for self-sacrifice, is there a higher form of heroism? It is the ultimate expression of love and as such is about the most powerful action a character can perform. It is as rare in fiction as it is in life. In 1942, Lloyd C. Douglas published an inspirational novel, *The Robe*, that became one of the greatest bestsellers of the twentieth century.

The Robe is the story of a prominent young Roman centurion, Marcellus, who due to a small social gaff is exiled to the remote backwater of Palestine, where he is given command of a rough and undisciplined detachment of soldiers. He wins their respect. Later, though, he winds up overseeing the execution of a local revolutionary, Jesus of Nazareth.

The events around the crucifixion convince Marcellus that Jesus was innocent. Haunted by the injustice of the execution and by the strange power of the robe Jesus wore on the day of his death, Marcellus returns to Rome in a suicidal depression. His father, a powerful senator named Gallio, turns to Marcellus's Greek slave, Demetrius, for help and advice in restoring his son to sanity. Demetrius, a Corinthian captured during war, is warmly portrayed as the equal of Marcellus in all but station. He is a slave, but he is also one of the most memorable characters in epic fiction.

Demetrius explains to Gallio the circumstances that brought on Marcellus's morbid state of mind. They agree that Demetrius should accompany Marcellus to Greece for a rest cure. Their discussion of the arrangements for the coming trip leads to one of the many moments in *The Robe* in which Lloyd C. Douglas powerfully builds his readers' sympathy for a character using the emotional power of self-sacrifice:

> "Take my son to Athens, Demetrius, and help him recover his mind. But no man should ask a slave to accept such a responsibility." He handed the document to Demetrius. "This is your certificate of manumission. You are a free man."
>
> Demetrius stared at the writing in silence. It was hard for him to realize its full significance. Free! Free as Gallio! He was his own man! Now he could speak—even to Lucia—as a freedman! He was conscious of Gallio's eyes studying him with interest as if attempting to read his thoughts. After a long moment, he slowly shook his head and returned the document to the Senator.
>
> "I appreciate your generosity, sir," he said, in an unsteady voice. "In any other circumstance, I should be overjoyed to accept it. Liberty means a great deal to any man. But I think we would be making a mistake to alter the relationship between my master and his slave."

It is the first of many sacrifices that Demetrius will make for Marcellus. It is a gesture that foreshadows the conversion to Christianity that both men will undergo. Millions of readers have found in Demetrius and Marcellus qualities that make them memorable, sympathetic and inspiring. Chief among those is the self-sacrificing love of one's fellow man.

Building a Cast

The construction of your main character is important, no doubt about it, but so is the construction of your cast. A solidly built cast will not only amplify the work you have done on your protagonist but will add dimensions to your novel that can make it feel like a candidate for a breakout.

A cast does not have to be large to feel deep. The guiding principle of cast construction is contrast. What good are secondary characters who simply stroke your main character, reflecting his attitudes and sympathizing over his conflicts? Secondary characters can serve to amplify what is going on, of course, but they are more useful still when they disagree or produce friction with your main character or, even better, add unforeseen complications to the main problem.

Needless to say, the more complex you make your secondary characters, the more lifelike and involving your story will be. Most interesting of all are secondary characters that have their own trajectory and outcomes, meaning subplots.

What if your story calls for a large cast, though? How do you orchestrate it? How many is too many? How much time should you spend on each character's story line? Are there guiding principles?

The most common mistake I see in large cast novels is not cast number but poor focus. Portraying two or more equally balanced points of view results in an equally diluted sense of reader identification. To put it another way, if you give your reader too many characters to care about, your reader may wind up not caring very much about any of them.

There is an exception to that rule in group and generational novels. Here the object is to portray a cross section of society or perhaps a friendship with a special lasting quality. Mary McCarthy's seminal 1963 novel *The Group*, discussed in chapter nine, demonstrates how a split focus can nevertheless result in a strong bond with the reader. The technique, briefly put, involves creating such a strong group identity that the group itself becomes a single character.

The Group opens in 1933 at the wedding of one of eight Vassar graduates, Kay Leiland Strong, to budding theatre director Harald Petersen. McCarthy quickly establishes the group identity in a passage exploring the friends' feelings about the change Kay underwent as an undergraduate from shy, pretty Western girl to hard-driving theater sophisticate.

> To her fellow group members, all seven of whom were now present in this chapel, this development in Kay, which they gently labeled a "phase", had been, nevertheless, disquieting. Her bark was worse than her bite, they used to reiterate to each other, late at night in the common sitting room in the South Tower of Main Hall, when Kay was still out, painting flats or working on the electricity with Lester in the theatre. But they were afraid that some man, who did not know the old dear as they did, would take her at her word. They had pondered Harald; Kay had met him last summer when she was working as an apprentice at a summer theatre in Stamford and both sexes had lived in a dormitory together. She said he wanted to marry her, but that was not the way his letters sounded to the group.

Note how McCarthy's group thinks as one. A similar unity underlies the group identities in novels like *The Last Convertible* (1978), Anton Myrer's novel of the World War II generation at Harvard, Kaye Gibbons's best-selling 1993 novel of three generations of women, *Charms for the Easy Life*, and Joanna Trollope's 1995 novel about two lifelong friends, *The Best of Friends*. As I say, though, these are special cases.

Overall, most novels need to be about one main character. Partly this is because most novels really only have one story to tell. Even when the subject of a novel is an entire historical era, say, the plot is usually best focused through the lens of one individual whose life touches, at one time or another, all the aspects of the era that are important to portray. Consider James Clavell's 1975 epic *Shōgun*. This best-seller covers an enormous amount of ground, but it is essentially the story of one man, the Englishman John Blackthorne, and his rise from shipwrecked pilot-major to the highest level of feudal Japan, the court of the shogun.

There are exceptions to the one novel, one story rule. E.L. Doctorow's great saga of turn-of-the-century America, *Ragtime* (1974), does have many characters and story lines. Even so, the *principle* story lines and characters are relatively few. The same is true of Larry McMurtry's *Lonesome Dove* (1985). I have noticed even in those novels that successfully present multiple well-developed story lines, and they are pretty rare, there tends to be an identifiable hierarchy among the plots.

Which plot is primary? Generally it is the one with the broadest scope and which captures the sympathy of the greatest cross section of readers. In most cases that will also be the story line belonging to the character who is the largest; i.e., the one who is above all others larger-than-life.

Advanced Character Relationships

How simple are your relationships with your friends? In many cases, fairly simple. You have office mates, tennis partners, distant relatives, service providers (a doctor, a lawyer, a literary agent), neighbors and enemies—who are a sort of friend, after all, insomuch as they provide a type of familiar comfort.

A smaller number of relationships may be more complex: longtime friends, business partners, your psychotherapist, creditors and parents (those last two at times being one and the same). And then there may be those few special relationships that involve long and not-easy-to-summarize histories: spouses, ex-spouses, close lifelong friends, children.

Now, which of these relationships occupy most of your time,

energy and thought? Which demand the most work and sacrifice, yet yield the greatest rewards? Which are the most important to you? The most complex ones, right? Yes, I thought so. That type of relationship will also be the most absorbing in your novel. A relationship that has a life and changing dynamic of its own is inherently more fascinating than one that is simple and easy to explain. It has more places to go.

How can you construct such relationships for your protagonist? One method is to combine roles, as in the lifelong friend who is also a doctor, or the ex-spouse who is also a tennis partner. Chart your cast. See if there are characters that could be combined. Doing so will lend your novel a measure of the richness and complexity of real relationships, and at the same time strengthen and deepen its hold on the reader.

Another technique of breakout character building is to make moments when characters measure each other, that is, when they voice to themselves or to others their opinions of the other characters in the story. A character viewed from different angles is automatically a richer creation. Not every other character will see the subject character in the same way.

A breakout novelist will also make moments when characters measure how their opinions of others have changed. Such moments reinforce the sense of passing time and the effect of a novel's events on their lives. Such moments contribute to the layering of character and story lines that is so central to making a breakout novel.

Sidekicks and Narrators

It is hard, now, to imagine F. Scott Fitzgerald's *The Great Gatsby* told from the point of view of Gatsby. The narrator, Nick Carraway, is indelibly a part of the story, though in truth the tale could have been told without him. (Yes, it could have. Objective third-person narration would have gotten the job done.)

Still, Nick Carraway proved to be a highly effective device. How do you know when you would be better off with a narrator?

Are not objective narration, first-person and close third-person point of view the nearly universal choices for novels today?

The option to use a narrator is probably a personal one. A story may feel more natural to you told in the first person, but for one reason or another, you may not want to adopt the main character's point of view. (Perhaps you want to keep him mysterious, or possibly he is going to die in the course of the story.) Whatever your reasons, I am less concerned about the option itself than about the choice of your particular narrator.

Who is the best narrator for your story? It would seem to be the person who is closest to your protagonist and the one therefore who is in the best position to witness the story's key action.

But there is more to it than logistics. What is the quality of that relationship? Does the narrator have rich and varied feelings about your hero? I hope so, and *if* so consider this: The best narrator may not be the hero's best friend or even a peer. Sometimes it can be a person removed a few steps from the hero. Harper Lee's *To Kill a Mockingbird* (1960) is thought of as a coming-of-age novel, but in reality it is the story of an adult, Atticus Finch, filtered through the innocent eyes of his daughter, Scout. Scout does not understand everything that is happening to her father, but the plot events have all the more power for that. Scout's awakening to the realities of prejudice make the pain of growing up more poignant than it would be from an adult's point of view.

What I am getting at here is a pairing not of narrator and protagonist, but of narrator and theme. Who is in a position to learn most from the events of the story? Who will be the most changed by them? That character may be your best choice.

If you have not yet made the choice of narrator, consider charting out your cast and thinking about who, besides the protagonist, will be transformed the most in the course of the story. (That could be the antagonist, though there are obvious problems in working through that point of view.)

If you are already working with a narrator and it is too late to change, then give some thought to ways in which your narrator might be more affected by the hero's story. If the answers do not come, consider working instead from objective or close third-person point of view. You may not need your narrator.

Sidekicks can be fun. They are a staple of crime fiction. Sidekicks provide a foil and counterweight for the detective; plus, the distance provided by the sidekick magnifies the magical qualities of the detective's logical mind. Think Watson to Holmes or, in a reversal of the usual hero worship, Archie Goodwin to Nero Wolfe.

Are sidekicks useful in other types of novels? Young adult novels are replete with best friends, which is natural to the social structure of high school. Epic or quest fantasy is another type of story that can hardly seem to do without sidekicks.

In other types of novels, though, I have found that sidekicks do not often fit in. Why? Because for the most part, the hero's problems are personal; or at any rate the plot is more effective when it is the hero and the hero alone who can solve the main problem. Isolating your hero is generally a good idea.

Depth and Differentiation of Character

Just as detailing is the secret of a memorable setting, so depth is the secret of memorable characters. Depth is the degree of detail you bring to your people. Quick brushstrokes are fine in openings, but in the body of the breakout novel, characters can only grow rich if they are examined from many angles. Read just about any breakout novel and you will find its characters are revealed in a number of ways.

One-dimensional characters are flat, simply motivated and always act "in character," that is, predictably. Fully rounded, three-dimensional characters have many sides, complex motives and act in ways that surprise us. Not every type of novel requires depth of characterization; comic novels and pastiches, for instance. Certain plot-driven thrillers also seem to do just fine without fully rounded characters. However, in most novels nothing is lost, and everything is gained, by enriching the inner life of one's cast.

Many time-tested tools are available for character development: backstories, life chronologies, cast diagrams, out-of-story dialogues between author and character, and so on. Find the tools that work for you. Needless to say, the greatest character resource is life itself. Biographies, bar mitzvahs, business meetings . . . we meet "characters" all the time. Developing fictional people is mainly a matter of opening oneself to real people, most of all to ourselves.

By far the most useful technique for character development is a simple principle that Anne Perry, among others, keeps in mind when building characters: "Like them." It is hard to write someone you don't know, harder still if you do not care for them. Eliminate characters whom you do not regard with warmth, to whom you are not drawn. The coldness you feel toward them will show in your writing.

By the way, the same mandate to like your characters may also go for your villain. Don't you find the most interesting villains are the ones whose motives we can understand? The ones who are made evil by circumstances, rather than the ones who simply are born bad? Depth of character in your opposition will make your writing more richly textured.

Character differentiation is the technique of making the characters in your cast different and distinct from one another. Here is where diagrams and charts can help. Contrast is the key. When characters are hard to keep straight, it is often because they are not sufficiently individualized.

One technique frequently employed by novelists is the "tag," a distinct identifier such as an eye patch or a special gesture. I am suspicious of tags. They definitely help me keep characters straight, but they can substitute for real, substantive character development. So can unusual names. While I have become inured to romance hero names like Stone, Cash and Buck, in other novels gimmick names can be distracting, like an eye tic. True characters do not need tricks.

One of our greatest practitioners of character differentiation is Anne Tyler. Her people are always highly individualized. Who can forget Macon Leary, the travel writer who hates to travel, in her 1985 triumph *The Accidental Tourist?* When Leary's wife leaves him at the beginning of the novel, his embrace of systems for happy living is not only a comic delight, it is an introduction to an utterly unique character:

> Well, you have to carry on. You have to carry on. He decided to switch his shower from morning to night. This showed adaptability, he felt—some freshness of spirit. While he showered he let the water collect in the tub, and he stalked around in noisy circles, sloshing the day's dirty clothes underfoot . . . At moments—while he was skidding on the mangled clothes in the bathtub or struggling with his body bag on the naked, rust-stained mattress—he realized he might be carrying things too far. He couldn't explain why, either. He'd always had a fondness for method, but not what you would call a mania.

I am sure you have your favorite characters, too. Examine them with an objective eye and you will probably find they are strong, sympathetic, multidimensional, larger-than-life, yet all too human. Their words and actions express the inner conflicts and desires with which we all can identify.

Creating character in the breakout novel is not simple. It involves going deep inside, right to the heart. Breakout characters get to us because they *are* us, only bigger. Build your characters carefully and completely using breakout techniques, and they will spin you a story that we will not soon forget.

BREAKOUT Checklist: Characters

✓ All stories are character driven.

✓ Engrossing characters are out of the ordinary.

✓ Readers' sympathy for characters comes from characters' strengths.

✓ Larger-than-life characters say what we cannot say, do what we cannot do, change in ways that we cannot change.

✓ Larger-than-life characters have conflicting sides and are conscious of self.

✓ Dark protagonists appeal only when they have sympathetic sides; e.g., they struggle to change or have hidden sensitivity.

✓ The highest character qualities are self-sacrifice and forgiveness.

✓ Build a cast for contrast.

✓ Build complex character relationships by combining roles.

✓ Choose a narrator based on who is changed most by the story's events.

✓ Build depth of character with tools like character biographies, author-character dialogues, etc.

✓ Differentiate characters with character charts.

✓ Breakout characters are deep and many-sided.

CHAPTER SIX

Plot

Plot is the organization of a story: its events and their sequence. What events? Which sequence? The choices you make will mean the difference between a gripping manuscript and a dull pile of paper. In discussing the ins and outs of plot construction, let us first establish the underlying fundamental principle of all stories, next the five basic elements common to all plots, and finally progress to a discussion of the larger frameworks that structure a plot.

Beginning novelists tend to tell their stories in strict sequential order, following the protagonist through her every day from sunrise to sleep, over and over again until the novel is completed. That can make for some dull reading. Not every moment of every day is dramatic. There are lulls, such as showers, meals, driving, getting up and going to bed.

This flaw in strictly sequential plotting seems obvious once it is pointed out, yet novice after novice makes this mistake. Why? I believe it is because many writers visualize their stories in the way that a film unspools on a screen. They write travel between scenes, establishing shots and incidental action (dropping ice cubes into a glass, flicking a lighter into flame) in order to "pace" their novels and make them feel more realistic.

That method is sometimes misguided. A novel is not a film. The compression inherent in film often demands its action be paced out; otherwise, the unrelenting tension of the film's back-to-back scenes would hammer the audience into insensibility. Novelists do not have that worry. A novel's pace is already slow. For novelists the challenge is just the opposite: to keep the tension level constantly high.

When 100,000 or more words are involved, it is a trick to make every one of them highly interesting. In truth, it cannot be done. Words alone cannot hold onto us for the many hours it takes to read a novel. More is needed: action, but not just any action in any order. To hold our attention a novel's action needs to compel us to read every word.

Conversely, in constructing the novel, the novelist needs to leave behind as few lulls as possible. Fortunately, there is a tool that can make that job easier. So powerful is this tool that it can gloss over many faults and, if properly applied, will keep readers glued to a novel's pages. What's the tool? Conflict.

Conflict

The essence of story is conflict. That principle is so well understood, so often espoused and so universally taught, it is easily the underlying and fundamental component of plot, wouldn't you agree? I do not think there is any doubt about it. However, it is worth taking a few minutes to understand *how* conflict makes a story a story, while in other contexts, it creates only anecdote, episode or news.

You would think that conflict is something we would avoid. Do you go out of your way to pick fights? I assume not. When a couple in a restaurant begins to argue loudly at a nearby table, does everyone turn to them with interest? Yes, at first, but soon the other patrons turn away in embarrassment. Does our nation lust for battle? Sometimes, but generally we debate a good deal before we take up arms.

Conflict hurts. If that is so, why does it grab our attention on the street, on TV and in novels? First, it is worth noting that the interest level generated by conflict varies. On the street a commotion will cause us to turn, perhaps even to pause for a moment to watch. On TV, a news item will hold our attention for a minute or two. A novel is different. Novel readers expect their attention to be held for hours.

That expectation is a tall order. Not just any commotion can do that. To hold us for so long a span, conflict must be rich and highly involving.

To achieve that level of involvement, the conflict must matter to us; equally, our interest level will decline in ratio to how removed we feel from those involved in a conflict. Take TV news: How do you react when you hear about war in the third world? If you are like me, you probably furrow your brow and feel bad for a moment but quickly put it out of your mind. On the other hand, how did you react to the shooting of Presidents Kennedy or Reagan, or to the Challenger explosion? Did you watch TV for hours, flipping channels for fresh information?

I did, too.

Only a few news stories have the power to maintain our attention for days, weeks or even months. Think of the shootings at Columbine High School. Why did that last in the news? The first reason is obvious: It happened close to home. We could easily imagine it happening in our own town, to our own kids. But that is also true of highway wrecks, house fires, robberies and other news staples. Columbine also gripped with its scale and surprise. It was large and unexpected.

The shock and proximity of that tragedy do not fully explain why it held our attention, however. What really made Columbine a long-lived news story were its layers, the questions it raised and, most significantly, the media's personalization of its victims. The pain of Columbine really hit a few days after the event when the funerals started.

Who will ever forget the playful, pretty and much-loved seventeen-year-old high school actress, Rachel Scott? She also was a budding playwright who was already talking about how she would decorate the apartment she would one day have. But she was not pretentious or snooty. She had to jump-start her car in the school parking lot. She dressed to please herself, wearing a sailor hat or pajama bottoms to school. (It showed her who her friends really were.) Her smile was like the sun shining. Then one day she was gunned down. Her prom date, Nick Baumgart, cried at her memorial and thanked her for sharing her life. Her car remained in the school parking lot for a time, buried beneath a mountain of flowers, cards, balloons and stuffed animals.

Details like that made Columbine matter, and a whole nation searched for an explanation for the tragedy. The most significant reason an incident like Columbine makes us care, then, rather than causing us to turn away, is that we feel deeply for the people involved. We feel sympathy for someone.

Conflict is an easy principle to understand. We all experience it every day. Most of it is quickly forgotten. Conflict that holds our attention for long periods of time is meaningful, immediate, large scale, surprising, not easily resolved and happens to people for whom we feel sympathy.

Thus, in building a novel, not just any conflict will serve. The breakout novelist needs a discerning feel for the friction in her story. Problems that are abstract, remote, trivial, ordinary, easily overcome and/or happening to someone for whom we feel little may be fit for casual conversation or perhaps the evening news, but they cannot fuel a gripping novel.

The Five Basic Plot Elements

When a novel does not begin by engaging our sympathies—as when, say, a novice thriller writer opens with a "grabber" scene in which an anonymous victim is slain by a nameless assailant—then the reader's interest level is only mild at best. Strong reader interest results from a high level of sympathy, which is grounded in knowledge of character and enriched by personalizing details.

The first plot essential, then, is that a story concern a sympathetic character, one whom we know in some detail. Next?

Something happens to that character: a problem arises. Conflict appears. That is essential plot element number two.

But what sort of conflict? Go back to an aspect of our discussion in the last section: whether or not conflict is easily resolved. In other words: Is your novel's conflict complex? Is it easy to understand (and forget), or does it pose to the reader tough puzzles and difficult questions?

Easy-to-solve problems are easily forgotten. Complex conflicts, on the other hand, generate long study. They stick in our minds, nagging for our attention. If you want your novel to get off to a fast start, work with heroes and villains pitted against each other in simple contests of good vs. evil. If, however, you want your readers to think about your novel long after the last page is turned, consider motivating your main characters in mixed ways. Put them in situations that are strong but in which the right path is not obvious. Too much ambiguity will leave your readers confused, of course, but that said it is nevertheless true that complex conflict has the most lasting impact.

Let us return to Columbine for a moment. It has more to teach the breakout novelist. For one thing, it was an event rich in conflict of many sorts. Some found the most intriguing aspect of the incident to be the personalities: the trench coat mafia vs. the jocks. Others felt most keenly the intellectual tension generated by the larger issue: the right to bear arms vs. the need to protect our children.

Columbine's issues are interesting, I agree, but for me the most puzzling aspect of that tragedy is the human questions that remain unanswered to this day: How could two normal-seeming teenagers have planned and then enacted such a savage attack? Why did things start to go wrong? Was it poor parenting, personal vendetta, the influence of violent music lyrics and computer games, the ready availability of assault weapons?

Columbine raised questions that are not easy to answer. They are engrossing and important. Its victims are sympathetic. For all that, though, when was the last time you thought about

Columbine? It has faded from our minds and from the news due to a lack of fresh details and developments.

The third essential element of a plot, most agree, is it must be reinforced. In terms of fiction technique, we would say that conflict must undergo complication. It must twist, turn, deepen and grow. Without that constant development, a novel, like a news event, will eventually lose its grip.

Have you ever lost interest in an ongoing news story? Sure you have. A news organization, hoping to keep ratings high, interrupts regular programming with a news flash, and you think, *Oh, give it a rest!* But wait . . . how can real world conflict lose its grip even when fresh complications are offered? To put it another way, why do people bother with sitcoms, movies and novels when real-life conflict offers so much rich human strife and an unending string of fresh angles?

Here is the final lesson of Columbine for breakout novelists: The real world rarely provides a conclusion to conflict. News "stories" are not often real stories, in my opinion, because they hardly ever come to a head and finally resolve; or, if they do, it is long after the main event. They drag on, hammering us with ceaseless strife, and so eventually we lose patience. We wear out. Fiction—whatever its medium—has this huge advantage over news: it ends. Or rather, it ends satisfactorily. In the vocabulary of fiction technique, fiction reaches a climax and a resolution, the fourth and fifth essential elements of any plot.

There are many ways to conceptualize conflict: the problem, tension, friction, obstacle to goal, worries, opposition, inner warfare, disagreement, looming disaster, the opposite of happiness, threat, peril, hope, putting your protagonist through hell, yearning, whodunit, a ticking clock and so on. It all amounts to the same thing: It is the magnet that draws reader interest, the discomfort that demands our attention.

So, what is it about conflict that makes a story a story? It makes us care by bonding us to a character. It sustains our interest through constant development and escalation. Finally, at its unavoidable peak, it brings us face-to-face with our deepest anxieties. If we face them and prevail—and what choice do we have given the structure of a story?—our anxieties are relieved. In the resolution we enjoy peace.

Applied simply, as I said, conflict is little more than incident, anecdote or news. Made complex, active, climactic and complete, it becomes a plot. Developed in depth and with layers added, plot in turn enacts our human frailty and fears. It asserts the lasting strength of our dreams.

So, how can you begin to create or work on improving the plot of your breakout novel? Where do you start? What should you be thinking about? Think about this: Make conflict deeper, richer, more layered, more unavoidable and more inescapably true. Let us examine some of the ways in which that can be accomplished, starting at the beginning.

Bridging Conflict

Great first lines and gripping openings are an art understood by all fiction writers above the novice level. Not that they are art forms that are always practiced with diligence, mind you. You would be amazed, perhaps appalled, by the number of weak beginnings I get in submissions from midcareer novelists.

Still, it is probably not necessary to say much about the importance of the first line or the first page. Do you need examples? Go to your bookshelf. Here are a couple of examples from my shelves, pulled more or less at random:

> "I've never actually killed anybody before, murdered another person, snuffed out another human being."
> —Donald E. Westlake, *The Ax*

> "There once lived a man named Martin Dressler, a shopkeeper's son, who rose from modest beginnings to a height of dreamlike good fortune."
> —Steven Millhauser, *Martin Dressler*

"Three weeks after Granny Blakeslee died, Grandpa came to our house for his early morning snort of whiskey, as usual, and said to me, "Will Tweedy? Go find yore mama, then run up to yore Aunt Loma's and tell her I said git on down here. I got something to say. And I ain't a-go'n say it but once't."
—Olive Ann Burns, *Cold Sassy Tree*

"It was not complicated, and, as my mother pointed out, not even personal: They had a hotel; they didn't want Jews; we were Jews."
—Elinor Lipman, *The Inn at Lake Devine*

"I WILL NOT: Drink more than fourteen alcohol units a week."
—Helen Fielding, *Bridget Jones's Diary*

"It's a new elevator, freshly pressed to the rails, and it's not built to fall this fast."
—Colson Whitehead, *The Intuitionist*

"When your mama was the geek, my dreamlets," Papa would say, "she made the nipping off of noggins such a crystal mystery that the hens themselves yearned toward her, waltzing around her, hypnotized with longing. 'Spread your lips, sweet Lil,' they'd cluck, 'and show us your choppers!' "
—Katherine Dunn, *Geek Love*

"Any thoughts that you'd like to start with?"
—Michael Connelly, *The Last Coyote*

One aspect of great first lines that has application beyond the opening ten or twenty words of your breakout novel is this: bridging conflict. If you think of a first line as a "grabber" or a "hook" or a slick trick that somehow captures your reader's attention because it is clever, puzzling, colorful, lurid or in some way curiosity-provoking, then you are missing a key element of the opening line's inner workings and utility in the overall narrative.

There is, in any great opening line, a miniconflict or tension that is strong enough to carry the reader to the next step in the narrative. Its effect lasts, oh, perhaps half a page, a little more if it is really good. After that another electric spark of tension needs to strike us. If it does not, our interest begins to weaken and will pretty quickly fade out.

You can observe the technique of bridging conflict at work in just about any popular or classic novel. I happen to be writing this passage in a hotel room in Winter Park, Florida. With my own bookshelves unavailable, a few minutes ago I strolled down brick-paved North Park Avenue to a store selling used books, where I snatched a paperback classic from the one dollar bargain book cart. Let us look at its opening:

> It happened that green and crazy summer when
> Frankie was twelve years old. This was the summer when
> for a long time she had not been a member.

Pretty good technique, don't you think? There is tension all through these lines. The phrase "green and crazy" sets the tone, and immediately we meet a "she" named Frankie. Already, before we are aware of it, the questions have begun: Why is a girl called Frankie? What made that summer crazy? And for heaven's sake, what has Frankie not been a member of?

Carson McCullers obviously has learned the trick of starting a novel *in medias res*: that is, events are already in motion, things have already happened, and we readers are playing catch-up. McCullers presumes we know a bit already—and perhaps the title of the novel, *The Member of the Wedding* (1946), does indeed give something away—but really we know nothing. Between what we are supposed to know and what we do not—

questions unanswered—there is tension. Our minds strain to fill in the gaps.

The technique of this opening is relatively familiar. But watch what happens next. McCullers spends a paragraph describing what a hitherto unrewarding summer Frankie has had and ends it with:

> And then, on the last Friday of August, all this was changed: it was so sudden that Frankie puzzled the whole blank afternoon, and still she did not understand.

Understand what? Tell us! But McCullers does not, not right away. Having delivered a second jolt of tension juice, she relaxes the pace and even toys with us a bit:

> "It is so very queer," she said. "The way it all just happened."
> "Happened? Happened?" said Berenice.
> John Henry listened and watched them quietly.
> "I have never been so puzzled."
> "But puzzled about what?"
> "The whole thing," Frankie said.
> And Berenice remarked, "I believe the sun has fried your brains."

McCullers's teasing is beginning to fry my patience a bit, too. She is too smart a novelist to mess with our curiosity for too long, though. In the next paragraph, she introduces the notion of a wedding and shortly thereafter, after a touch of self-pity on Frankie's part, practical Berenice spits at Frankie both a rebuke and a lump of useful exposition:

> "Your brother came home with the girl he means to marry and took dinner today with you and your Daddy. They intend to marry at her home in Winter Hill this

coming Sunday. You and your Daddy are going to the
wedding. And that is the A and the Z of the matter. So
whatever ails you?"

For the next 153 pages, we find out exactly what ails Frankie,
and a moving and surprising story it is, too.

Here in a nutshell is the technique of bridging conflict.
Whether short and sweet, as in *The Member of the Wedding*, or
drawn out for many pages, it always works the same way: A
series of smaller conflicts serves to capture and keep our attention until the main conflict or first large event of the story
arrives.

By the way, notice also a key secret of working *in medias res*:
McCullers does not backtrack. She might have set up the situation like this:

> That morning Frankie's brother *had* brought home the
> girl he intended to marry. Frankie *had* listened, amazed,
> as he announced their plans to marry the next Sunday in
> Winter Hill. She *had* not been able to believe it.

McCullers's understood that the past perfect tense and its
evil facilitator, the word "had," will always rob a scene of its vital
immediacy. Even though we need to learn about events that have
already happened, she keeps the action always in the present. It
has more impact that way, don't you think?

A masterful example of extended bridging conflict can be
found in P.D. James's mystery *A Certain Justice* (1997). The novel
features James's familiar Scotland Yard inspector Adam Dalgliesh, but Dalgliesh does not appear in the first 150 pages of this
novel. Instead, James spends her first ten chapters introducing
the victim and a number of potential suspects, none of whom is
particularly sympathetic.

To make matters worse, there is little plot-advancing action
in those ten chapters. There is instead lots of background and

character establishment. James would seem to be breaking every rule of openings, yet she manages to keep us riveted. How? With bridging conflict. The process begins in the opening lines:

> Murders do not usually give their victims notice. This is one death which, however terrible that last second of appalled realization, comes mercifully unburdened with anticipatory terror. When, on the afternoon of Wednesday, 11 September, Venetia Aldridge stood up to cross-examine the prosecution's chief witness in the Case of Regina v. Ashe, she had four weeks, four hours and fifty minutes left of life.

As with McCullers's novel, questions immediately arise in the reader's mind: Why will Aldridge be killed? Who will do it? In the few seconds it takes to read those lines, we do not articulate those questions to ourselves. Even so, they underlie what we read, and for a moment we feel the tension they produce.

To keep our interest, James needs to personalize this future victim, but again she flies in the face of convention by making Aldridge a first-class bitch. Page one hints at just how unsympathetic Aldridge is (the italics are mine):

> After her death the many who had admired her *and the few who had liked her*, searching for a more personal response than the stock adjectives of horror and outrage, found themselves muttering that it would have pleased Venetia that her last case of murder had been tried at the Bailey, scene of her greatest triumphs, and in her favourite court.

Oh, dear. Why on earth should we care about the death of this unpleasant woman? We will, but until that change occurs, James retains our attention by raising unanswered questions of ever rising interest: How does a woman of such caliber come to be killed? Indeed, how can it be that the very courts of criminal justice can become the milieu of criminal violence? There is a paradox here that demands explanation.

Notice something else about James's opening: Her high blown language confers gravity upon the anticipated murder. You may not like her elevated prose, but whatever your preferred style, it does make the coming events feel important. We sense that in some respects this story will be about the system of justice itself, about maintaining its integrity. The stakes will be high. The outcome will matter to all of us.

By the way, notice also how James has begun to weave in a feeling of separate identity for the setting. She reinforces this in her second paragraph:

> Court Number One had laid its spell on her since she had first entered it as a pupil . . . she responded to this elegant wood-paneled theatre with an aesthetic satisfaction and a lifting of the spirit . . .

The setting lives all by itself, and thanks to all the other techniques that James has so deftly deployed, we are hooked.

Now, because a hero has not yet arrived, all that might be for naught. Since we feel no sympathy for anyone in the story, James is in danger of losing our attention. This master plotter solves that problem by making her victim, Aldridge, sympathetic . . . quite a trick, given that Aldridge is a vicious ice queen.

How does James manage to make her unpleasant victim compelling? This transformation occurs in chapter three, in which we get the sad story of Aldridge's childhood, her rearing by her cold and heartless father (a headmaster at a second-rate boys' school) and her heartbreaking friendship with Frog, the lonely teacher who introduces her to the drama and discipline of criminal court. Later Aldridge becomes a defense counsel and a cold mother herself, but by that time we well understand why. Through our understanding of her we gain sympathy.

Similarly, James's mastery of the first essential element of plot becomes evident as she introduces her cast of suspects in such depth and detail that they become sympathetic. Among the suspects is Aldridge's colleague Drysdale Laud, who anticipates becoming Head of Chambers, but who is shocked to learn that Aldridge has been appointed over him. This unwelcome surprise is sprung by John Langton, the retiring Head of Chambers. Does Aldridge have a hold on him? Questions multiply, keeping tension high.

We soon thereafter meet Gary Ashe, the sick and twisted murderer of his own aunt (herself no prize), whom Aldridge gets acquitted. There is also Aldridge's surly daughter Octavia, who hates her mother and yet is so love-starved she has fallen for Gary Ashe in a fit of romantic self-delusion.

The list goes on . . . Hugert Langton . . . Simon Costello . . . James loads these characters with motive, all of it lovingly detailed in chapters five through ten. Little "happens" in these chapters in a plot-advancing sense. The content is largely interior. Even so the scenes are suffused with the characters' inner tensions. Because we understand them, we are drawn to them and naturally enough wonder: Which of those inner conflicts is going to lead to murder?

At first it seemed that James was breaking the rules of openings, certainly in the 150-page delay in introducing her hero. But lavishing so many pages and so much detail on the victim and suspects is the only possible way in which she can sustain the tension and our interest long enough to begin the story in present action. If she had not, she would have found herself in a familiar mystery novel dilemma: How to make a murder truly matter when the body is discovered on page one, the victim now unknowable and the body already cooling?

Read A Certain Justice and you will notice something else: The cause of the inner tensions that keeps us riveted are not things buried in the past; rather, they are things that are happening now; things of which Aldridge is the obvious instigator. James knows conflict must be immediate, unavoidable and urgent, and she makes it so.

Finally, just when we have had about enough of this building of tension, just when we are ready for a break, at the end of chapter eleven, the name of Adam Dalgliesh is mentioned. Ah! James fans know that James's superlative and sensitive detective is coming. Even new readers can sense that a savior is on the horizon. Everything is going to be OK—eventually.

While I would not recommend James's approach for every novel, especially not first novels, that P.D. James can keep us hanging for ten dark chapters before her hero shows up is high testimony to her skill with bridging conflict. Review any of your favorite novels, and I guarantee you will find this technique at work.

What is the Worst That Can Happen?

The principle of bridging conflict applies equally to short stories, midlist fiction and breakout fiction. Let us now look at the main or central conflict in the breakout novel. What makes it different? Isn't conflict just conflict?

Is conflict in a breakout novel a matter of scale? Not really. A mediocre thriller can leave us yawning even when the stakes are save-the-world sized. What makes a breakout novel memorable are conflicts that are deep, credible, complex and universal enough so a great number of readers can relate.

How is such a conflict constructed? Let us begin with depth, by which I mean pushing your central problem far beyond what any reader might anticipate or imagine. To accomplish that you, the author, must first be willing to push your characters into situations that you would never go near in your own life.

That can be tough to do. As authors we like our protagonists. We are tempted to protect them from trouble. That temptation must be resisted. Indeed, it is better to drive full speed into dan-

ger, laughing as you do it. A breakout novelist is somewhat mani-
acal, possibly even sadistic. (Where her characters are concerned,
I mean.) She will discover what is the worst that can happen
then make matters worse still.

There are tricks to that. Setting the outer limits of trouble
somewhere short of their actual boundaries, then bursting
through them is one way to do it. Another is to stretch beyond
what is plausible, but first construct the circumstances in which
real-world checks and balances are taken out of operation. In
other words, take that which is improbable and make it look
possible; better still, make the impossible look real.

What happens in fiction rarely happens in life. Dramatic
plot situations demand some fudging. A breakout plot pushes
events to high extremes but nevertheless makes them feel utterly familiar.

An example of this can be found in Michael Crichton's *Jurassic Park* (1990). Everyone knows dinosaur DNA cannot be ex-
tracted from amber and used to grow real dinosaurs, at least not
yet. Some novelists may imagine that what makes Crichton's
premise work is that it is almost credible; i.e., that this near-
future technology feels chillingly close and real.

That is wrong. Rather, readers buy into Crichton's premise
because he painstakingly discloses it in stages, building up to it
by first acknowledging its implausibility via expert characters but
finally revealing to them, and to us, the incontrovertible truth
that the incredible has been accomplished: Dinosaurs live.
Crichton does not ask the reader to imagine; instead, he makes
the impossible highly believable.

Take a fresh look at Crichton's novel: Everyone knows from
the title and jacket copy what the story is about, but Crichton does
not take our acceptance of his premise for granted. He first carefully
captures us with a series of taut bridging scenes: At a clinic on the
Costa Rican coast, an American doctor (note her nationality,
which aids reader identification) treats a victim of a "construction
accident" whom she can see has been mauled. The daughter of an

American family traveling along the coast suffers a lizard bite. A pack of such lizards later devours a baby in her bassinet.

Analysis of lizard saliva samples further deepens the mystery and the plausibility of the premise:

> But among the salivary proteins was a real monster: molecular mass of 1,980, one of the largest proteins known. Biological activity was still under study, but it seemed to be a neurotoxic poison related to cobra venom, although more primitive in structure.
>
> The lab also detected traces of the gamma-amino methionine hydrolase. Because this enzyme was a marker for genetic engineering, and not found in wild animals, technicians assumed it was a lab contaminant.

Molecular mass of 1,980? Is that how molecular mass is measured? No doubt it is. Like best-selling techno-thriller writer Tom Clancy and horror writer Stephen King, Crichton loads his fiction with the details that make the unlikely seem realistic.

Finally Crichton introduces his hero, paleontologist Alan Grant, and his villain John Hammond. A storyteller with a simplistic sense of conflict would have set these two in opposition: Grant good, Hammond bad. Crichton is more sophisticated. He draws Grant to Hammond's dinosaur world, Jurassic Park, but instead of horror or apprehension, Grant feels, upon first seeing living apatosaurus, a sense of joyful wonder:

> Grant just shook his head, and continued to laugh. He couldn't tell them that what was funny was that he had seen the animal for only a few seconds, but he had already begun to accept it—and to use his observations to answer long-standing questions in the field.

Crichton's plausibility drive does not end there, by the way. A highly technical discussion of the dinosaur building process follows, complete with computer-generated inserts of "dinosaur" DNA sequences. Indeed, this detailing never lets up.

In fixing the main conflict, Crichton does not, as I said, set Grant and Hammond against each other. Instead, he constructs personal problems for each: Hammond needs to convince his backers that Jurassic Park is safe; Grant wants desperately to learn the secrets of the dinosaurs. Hammond's higher purpose in building the park is carefully developed. He is not evil, exactly; he has acted both to entertain and to advance science. He is Walt Disney crossed with Dr. Frankenstein.

Grant, meanwhile, good scientist that he is, longs to soak up the facts newly and uniquely available to him, even while others hold him back and sound alarms. Both Grant and Hammond are motivated by high principles, but they have blind spots: As we have already learned in the novel's opening, the dinosaurs cannot be safely contained. No good can come of this.

Thus, the central problem of *Jurassic Park*, that dinosaurs live and pose a danger, achieves breakout scale because Crichton develops it until it is credible, complex and universal. It is deep because, as we shall see, it is as horrible a problem as it can be. Its credibility, of course, is lovingly enhanced. Its complexity and universal quality show in the differing ways in which the central problem affects the story's main characters.

What about depth? Does the central problem of *Jurassic Park* have it? Yes. Having set the personal conflicts for his two key players, Crichton makes their external problems as bad as they could possibly be—and then makes them worse. Examples: Hammond has brought his grandkids to the park. The raptors get loose. The last boat leaves. A storm blows in. The dinosaurs have begun to breed on their own, which was thought to be impossible. The island's electrical power goes out. T-Rex gets through the electric containment fence.

Let us pause for a moment on the universal quality of *Jurassic Park*'s central conflict. Not only do the protagonist and the antagonist grapple with the problem from their own personal perspectives, the events of the story raise larger issues: problems, to put it another way, that affect us all.

For instance, in the novel we see scientific method compromised by our appetite for mass entertainment. Also, human hubris comes up against the primacy of nature. Those larger conflicts are embodied in two men, neither of whom is a wholly perfect hero or a thoroughly evil villain. They are both humans. Each finds that something out there is bigger than he is—literally. Crichton has taken the two sides of each of his larger issues and has embodied them in two characters.

Thus, Crichton layers conflicts that are both personal and public, germane to the hero and germane to humanity. Interwoven this way, public and private conflicts together have a powerful effect.

Back to making things bad: Just how bad do events get in *Jurassic Park*? Needless to say everyone winds up running for his life, but Crichton does not stop there. Hammond must confront the failure of his vision, though he does not learn. Grant is taught there are things he is not meant to know, although his expertise helps him to survive. In facing the dinosaurs, both men's inner conflicts reach an unavoidable climax.

In a larger sense, science will ultimately bow to nature. Man will learn his limits. When a helicopter pilot asks at the end, "Please, señor, who is in charge?" Grant answers, "Nobody." Are the conflicts in this novel small? No, they are large and layered, which is to say universal, important and interconnected.

Jurassic Park may be a B movie at heart, but in the end Crichton employs conflict to its full potential to make a breakout book.

What's that you say? You did not like *Jurassic Park*? OK, let's take a look at how these aspects of central conflict are developed in a completely different type of novel: Elizabeth Berg's *Joy School* (1997). This delicately written and critically praised literary novel tells the story of thirteen-year-old Katie, who must find a way to fit in and be happy when her single-parent father moves them to a new town. Katie seems to find her salvation one day when, after falling through the ice on a skating pond, she falls in love with the handsome guy who pumps gas at a nearby Mobil station.

Hundreds of paperback teen romances have covered similar ground. Why does Berg's novel stand out? First, because she deepens the conflict. The handsome guy, Jimmy, is not exactly a boy. He is twenty-three and married. Berg thus raises the danger factor for Katie; so much so, in fact, that this novel was not, and could not have been, published as a young adult novel. As the novel progresses, Katie digs herself ever deeper into her impossible romantic fantasy.

Alert plot constructors will see right away the plausibility problem with this premise: Why would any thirteen-year-old go for someone so much older? Or, if she does, why wouldn't her parents put a stop to it? Berg, however, does exactly what Crichton does: She makes her impossible central problem seem utterly real. Through the depth of Katie's feelings for Jimmy, as well as through Katie's obvious need for love and Jimmy's subtly revealed need for Katie's admiration, we quickly come to accept Katie's infatuation, perhaps even to cheer for it.

Here is how Berg handles the moment when Jimmy offers wet, shivering Katie some hot chocolate:

> I nod. The Queen of England has never felt better than this. It is something to be saved. And this man is shiver-handsome. He really is. He has brown wavy hair and blue eyes like Superman. He is wearing jeans and a red-checked flannel shirt, and the buttons are open at the top of his throat in a way I can't look at. Although I did see a V of very white T-shirt and some dark curly hairs reaching up. He puts some coins from his own pocket in a machine in the corner of the room, then hands me a thick paper cup. It is the too-dark, skinny kind of cocoa but I know that now it will taste delicious to me. Say I could even have marshmallows. "No thanks," I would say. "Don't need them."

Notice how Berg piles on the details that deftly capture an uncontrolled rush of teenage longing, then adds more. *Shiverhandsome. Coins from his own pocket.* Katie does not exactly gush; rather, every descriptive nuance (. . . *thick paper cup . . . skinny kind of cocoa . . . delicious to me . . .*) adds to the impression of a girl flipping head over heels. Berg's balance of teenage rush and mature restraint is masterful. It really, really is. Katie's unlikely love becomes credible.

All of that would be good enough, but Berg does not stop there. There are other conflicts in *Joy School*, all beautifully layered together. Katie's older sister Diane, who is estranged from their father, is coming to visit; a visit sure to be tenser still because she is pregnant. Katie's new friends are also problematic. Well-off Cynthia has an embarrassing Italian grandmother. Model-pretty Taylor is a shoplifter. Again, none of that would be any different than in your average teen problem novel, except Berg weaves these threads together by giving Katie a personal problem that thematically connects to and clearly magnifies everything else happening to her: She begins to lie.

Berg's mix of longing and lies, of change and chance, gradually builds into a story in which the personal stakes could not be higher. The tension becomes taut as she flings her heroine through a series of surprising turnabouts . . . which brings me to another couple of aspects of plotting the breakout novel.

High Moments, Turning Corners, Killing Characters
The directives in the subheading above are probably self-explanatory, but bear with me. They have useful depths for us to plumb.

And for Elizabeth Berg to plumb, too. As *Joy School* continues, she does not pull her punches. The pregnant sister Diane loses her baby and lands in a Mexican hospital. Cynthia's Italian grandmother dies. Taylor urges Katie to ever-riskier heights, or rather depths, in the backseat on their double dates and later in driving without a license.

Katie's longing for Jimmy reaches a high moment when he takes her for a ride in the restored Corvette ("A Blue Flame Six!") that he keeps under a tarp at the gas station, a secret even from his wife:

> It's cold with the top down, but it's fun, too. The heater will not exactly win any awards, but when you know in a little while you'll be warm again, you're all right. I love the sight of Jimmy's profile, his bare hands on the wheel.

The subtle suggestiveness of the language shifts the story into a higher gear, and immediately afterward Jimmy tells Katie he is moving away. Berg has Katie react with back-to-back grand gestures:

> Oh, now. No. No . . .
> "You are a very handsome man." My voice is wearing boots and marching.
> He looks up, smiles. "Well, thank you. And you are a very attractive young lady."
> "I think I love you."
> His look freezes.
> "No. I do. I can tell."
> "Oh, Katie. I didn't know . . . I didn't mean to—"
> "You didn't do it. You didn't do it. It just happened by its own self."

Two pages later she is in class, unable to read what her history teacher has written on the blackboard:

> "No," I say. "I mean, if you take the first line and go all the way to the last line, that is what I can't read." . . .
> "So what you are saying, Katie, is that you can't read any of this."
> "Yes, sir."

A kind-sized miracle has happened. The students in
Mr. Spurlock's class are sitting up, interested and alert.
"Well, do you need glasses?"
"No. A teacher would do."

Ah! One of those lines I wish I had popped off in high school,
except that Katie does it. Notice that in releasing Katie's confes-
sion of love, Berg also, in a way, releases Katie. She breaks
through barriers, sets her heroine free. That is the purpose of the
second grand gesture: The younger Katie would not have lobbed
an insult at her teacher. Now she has changed. Bigger things are
possible, even while (or perhaps because) her love for Jimmy will
now come to nothing.

Berg is generous with her high moments and is not afraid to
put her heroine through not just painful humiliation but permanent
change. Katie's heart breaks, the grandmother's funeral reveals the
eccentric woman's hidden depths, Katie's sister's marriage ends just
as Katie's father finds new love. Finally, Berg ties up the whole
funny, sharp and painful story with a symbolic gesture involving a
special, smooth stone that Jimmy once gave Katie, and with a fond
nod to an Italian grandmother's indomitable voice:

> I put the stone against my face, right where he
> touched me. And then I fling it far out into the pond.
> It lands right about where I fell through the ice on the
> day I met him. I didn't mean to throw it. I wish I hadn't
> done that. I would like to have the stone back. I could
> carry it in my pocket no matter where I was or who I
> was, it would always be there. I could use it like he said,
> pull it out to soothe a troubled time. I stare out at the
> closed water, curl my fingers around nothing.
>
> Well, whattya gon' do, go complain-a city hall?
>
> I'm cold. I start for home. Winter will pass. It may seem
> that it won't, but it will. And that stone isn't leaving, it's
> just waiting. In the spring, I'll come back and find it again.

Think about the boxes of mementos you have stashed away, the love letters left unburned, the tattered photos lying unrestored. Our real lives are chockablock with confessions unspoken, gestures delayed and impulses stifled. That is why real life is dull and forgettable. The reverse is why breakout novels excite and stay in mind for days.

What are the high moments in your novel? What exactly happens at the climax? If it is an action climax, is its emotional component sharp enough to make your reader catch her breath? If it is an emotional climax, what external action does it provoke? Can the inner and outer climaxes of the story be unified? What symbols can come into play?

Think about it: People do not change without in some way acting out. Once you have ripped out your protagonist's heart, opened her eyes, moved her with the force of an earthquake, what do you have her do? Fix a cup of tea? Please! Have her run hell-bent for leather! Make her do something big, dramatic and loaded with meaning. Symbols are symbols for a reason: They wrap a ton of significance in a tiny package.

Better still, make the changes you craft for your main character permanent and irreversible. There are a million ways to do that—pick your favorite—but whichever way you go, make sure when the dust settles, your hero will never be the same again.

Structuring Plot

At this point you may be thinking, *All that sounds great but what about structure? How can I be sure that my conflicts will escalate in a powerful way, that they will provide a sense of rising action?* Good questions. Let us step back and study the blueprints that can organize your conflicts, high moments and irreversible changes into a breakout novel.

Are you working on a genre novel, such as a mystery, thriller or romance? If so, organizing your plot may not be much of an issue. *Whodunit? Can it be stopped? Will they ever get together?* These are three of the most durable and easy-to-understand story structures around. Are they sturdy enough to support a breakout novel? Certainly. Set these problems in motion, build them in rising steps to a climax and you have a novel.

But a breakout novel? Ah. There is an art to spinning a simple plot structure into a powerful novel. Some of the techniques for doing so have already been covered in this chapter. Remember if the plot is simple, the stakes had better be high, the characters had better be complex, and the conflicts had better be layered like a wedding cake. If they are not, chances are that reader involvement will be low.

A simple tale simply told is a fable. Novels of this type are published from time to time, and some have entered the canon of classics. Robert Nathan's 1939 novel *Portrait of Jennie* comes to mind, as does Daniel Keyes's 1965 novel *Flowers for Algernon*. Such novels generally have a simple idea at their core. Their stories are metaphors with a poetic and lasting resonance. The key is to keep them simple, yet infuse them with sincerity of feeling. Deeply felt fables with a rich enough premise can achieve universal meaning.

Fable-like settings can help accomplish the same thing: Think of the imaginary worlds of James Hilton's *Lost Horizon*, George Orwell's *Animal Farm*, Ray Bradbury's *Fahrenheit 451* or William Golding's *Lord of the Flies*. The simple, inflexible rules in these societies make it easy for their authors to convey a moral point. Of course, all the other rules of breakout storytelling apply to fables, too, though generally the plot layers are fewer. Not just any old fable can break out.

What about plots organized in more complicated ways? One structure that does not easily support a breakout novel is the surprise ending. A sudden twist at the last minute is a great device for a short story, but keeping a secret from the reader for hundreds of pages is a trick almost impossible to pull off. Writers either make the surprise too unpredictable or too obvious. How many times while reading a novel have you thought to yourself, *I saw that coming a mile away!* Those authors have not succeeded in structuring a surprise.

There are exceptions. William Hjortsberg's novel *Falling Angel* (1978) is about a private eye in 1940s New York, Harry Angel. Angel goes in search of a missing person: a crooner named Johnny Favorite who has sold his soul to the devil but who now seems to be trying to slide off the hook. The question of where Johnny Favorite has disappeared to comes down to the final pages and a surprise ending that thrills most first-time readers.

Will it shock you to learn that Johnny Favorite is actually Harry Angel, who lost his memory during the war? It seems pretty obvious when set down plainly. How does Hjortsberg keep this "secret" from becoming obvious over several hundred pages? By employing a huge and effective distraction: a noir novel set in an underworld of black magic and voodoo cults in a wonderfully evoked "modern" Gotham. Thus, a mystery novel becomes the means of keeping the reader's mind off of what is actually a cheat-the-devil tale with a reverse outcome.

Slightly more complicated than that, and a plot structure with a proven track record, is the *frame story*, sometimes called a *tale told in flashback*. In its simplest form, the novel opens at the end of the action and the author then flashes back to show us how we got to that (hopefully) striking state of affairs. The advantage of this structure is it gives both author and reader an end point for which to shoot, a question to answer: *How did we get here?*

Novels as heavy-hitting as Joseph Conrad's *Heart of Darkness* and as lightweight as Robert James Waller's *The Bridges of Madison County* have benefited from the natural organization imposed on a story by this flashback structure. Another classic example is Thornton Wilder's *The Bridge of San Luis Rey*.

When should you apply a frame structure to a novel? Just about any novel can be built that way, but it is most useful for novels that need long setup (that is, novels in which the central conflict will not quickly emerge) or that span long periods of time. The biographical novel—that is, the story of a whole life (discussed in more detail in chapter nine)—is an example. Generally the action of a novel takes place over a short period of time: days, weeks or months. A frame plot structure can lend connection to events that span years or decades.

Another proven plot structure is the *façade story*, in which what at first seems real is shown to be untrue. Façade stories work especially well when told from a narrator's point of view, especially when the narrator is young or offbeat. A naïve narrator's eyes can gradually be opened, as in the coming-of-age novel; alternately, the first-person protagonist can prove to be the deceiver, the so-called unreliable narrator. The gloating antihero of Nabokov's *Lolita*, Humbert Humbert, is both naïve *and* unreliable: He believes that he knows the truth about the object of his twisted desire, succulent Lolita, yet his ultimate undoing is as big a surprise to him as it is to us.

If you are going to peel away the layers of an onion to reveal a hidden secret or truth, it is a good idea to escalate as you go. Raise the stakes, ratchet up the urgency, make the answer to your puzzle seem progressively farther away. What is the point, in a novel, of getting closer to a solution only to find, guess what? That's it! Where is the fun in that? It is far more effective to keep your reader in suspense, taking her down blind alleys as time runs short.

All of the above plot structures usually produce a fairly tight novel; i.e., one in which the focus and time span of the action is relatively short. That is also usually true of the *visitation story*, sometimes shorthanded as "a stranger rides into town." Generally the stranger is an agent of change. The plot is built out of the singular changes brought upon the static residents by the arrival of the stranger.

Larger Plot Structures

What about more expansive plot structures? In a later chapter on advanced plotting, I will discuss some highly complex story patterns, but one common form of expansive plot is that in which a span of time, typically one year, provides the framework for the story. Donna Tartt's successful debut, *The Secret History* (1992), which chronicles a year in the life of a group of classics students, is an example.

The inverse of the visitation story is the expansive quest or journey. Many writing teachers teach only this form, as if Joseph Campbell's *The Hero With a Thousand Faces* (1948) and Christopher Vogler's distillation of Campbell's work *The Writer's Journey* (1998), were the only workable blueprints for a novel.

To be sure, the elements of this mythic structure, strung together, can make for a powerful story: the call to adventure, the call refused, the mentor, the outset, allies and enemies, the test, the innermost cave, the supreme ordeal, the reward, the road back, death and resurrection, and so forth. Its utility in epic or quest fantasy is particularly striking, but these elements can be applied as a template to almost any novel to test its strengths and reveal its weaknesses.

Many writers have benefited from the methods taught by Robert McKee in his screen writing seminar and book by the same name, *Story: Substance, Structure, Style, and the Principles of Screenwriting*. McKee's approach to plot construction involves many elements of the hero's journey. Along with those elements, he teaches principles such as character arc, story logic, scene linkage, setups and payoffs, beats and scenes, and so forth. His overall three-act structure is a powerful tool for building screenplays, although its usefulness in plotting a novel is a little less clear to me.

That said, I have come to feel that the hero's journey is not a universal plot cure. The novel is too fluid a form to have only one basic structure. Same with film. Indeed, I sometimes wonder if the pervasiveness of McKee's seminars does not explain why many Hollywood movies seem to be the same action story relocated in outer space, eighteenth century Scotland, the lethal streets of Los Angeles or wherever you please.

Do those familiar plot structures serve your purpose, or are you after something that does not follow established patterns? What if you are not writing a genre story or working a variation on a classic novel form? What if your novel is not plot driven at all, but rather is a novel that deals with people and their inner lives more than with cooked up action?

Can a novel break out even when it is not highly plotted? Is there a contemporary plot structure that is flexible enough for any literary or mainstream story, yet powerful enough to break out?

In the next chapter, I'll discuss the answers to these questions by examining the shape and structure of contemporary novels.

BREAKOUT Checklist: Plot

✓ Plot is the organization of a story.

✓ The essence of story is conflict.

✓ Conflict in the breakout novel is meaningful, immediate, large scale, surprising, not easily resolved and happens to people for whom we feel sympathy.

✓ The five essential plot elements are sympathetic character, conflict, complications, climax, resolution.

✓ Breakout plots are layered.

✓ Bridging conflict carries the reader from the opening line to the moment when the central conflict is set.

✓ In breakout fiction, the central conflict is as deep and as bad as it possibly can be.

✓ Employ high moments, plot turns and death to change characters or set them free.

✓ To break out, simple plot structures need high stakes, complex characters and layered conflicts.

✓ Simple plot structures produce tight stories; expansive stories come more easily from open-ended or complex plot structures, such as the hero's journey.

CHAPTER SEVEN

Contemporary Plot Techniques

In the long history of literature, the novel is a relatively recent development. It arose during the Enlightenment, flowered during Victorian times, and in more recent decades has shortened and grown more intimate in response to our faster pace of life and in reaction to the dehumanizing aspects of our times. The novel today has downsized, grown more direct and has made character supreme.

The New Shape of the Novel

The transformation of the contemporary novel can be seen in the progressive narrowing of point of view. Once essential, the *author's voice* gave way to *omniscient narration*, which in turn gave way to *objective narration*, which in turn lost ground to *first-* and *third-person narration*, which in turn has been eroded away somewhat by what can be called *close third-person point of view*.

It seems in our postmodern era, readers are only willing to trust stories that are told strictly through the eyes of a story's characters. Perhaps we have been too manipulated by the media? Maybe in our stressed out age we search for authentic experience? Whatever the sociological reasons, it seems that nowadays readers' preferred routes into a novel are through its characters, especially the protagonist. Hence, narrative content—what goes into a story—often is limited to what can be directly experienced by a novel's point-of-view characters. There is no story without them.

In the publishing business one often hears the term *character-driven story*. Like the adjective "edgy," it is a vague term tossed about with assurance and accepted with an equal confidence that it means something. But what, really, is a character-driven story? Is it a concrete plot form? Is it solid enough to serve as the basis for a breakout novel?

The Character-Driven Story

Simply put, a character-driven story is one in which the character's own impulses, desires or needs drive the plot. The protagonist in a character-driven story is not an Everyman prodded into action by outside forces. Rather, he is a dynamic player who impels himself forward, backward, downward or any direction at all, as long as it involves change.

The simplest and least exciting form of this story pattern is one in which a character must uncover a secret in the past in order to become whole in the present. Countless crime novels have employed this pattern, and in my office we see at least one example every week in a query letter from a novice mystery writer. Inevitably we are pitched a detective figure haunted by the past murder of his wife (never husband) which somehow he was unable to solve. Some new clue or information arrives and with it a chance to uncover the truth and at last lay the hero's guilt to rest.

Actually, the hero's inner conflict is rarely identified with a concrete word like "guilt"; instead, it is usually vaguely described as "his demons." So common is this cliché, when I come across it in an outline or a manuscript, I itch to set the pages aside right then, and frequently do.

A more flexible and frequently employed form of the character-driven plot is the *journey of self-discovery*. It may be a journey into marriage or across Nepal, but whether short or long, inward looking or outward bound—or, in many cases, both—the journey of self-discovery is like the hero's journey, except the prize to be won is not an object that will save the world but a transformation that will save one soul.

There are a great many ways to send a character on a journey of self-discovery. It need not involve actual travel. In one form or another, it involves being lost, then found.

In Jennifer Chiaverini's 1999 debut novel, *The Quilter's Apprentice*, young wife Sarah McClure is adrift due to nothing more profound than her inability to find a job after moving with her husband to a small Pennsylvania town:

> Funny how things had turned out. In college she had been the one with clear goals and direction, taking all the right classes and participating in all the right extracurricular activities and summer internships. Her friends had often remarked that their own career plans seemed vague or nonexistent in comparison. And now they were going places while she sat around the house with nothing to do.

No dark angst here. No depression or drinking to make her unsympathetic. Sarah is merely adrift. Although she wonders whether she is unconsciously sabotaging her job interviews, it is not a deep worry. Sarah occupies herself by taking quilting lessons from master quilter Sylvia Compson. As Mrs. Compson stitches together the story of her life, Sarah finds herself increasingly drawn to the quilters' world. In the end, she uses her hated accounting skills to save Mrs. Compson's endangered home, Elm Creek Manor, and turn it into a quilting retreat center. Her life achieves meaning and purpose.

Fictional protagonists today are frequently at sea following the loss of a loved one. Contemporary literature is littered with dead children, spouses and parents, and with the survivors who must put their lives back together following family tragedies. Jane Hamilton's *A Map of the World*, mentioned in chapter four, opens

with an eloquent statement of a woman's despair after the drowning of her friend's daughter:

> I used to think that if you fell from grace it was more
> likely than not the result of one stupendous error, or else
> an unfortunate accident. I hadn't learned that it can hap-
> pen so gradually you don't lose your stomach or hurt your-
> self in the landing. You don't necessarily sense the motion.
> I've found it takes at least two and generally three things
> to alter the course of a life: You slip around the truth once,
> and then again, and one more time, and there you are,
> feeling, for a moment, that it was sudden, your arrival at
> the bottom of the heap.

Here is a woman not only adrift but in need of total renewal.
Notice, though, how Hamilton uses her heroine's self-awareness
to keep her sympathetic. Her heroine is lost but not weak. She
has fallen from grace, but she has tracked her downward path.
Because she has perspective on her fall, we know she will find a
way back to happiness, a trail to a restored self.

Jacquelyn Mitchard's 1996 novel *The Deep End of the Ocean*
concerns a similar tragedy, the disappearance of photographer
Beth Cappadora's three-year-old son Ben from a Chicago hotel
lobby while she has her back turned for a minute to check in. In
the framing prologue, Beth looks at photographs of her son for
the first time in eleven years and contemplates the extent of her
loss, the cost of grief which has not yet healed:

> Beth had once put stock in such things. Signs and
> portents, like water going counterclockwise down a sink
> drain before an earthquake. When she was seventeen, she
> believed that missing all the red lights between Wolf Road
> and Mannheim would mean that when she got home her
> mother would tell her that Nick Palladino had called. She
> believed, if not in God, then in saints who had at least

once been fully human. She had a whole history, a life
structure set up on luck, dreams, and hunches.

And it all went down like dominoes in a gust, on the
day Ben disappeared.

The collapse of a life's architecture is powerfully expressed in
this passage. Hamilton's and Mitchard's heroines yank us almost
against our wills into their journeys toward restoration and
wholeness. It is through these characters that the narrative drive
is formed. The story of their inner journies is the story of the
novel.

In cases of lost identity, the journey of self-discovery becomes
literal. Anne Perry's *The Face of a Stranger*, mentioned in chapter
five, is one example. Another is Robert Silverberg's highly successful 1980 science fiction novel *Lord Valentine's Castle*. In this
epic tale, Valentine is a young man with no memory. He becomes
an apprentice to a troupe of jugglers and journeys across the
planet Majipoor, through the city of the Shapeshifters, the temple of the Lady of Sleep and the Isle of the King of Dreams, in
a quest to regain his identity and his rightful claim to royalty.

Turning an inner journey into an actual sojourn provides not
only a durable metaphor but also a useful framework for plot.
Mona Simpson's 1986 mother-daughter road trip, *Anywhere But
Here*, is one example. Cormac McCarthy's 1992 National Book
Award-winning novel *All the Pretty Horses* sends its young protagonist, John Grady Cole, on a horseback journey across the border
to a Mexican hacienda, where he breaks horses and is in turn
broken when he falls tragically in love with the hacienda owner's
beautiful daughter.

Journeys into the past to uncover a long-hidden secret are
not my favorite type of self-discovery story. It is difficult to make
long ago events seem truly urgent in the present. Even so, it can
be done. The key, I believe, lies in tying some present problem
to the past. In Margaret Maron's Edgar Award-winning 1992
mystery novel *Bootlegger's Daughter*, South Carolina attorney

Deborah Knott delves into an eighteen-year-old murder. There is nothing special in that. The novel's high stakes come, rather, from Deborah's simultaneous run for a judge's seat. The injustices she has witnessed in court stoke her desire to win, but digging up the past stirs up unwelcome legacies, not least of which is her father's shady history. Maron does not try to build a novel only on the past; rather, the past bears heavily upon the present.

Another outstanding link between past events and a present journey can be found in A.S. Byatt's 1990 tour de force *Possession*, in which two literary scholars, Maud Bailey and Roland Mitchell, search for the truth about a love affair between two Victorian poets. By all rights this story ought to be a snore. The truth about a love affair between two fairly minor, long-dead poets? Who on earth cares about that?

Byatt makes it matter because as their academic detective work deepens, Maud and Roland find themselves coping with professional rivalries as well as challenges to their ideas about their subjects, themselves and their own relationship. Separately, neither the research nor the relationship are of high consequence, but by joining them Byatt is able to make the past important to the present, and vice versa. Byatt breaks the rule about a journey into the past by tying it to a sojourn—in this case, toward love—in our own times.

What sort of journey are the characters in your current manuscript on? Protagonists can be driven from their static situations into action by all manner of outer forces and inner motives. The propellant for the journey is a fuel as varied as human experience itself. What moves you to get out of bed in the morning? To take the bus instead of the train? To leave your wife? To take holy orders? To paint yourself blue and ride a bicycle backwards across British Columbia?

You do not do things like that? Clearly you are not on a journey of self-discovery.

Why are journeys of self-discovery so compelling? Because they take us to interesting places? Bring us into contact with people we would not otherwise meet? I do not think the people and places encountered along the road are adequate to explain the appeal of this type of story, although obviously that is part of it. Neither is it wholly the resolution of an inner conflict that satisfies. Think about it: You do not have to propel yourself any farther away than church, an AA meeting or a therapy session to find healing and wholeness.

No, I think what gives the journey of self-discovery its deep-rooted attraction is the promise of transformation. At the end of the trip, you—sorry, the hero—is not the same as at the beginning. The hero is different. Better. Stronger. Wiser. Happier. At peace. All in 350 pages! It takes most of us decades to shake off our doubts, fears, self-defeating habits, self-image problems, money worries and so on. We long to wrestle the problems of life into a healthy perspective. We dream of rising above it all. But who has the time or the energy?

The protagonists of self-discovery novels do have the time and energy. They seek the inner light that to us looks dim. They embark upon the journey and complete it. They change themselves in ways the rest of us would dearly like to. They are the new heroes of our age.

So profound is our Postmodern dream of becoming something different, as opposed to the Modern Era's existential mandate to accept ourselves the way we are, that our current period's central purpose seems to be to alter everything radically and completely, and to do so at high speed.

With regard to fiction, I am not talking about old-fashioned character growth but the Big Transformation. Changing Everything. The mutation that means we will never have to go back to the ugly old place or be the ugly old self ever again: deep-down, soul-shaking, irreversible transformation for good and for always.

Self-Discovery in the Plot-Driven Novel

Of course, the journey of self-discovery can be a narrative line in an otherwise plot-driven novel. Indeed, so powerful is the grip of self-discovery on novelists today, it is rare to read a breakout novel in which the protagonist is *not* on an inner journey, searching for a better self while also searching for true love, whodunit, a way to prevent The End of the World as We Know It, or whatever.

Once a hero was a red-blooded, steady-as-a-rock guy, sure of himself, strong and unchanging. Think James Bond. Today a hero is strong but to some extent is uncertain of himself. Think Harry Potter. In a breakout novel today, the hero may save the day, but he is also likely to save himself in the process.

Character transformation is a particularly tricky business for authors of series novels, such as mysteries or science fiction sagas. Indeed, so popular is the series format even romance publishers have invented ways to stretch one-in-a-lifetime love to once-a-month visits with communities of familiar characters.

A client of mine, the John W. Campbell Award-winning science fiction writer David Feintuch, faced this sort of problem at the conclusion of his popular four-book saga of space-navy hero Nicholas Seafort. The first volume in the series, *Midshipman's Hope* (1994), thrusts junior officer Nick into an impossible, but ultimately heroic, situation. By the fourth volume, *Fisherman's Hope* (1996), Nick has become an old man and a world leader, saving human civilization while reconciling with his father.

The problem? Readers wanted more. So did Feintuch's hero Seafort. He would not die. But how many times and in how many ways can one transform a man who has been through it all? Feintuch has solved this problem by finding smaller but nevertheless significant aspects of Nick's character to change. For example, in the sixth novel in the sequence, *Patriarch's Hope* (1999), Nick has become SecGen of the United Nations. He has diverted Earth's resources into the construction of a heavily armed space navy, leaving the planet a wasteland pocked with toxic swamps. The radical Enviro movement protests, but Nick cannot abide its violent methods. Clearly, Nick is in the wrong, but he mightily resists any change.

Nick's son, Philip, attempts to turn his father's heart by taking him on a tour of the decimated Earth. He is not successful until they arrive at the final stop on the tour, where Nick (temporarily confined to a robotic chair) narrates his epiphany:

> Danil took his place. "Sir, where are we?"
>
> "Some godforsaken hellhole. No doubt [Philip] picked the worst place on the planet, to impress me." I blinked; my vision began to clear. Brown, unhealthy grass. A neglected fence. A few scraggly trees, struggling against impossible odds.
>
> "It's just a farm," said Danil. "A ratty old place, if you ask me. Mr. Winstead could show you a thousand—"
>
> A cry of despair.
>
> He leaped, as if galvanized.
>
> "No. Not here. *NO!*"
>
> "Sir, what—"
>
> "Take me away!" My fists beat a tattoo on the chair.
>
> He drew back, stared at me in shock.
>
> Father's farm, the home of my boyhood.
>
> Cardiff.
>
> The remains of blistered paint hung from sagging siding.
>
> A quarter century, since I'd last been home. Not since my wife Annie . . . I'd left her here with Eddie Boss, and fled to the monastery. Eventually she divorced me. The farm was a last gift. I hadn't wanted to see it, see her, recall life's promise I'd squandered.
>
> The gate I'd oft vowed to fix lay rotted across the walk.
>
> The hill behind, down which I'd run, arms spread wide to catch the wind, was gray and dead.
>
> In my mask, I began to weep.

Transformed, Nick becomes an environmental reformer at great political and personal cost. The rebellion that Nick must single-handedly put down at the novel's climax is all the more powerful because it was provoked by his own new convictions.

One further word about mixing a character-driven narrative line with plot-driven narrative lines: A depth and emotional power will be added to your story if you can unify the inner and outer climaxes. The logic of this is probably clear, but putting it into practice will take careful orchestration. Commit to it, though, and it can be done.

Whatever drives the main character in your character-driven story, make sure it is an inner conflict as powerful as any outer conflict could hope to be: urgent, unavoidable and full of an emotional appeal that anyone can feel. Setting your character on such a journey is often the key to breaking out.

Nonlinear Narrative

As I said ours is the Postmodern Age in which absolute certainties are suspicious and only one's individual outlook is trustworthy. Authority is obsolete. Language is a social construct and therefore unreliable—unless it is deconstructed, in which case I guess we are OK. The one constant and worthwhile fact of contemporary life is change.

Given those sentiments, it is perhaps not surprising some novelists are drawn to story structures that undermine the whole notion of story itself. Experimental fiction and hypertexts take this intention to an extreme with which most readers are uncomfortable. (Although I would recommend to anyone a look at the work of British novelist B.S. Johnson, the most accessible experimental novelist that I have found.)

Fortunately for me, most novelists do not want to completely tear down their art form. An adventurous mainstream novelist, however, may find himself at one time or another drawn to a story that plays with time, reality and/or identity.

The great paradigm of such experiments is *Tristram Shandy*

by Laurence Sterne, which was written in about 1750. A more recent example might be Philip K. Dick's *Valis* (1981), a novel that sends its protagonist, Horselover Fat, on a search for sanity in an insane world. As with so much of Dick's fiction, a central conceit is that reality is not what it seems. In *Slaughterhouse-Five* (1966), Kurt Vonnegut presents us with a protagonist whose life is lived in a scrambled order.

The guiding principle of any nonlinear plot is that the story is not organized in terms of chronological time but according to some other logical progression. For example, if the purpose of your story is to unfold the secrets at the center of your hero's life, then there is no reason the key events or revelations need to be presented in the calendar order in which they occurred. What is more important is that there is a march toward understanding, a sense we are drawing ever closer to the truth wherever it may lie.

That said, not just any time-hopping plot pattern will result in a satisfying novel. It is still important for tension to escalate. Rising action is the key. If going backward through time makes things progressively more exciting, then by all means deliver your chronology in reverse. If a mystery grows more puzzling by moving from B to D to C to A, then experiment: Shuffle around the sequence of scenes.

If you do embrace a nonlinear structure, though, you might consider the use of a *marker*; that is, a touch point in time to which the novel periodically returns. It is like home base, or better still a front porch: a familiar place to which the reader can ascend to get a view of what has been happening.

When is a nonlinear novel over? As with any story, it is over when conflict ends. Can a nonlinear plot structure be the basis for a breakout novel? I suspect that it can, but if so it will be a special case. People still want to be told stories. Beginning, middle and end are powerful cultural conveyors, and even in our relativistic Postmodern Age, there is a longing for the grounding of a moral declared and a resolution found.

Tension on Every Page

Conflict is the unsettling core of events that makes us stop and look, wanting to understand, wondering what will happen, hoping for the best, fearing the worst. When the conflict level in a novel is high—that is, when it is immediate, credible, personal, unavoidable and urgent—it makes us slow down and read every word. When it is low, we are tempted to skim. We do not care. We wonder, *what's on TV?*

Have you noticed how an audience fidgets during the love scenes in a romantic movie? That is because sex usually is a release of tension. From the moment conflict is over, we restlessly long to move on. The same is true in a novel. The moment tension slacks off, reader attention slacks off, too. It is as if the derivation of the word is "at-tension."

Without a doubt the most common flaw I see in manuscripts from beginners and midcareer novelists alike is the failure to invest every page of a novel with tension. Low tension equals low interest. High tension equals high interest. The ratio is mathematic, the result positive, so why do so many writers believe they can ignore the equation?

Certain types of scenes are so reliably low tension that when reading a manuscript, I count them in my notes with hatch marks. They include: mulling things over while driving from one place to another, relaxing in the shower, fixing a cup of tea or coffee. Category romance writers are especially prone to these time wasters. When they complain to me at conferences that they cannot seem to break "out of category," it is a pretty good bet that their heroines are tea addicts.

How many coffee breaks does your protagonist take in your current manuscript? Any? Cut them out. Now. And eject him from his car, too. (Unless, perhaps, it is hurtling off a cliff or the passengers inside are in some other way careening out of control.)

Another way to avoid slack tension is to build a novel in scenes. A well-constructed scene has a mini-arc of its own: a beginning, rise and climax or reversal at the end. Jump cutting from the close of one narrative development, one unit of complication, to the beginning of the next moves a story along at an efficient clip.

The so-called "aftermath" scene, in which the hero digests what has just happened to him and settles on his next step, is an outdated technique. Low tension breeds in the space between confrontations and other high moments. Today, breakout novelists frequently use exposition—that is, interior monologues in which there is no action—not to propel their protagonists in new directions but to deepen dilemmas and increase tension.

Exposition can be tricky, needless to say. It trips up beginners all the time. Irresolution and mixed feelings are by definition tense, but getting that across in words is something else again. If your protagonist is merely going to wallow or rehash what we already know, I suggest leaving such passages out of your book. In first manuscripts those are more often than not the passages that I skim.

For the same reason, it is wise to avoid a strictly sequential narrative. By that I mean the narrative pattern that follows a protagonist's movements through a day, from waking in bed and everything in between. It is easy to accumulate pages that way but hard to make every waking moment gripping.

One of the greatest crafters of high-tension stories working today is John Grisham. As with many best-selling authors, it is fashionable to put down his writing: *His prose is plain . . . his scene setting is perfunctory to nonexistent . . . his characters are cardboard cutouts.* There is some truth to those charges, but one cannot deny that Grisham compels his readers to turn the pages. His gift for building tension has made him the country's best-selling author.

What is even more amazing to me is that Grisham has done that while breaking one of the biggest and most fundamental rules of plot construction: Grisham's protagonists frequently do not fully reveal themselves to the reader until late in his novels. Think about it. . . . In his 1996 novel *The Runaway Jury*, the plot revolves around a mysterious juror in a high-stakes court case in which the big five tobacco companies are being sued. The juror, Nicholas Easter, has maneuvered to have himself selected. He is highly savvy about the jury-fixing tactics employed by the tobacco companies. He has a purpose, a mission. But what is it? For two hundred pages, we do not know, nor is there any other sympathetic character, let alone hero, in sight.

Grisham's 1997 novel *The Partner* is focused around the capture of a lawyer, Patrick Lanigan, who faked his own death and disappeared with a $90 million settlement from his firm's bank account. He is apprehended in Brazil, tortured, turned over to the FBI. The money has vanished to tax havens unknown, but we learn that *he has not spent a penny of it*. Why not? In faking his death, it seems that he murdered someone to leave behind a body. He deserted a beautiful wife and small daughter. Sympathetic his actions are not. So what is Patrick Lanigan up to? What motivates him? It is not until very late in the novel that we find out.

Grisham is a master of holding back information from his readers. He leaves us without a conventional hero for whom to cheer for hundreds of pages. Only an author with great skill in the art of generating tension can do that. Grisham is such an author.

But how, exactly, does he do it? First, let us acknowledge that the premises of his stories have inherent tension, originality and gut emotional appeal. For instance, take *The Partner*: A fugitive hunt and the fugitive's subsequent prosecution proves, not surprisingly, to be a milieu shot through with conflicting interests. Patrick Lanigan's spectacular escape from the grind has emotional appeal; indeed, in the story he becomes something of a folk hero among lawyers. At the same time, Grisham does not make his motives obvious or his circumstances appealing; in fact, Grisham disguises them. It is a tactic with tremendous originality.

The mystery of Patrick Lanigan's motives underlies much of our interest in *The Partner*. Grisham keeps the pot boiling, though, by building extremely high stakes for all those who need to find Lanigan or, perhaps, keep him dead: the bounty hunter

Jack Stephano, Lanigan's bankrupt ex-law partners, Lanigan's insurance-dependent "widow" Trudy, and his beautiful Brazilian lawyer and lover Eva Miranda. Grisham also drops little hints along the way that Lanigan is not a bad man. Eva loves him. He has not spent the money. He also has anticipated everything that is going to happen to him. He planned for it. He fully expected to get caught.

Even so, it is hundreds of pages before we have enough information to fully understand Lanigan and to sympathize with him. Grisham keeps us going by making sure every scene advances or sets back Lanigan's friends or enemies. His prose is plain but direct. He does not waste words. His scene setting is perfunctory but efficient. His characters may be cardboard, but each has a clear, uncomplicated purpose. Every moment of the story contributes to building conflict.

Flip to any scene in *The Partner* at random, and you will find Grisham building tension. The end of chapter twelve finds Patrick Lanigan winding up a meeting with the law school buddy Sandy McDermott whom he has chosen to defend him. Lanigan describes his torture and instructs McDermott to file a lawsuit against the FBI, a gesture of hopeless defiance since Lanigan knows perfectly well it was not the FBI who abused him. He tells McDermott: "It's strategy. A little sympathy won't hurt." In their closing exchange, Grisham simultaneously ratchets up the danger for McDermott and buoys Lanigan's sympathy quotient with a larger-than-life bit of bravery:

> "Be careful," Patrick said. "As soon as you're identified as my lawyer, you'll attract all sorts of strange and nasty people."
>
> "The press?"
>
> "Yeah, but not exactly what I had in mind. I've buried a lot of money, Sandy. There are people who'll do anything to find it."
>
> "How much of the money is left?"

"All of it. And then some more."

"It may take that to save you, pal."

"I have a plan."

"I'm sure you do. See you in Biloxi."

A couple of pages later, FBI exec Hamilton Jaynes learns about Lanigan's lawsuit against the bureau. After learning it was the bounty hunter Stephano who captured Lanigan, Jaynes applies pressure to Stephano to tell him everything about how Lanigan was apprehended and what was done to him afterward, and by whom. He threatens to arrest Stephano's clients for paying for torture, which unfortunately failed to disclose the location of the stolen money. Their exchange briskly and efficiently clocks up the stakes for both of them:

"It'll kill your business, you know," Jaynes said, feigning sympathy.

"So what do you want?"

"Well, here's the deal. It's quite simple. You tell us everything—how you found him, how much he told you, etc., everything. We have lots of questions—and we'll drop the charges against you and lay off your clients."

"It's nothing but harassment then."

"Exactly. We wrote the book. Your problem is that we can humiliate your clients and put you out of business."

"Is that all?"

"No. With a bit of luck on our end, you could also go to jail."

* * *

"I'll have to talk to my attorney."

Tick, tick, tick: the tension goes up, up, up. Pick any scene in the novel, and you will find Grisham piling it on. On page

197, Lanigan's enemies are setting up camp in Biloxi (site of the coming trial) on the theory that the Lanigan's accomplice Eva Miranda, who can lead them to the missing money, will sooner or later have to surface there. On pages 197-201, Grisham delivers the backstory of Benny Aricia, the whistle-blower whose revelations about overbilling by a government contractor resulted in the $90 million jury award that Lanigan took; a backstory that, for the moment, makes the money look like a well-deserved reward.

Criticize Grisham if you must, but there is this to learn from him: Tension on every page is a technique that keeps readers glued to a novel, even in the absence of artistic prose, rich atmosphere, complex characters and lofty themes. It is the application of macroconflict on a microscale.

It is a key breakout skill.

BREAKOUT Checklist: Contemporary Plot Techniques

✓ The new shape of the novel is the character-driven story.

✓ Character volition propels the character-driven story.

✓ Breakout fiction frequently involves journeys of self-discovery.

✓ Breakout protagonists transform, even in series fiction.

✓ In nonlinear narrative, rising conflict or unfolding secrets dictate scene order.

✓ Build a novel in scenes, but avoid "aftermath" scenes.

✓ The secret of breakout plotting is tension on every page.

CHAPTER EIGHT

Multiple Viewpoints, Subplots, Pace, Voice, Endings

Multiple Points of View

Most authors think of multiple points of view as a requirement of the breakout novel. More ambitious still is the spinning of subplots, extra narrative lines with their own conflicts, complications, climaxes and resolutions. Does breaking out depend on these techniques? Is a "big" book big only if it has multiple viewpoints or subplots?

You would think so given how often the subject comes up at writers conferences. Authors who want to convince me of the breakout potential of their novels almost invariably assure me, "Of course, it has multiple points of view." It is as if those extra angles on the action will magically conjure larger advances.

The truth, needless to say, is not so simple. Plenty of bestselling novels are told from one primary point of view, while scads of failed novels have subplots galore. Multiple points of view and subplots can enhance your novel or they can detract from it. It is all in how you build them—or don't.

That said, I must admit there is something satisfying about reading novels with multiple points of view. These views provide diversion from, and contrast to, the protagonist's perspective. They can deepen conflict, enlarge a story's scope and add to a novel the rich texture of real life.

Subplots carry those effects even further. In our workaday world, we do not live in isolation. Our lives intersect, collide and overlap. Subplots lend the same sense of connectivity to a novel. They remind us of our mutual need, our inescapable conflicts and our intertwined destinies.

Subplots and multiple points of view make novels longer to be sure, and more work, but rewards for that effort are there for writer and reader alike; that is, if they are successful. Let us look first at subplots and how to build them in the breakout novel.

Successful Subplots

A subplot is still a plot. The same five elements that we have identified as plot essentials will need to be present in every subplot in order for it to be complete. Choosing a subplot, then, begins with choosing characters with which to work. Who among your secondary characters is sufficiently sympathetic and faces conflicts that are deep, credible, complex and universal enough to be worth developing?

If none are to be found, it might be worthwhile to grow some of your secondary characters, depending on the nature of your novel. Do you intend it to be a sweeping epic? If so you certainly will want to construct a cast with plenty of subplot potential. Is it a tightly woven, intimate exploration of a painful period in one character's life? In that case subplots will only pull you and your readers away from your main purpose. You may not even want to clutter your novel with multiple points of view.

Subplots will not have the desired magnification effect unless there are connections between them. Thus, the main characters in each subplot need to be in proximity to one another; that is, they need a solid reason to be in the same book. Therefore, in searching for subplots, I recommend breakout novelists first look to those characters already in the main character's life: family, classmates, colleagues and so forth.

One of the most difficult subplot tricks to pull off involves creating story lines for two characters who at first have no connection whatsoever, then merging those plotlines. For some reason, this structure is particularly attractive to beginning novelists. While such a feat can be pulled off, again and again I find that novices fail to bring their plotlines together quickly enough. Beginners often feel the need to present scenes from each plotline in strict rotation, whether or not there is a necessity for them. The result is a manuscript laden with low-tension action.

Joining together story lines from two different eras has similar challenges. A time-traveling character is one easy solution, but that gimmick is not for every novel. Absent that, forging tight connections between two times, and forging them quickly, is essential. Some successful examples can be found in *The French Lieutenant's Woman* (1969) by John Fowles, Katherine Neville's *The Eight* (1988) and A.S. Byatt's *Possession* (1990).

In such novels you will see that the connection between past and present is established almost immediately; or, if it is not, then one era or the other simply is not introduced until it is needed. In truth, it seems to me that many such stories I see on submission do not need a second era at all.

In his 1999 breakout *Cryptonomicon*, science fiction writer Neal Stephenson tells the story of World War II cryptographer Lawrence Pritchard Waterhouse, and of his present day grandson, Randy, who is attempting to create a "data haven" in Southeast Asia. (Note the contrast in their purposes: One seeks to hide information, the other to keep it free.) What connects the two stories is a sunken Nazi submarine that holds the secret to an unbreakable code called Arethusa. It is the binding that holds sprawling *Cryptonomicon* together.

A second requirement of subplots is that they each affect the outcome of the main plotline. If a subplot can be cut with no consequence to the outcome of the story, then question whether it belongs in the novel to begin with. Subplots widen the scope of the novel's action, but if that is all they do then, once again, the result is likely to be a sluggish volume.

A third quality of successful subplots is that they range. In nineteenth century sagas this often meant ranging high and low over the strata of society, from princesses to beggars, from the palace to the gutter. Social scale is a bit harder to pull off today. More helpful, I think, is to think of portraying a variety of experience. Your setting may be restricted to one milieu, but ranging over that milieu in all its aspects will enrich the world of your novel.

How Many?

How many subplots are too many? Novels swimming in subplots can feel diffuse. Two or three major subplots are about all that even the longest quest fantasies can contain. With more than three subplots, it becomes difficult to sustain reader involvement. Focus is too scattered. Sympathy is torn in too many directions.

Readers of overcrowded novels frequently complain, "It was hard to keep the characters straight." That is often due to the author's failure to maintain strong character delineation. Great saga writers have a gift for creating large and varied casts, but it is a rare author who can make more than twenty characters highly individual and distinct. In truth, only giant sagas need that many characters. Novels begin to take on breakout expansiveness with little more than two points of view and as few as one, possibly two, subplots.

Proof of this can be found in some of our era's greatest sagas. James Clavell's 1975 blockbuster *Shōgun* is a doorstop of a novel, 1,200 pages in paperback. It is a massive and immensely detailed journey through feudal Japan. Scores of characters appear, many of them with points of view. For all its heft, though, there are really only two principle points of view: John Blackthorne, the shipwrecked English pilot-major who saves the life of powerful *daimyo* Toranaga, and the beautiful and courageous married woman with whom Blackthorne falls in love, Mariko. Even so, most of the book belongs to Blackthorne.

Similarly, Larry McMurtry's 1985 sprawling cattle-drive of a novel, *Lonesome Dove*, tells dozens of colorful tales—of cowboys, whores, swindlers and such—but without a doubt the novel's primary focus is cattleman Augustus McCrae. James Jones's gigantic 1951 epic of World War II, *From Here to Eternity*, is built around just two men, Pvt. Robert E. Lee Prewitt and 1st Sgt. Milton Anthony Warden; this in a novel that fills 850 pages in its current trade paperback edition.

What these master storytellers know is that a large-scale story is nevertheless still just a story. Overcomplicate it and you lose the essential simplicity of narrative art. Readers identify primarily with one strong, sympathetic central character; it is that character's destiny about which they most care. Have you ever skimmed ahead in a novel to find the next scene involving your favorite character? Then you know what I mean. Enrich your novel with multiple viewpoints, but keep subplots down to a minimum.

In fact, many breakout novels that seem to have lots of subplots are really only telling the same story from different points of view. In chapter five I mentioned Sandra Brown's best-seller *Where There's Smoke*. In this busy novel, there are many major points of view: Dr. Lara Mallory, the newcomer with a past; Key Thackett, bad-boy brother of Lara's dead lover; Jody Thackett, ailing but imperious head of Thackett Oil; Janellen Thackett, her repressed daughter; Bowie Cato, the ex-con whom Janellen hires to work the rigs and with whom she falls in love; Darcy Winston, the local society slut who lusts for Key; Fergus Winston, Darcy's calculating husband; Heather Winston, Darcy's calculating cheerleader daughter; Tanner Hoskins, Heather's hapless boyfriend.

Have I missed any? Probably. All of the point-of-view characters have lines of action that are sewn up by the end of the novel: Jody Thackett is dead. So are Heather and Tanner. Fergus Winston is in jail. Janellen and Bowie have married despite likely public disapproval. And as for Lara and Key, the revelations and changes they undergo are too many to summarize. One certainty, though, is fulfilled: By the end they are together.

In fact, *Where There's Smoke* essentially is a romance. All the other characters are there in some way or other to keep Lara and

Key from getting together, a juggling act that Brown manages splendidly.

Only two subplots in *Where There's Smoke* reach conclusions: the against-the-odds romance of Janellen and Bowie, and the tragically misguided teenage love affair between Heather and Tanner. Why does Brown give them both endings? Because they serve to comment upon the novel's main romance. Janellen and Bowie's love transcends pubic pressures, a strength that Lara and Key must learn. Heather and Tanner die as a result of meddling by Heather's mother. This parallels the destructive role played by Key's mother, Jody. In other words, the subplots amplify themes running through the main plotline. They are supportive, not wholly separate.

How can you be sure the subplots in your novel either support or parallel your main plotline? Here is where your purpose in writing your novel needs to be clear in your mind. Most authors launch into their manuscripts without giving any thought to theme. Breakout novelists, on the other hand, generally are writing for a reason. They have something to say. Identifying that something will be covered in chapter ten. For now, let us stipulate only that you cannot fully grasp the relationship of your subplots to your main plot until you know what they all really are about.

If you do not know—if, say, you are an organic writer—then perhaps it is best not to plan subplots but simply to allow multiple points of view into your story, then see which points of view grow into subplots. (In fact, it is not uncommon for organic writers to find that a minor story line has mushroomed out of control and has become their novel's main plot.)

Finally, it is worth repeating that not all novels need subplots. There are, for instance, a great many point-of-view characters in Grisham's *The Partner*, analyzed at the end of the last chapter. Yet out of perhaps a dozen major points of view, no other character than Patrick Lanigan has a truly separate story line. The entire novel is built around the desperate situation of this runaway lawyer with the $90 million in stolen money. Every-one else in the novel either supports him or tries to tear him down.

The Partner feels like it is elaborately plotted, but in reality its structure is simple: It is about a man digging himself out of the worst imaginable trouble. To be sure, there are endless com-plications, but *The Partner* has no true subplots.

Group and generational novels such as Mary McCarthy's *The Group*, Philip Rock's *The Passing Bells* (1978) and Anton Myrer's *The Last Convertible* (1978) are exceptions to the rule on limiting subplots. Here, though, diversity of experience is the point. In this plot pattern, a group begins in a common place, diverges, then reassembles again so that we can measure the variety of its experience. It is a pattern that demands subplots but also has a powerful unifying element to glue it together: the generation or group itself.

Before you get carried away with subplots and points of view, remember it is perfectly possible to write a breakout novel from the protagonist's perspective alone. How do you know whether to include a particular subplot or let it drop? The answer lies in a subplot's contribution to the overall novel. Is it mere diversion, as in the oft-attempted-but-rarely-successful "comic relief" sub-plot? If so, it should be cut.

On the other hand, if it complicates, bears upon, or mirrors or reverses the main plot, then it adds value.

Building Subplots

How, then, do you build a subplot? How should it be weighted? How many scenes should it entail? Go back to the three aspects of a successful subplot: connections, added complications and extra range. These dictate the size and, to some extent, the struc-ture of subplots. Let us look at how.

In forging connections between plotlines, character lists and plotline chronologies can be helpful. There are probably unused connections between the plotlines in your current novel. Look for nodes of conjunction, such as settings. For instance, suppose in your main story line you have a wedding, while a subplot involves a breakup. Why not have both occur at the same time and in the same place?

Other nodes of connection can be built in backstory. It is a shame when paired characters have only one point of common reference, say childhood or college. A novel's texture is generally much richer when there are multiple connections between characters. Why should a wife's best friend be only her best friend? Cannot she also be the co-worker who is causing the wife's husband a problem at his office? Cannot the co-worker's own husband be the first wife's doctor, who must inform her that she has cancer? Can the two men be old army buddies? Can the women have an old high-school rivalry?

Interwoven character relationships almost create plot complications all by themselves. They can help make plot outcomes dependent upon each other. In the above example, for instance, the office politics are going to change when the office exec learns that her best friend has cancer. The two army buddies—let's say that they saved each other's lives in Vietnam—are bound to fall out to some extent when the doctor can do nothing to cure the cancer killing his buddy's wife.

Did you follow that hypothetical example? You did? Wow. A four-way plot like the one above poses big challenges. Do all four characters get their own full plot or even point of view? If so, the novel runs the risk of being too diffuse. In a three- or four-way situation, it may be better for the novel to be primarily about only one person. Which one? Hmm. The answer probably will depend on your own personal interests.

Anne Perry has built her longest-running Victorian mystery series around a pair of characters, Thomas and Charlotte Pitt, whose marriage and contrasting backgrounds provide rich connections between plotlines. Thomas is the son of a groundskeeper wrongly convicted of a crime. He is lowborn and burning with a desire always to know the truth. Charlotte is a highborn woman offended by social inequalities and injustices that she sees around her—and there are plenty in 1890s London. They are married, but neither can wholly cross into the other's world. They can, however, investigate crimes from differing angles, and it is the clash and connections between society and the street that lend this series its interwoven plots and storytelling range.

Connections between characters can sometimes feel a little contrived, of course, but I find most readers willing to accept them provided the connections are drawn in enough detail to make them convincing. If plot connections do not feel natural, it is important to work on them until they do. Take Anne Perry: How does she keep Thomas and Charlotte's marriage from seeming a contrivance? She does this by making their love for one another warm and wholly genuine.

Range can be added to a novel not only by selecting a cast from different levels of your world but by having characters leap between story lines, possibly even change places. Great plot twists come from a sudden elevation, or fall, from one level to another. Altering a character's role can make a plot twist, too; for example, as with the mystery benefactor who is revealed as the bum sleeping in a cardboard box in the park. Look in your current manuscript for underutilized characters who can cross plotlines. Put them to work. Your novel will be richer for the interweaving that you do.

Contrast is also essential in constructing subplots. What use is it to rehash the main story line's conflicts or its circumstances? Be sure your subplots are truly different from your main story line in purpose, tone and substance. Only then will your manuscript have the multidimensional feel of a breakout novel. Repetition adds nothing.

Finally, how many scenes should you give your subplots? As many as they need, but far fewer than the main plotline. If, no matter what you do, a given subplot outweighs the main plotline, then obviously it is richer in inherent conflict and other qualities. It probably ought to be the main plot.

None of the techniques I am talking about are easy. Adding subplots multiplies the work involved in writing a novel. It can also multiply the rewards, both for the reader and the writer. Think big. It pays off in many ways.

Narrative Pace

The number one mistake I see in manuscript submissions is a failure to put the main conflict in place quickly enough; or, perhaps, a failure to use bridging conflict to keep things going until the main problem is set. In fact, it is the primary reason I reject over 90 percent of the material I receive. Why do so many writers fail on this point? It is such a simple flaw to fix!

No doubt about it, high-tension openings are job number one. What about after that? How fast should a story clip along? Where should the high points and low points fall? When should a subplot scene be inserted? Are cliff-hangers clunky and obvious, or do they serve a real purpose?

Narrative pacing is the novelist's biggest challenge. Hundreds of pages and several years into a complex novel, it can be impossible to know whether it is "working." Is there too much material? Too little? Are some elements too strong? Others too weak? Trusted readers are essential, of course, but so is instinct—that, plus an iron conviction with respect to the purpose of the novel. A determination to portray a particular time, place or person, or perhaps to say something of importance to the reader, is the strongest test of whether a particular scene or sequence belongs. Is the material utterly necessary to your purpose? Yes?

There is your answer . . . unless, of course, we are talking about setup or backstory. Here are two major traps. So fatal is the business of "setting up" something in a novel that I believe the very idea should be banned. "Setup" is, by definition, not story. It always drags. Always. Leave it out. Find another way.

Backstory can be essential to understanding a plot point or character; in particular, it can deepen inner conflict, motive and other factors that affect sympathy. But which backstories are important? When should they be presented? Novice authors begin their novels with backstory or drop it in too soon. Backstory delivered early on crashes down on a story's momentum like a sumo wrestler falling on his opponent. Because it is not yet necessary, I usually skim it. Remember that backstory is, for the most part, more important to you, the author, than to your reader.

Once the main plot problem is focused and the characters have been launched on their trajectories, however, backstory can be a development, a deepening, of what is happening. Breakout novelists hold it back for just the right moment, which can sometimes be quite late in the novel. That is especially true if backstory holds a buried secret.

What about the novel's ups and downs, its high moments and low points? Where do they go? Mystery, thriller and romance structures provide ready-made frameworks. Covering suspects and clues, running through the developments that will prevent a looming disaster (or make it more likely), or laying out the factors that keep a couple apart all will provide you with at least a basic body of plot which you can shape. Just remember this: It is always darkest right before the dawn. In commercial fiction, in other words, the central problem generally grows and grows until it seems to have no solution.

What about the more fluid form of the literary or mainstream novel? What if your story is about, say, a family's disintegration or survival? How is that organized? Go back to these basic plot elements: high moments, corners turned and deaths. These are some of a novel's milestones, the dramatic developments to which you are building and whose passing you want to mark. Each scene in a novel ought to move us closer, or farther away, from such milestones.

When one goes by, things ought to feel different. A transition has happened. Something has changed, and the change can be marked by a shift in tone, time, setting, a character's fortunes or whatever you please. If it is big enough, it can even demand a major division in the novel (Book One, Book Two, etc.).

The scene immediately after a high point is often a good place to introduce a subplot scene. The contrast gives the reader a change of pace and adds texture to the overall story. Scrambling up main plots and subplots, though, can overcook a novel. It is important that the main story line never be far away. Narrative momentum resides in the main plot; subplots put on the brakes. They skew the novel sideways. That can be fun, but readers basically want to be hurtling straightforward at fairly high speed.

Is a "leisurely" pace ever justified? If by that you mean scenes or sequences that deepen rather than develop a story, yes, at times. Journey novels like J.R.R. Tolkien's *The Lord of the Rings* really only have one plot problem: get from here to there. (Or, perhaps, go there, find "it" and bring "it" back.) Travel is not plot, as such, and so the episodes in a road or quest novel serve primarily to test the heroine's mettle, deepen her motives, raise her stakes, and so on. Enemies can be added, allies subtracted, but the basic question is always the same: Can she make it from here to there?

It is worth remembering that even when deepening some aspect of a story, rather than moving the plot forward, it is essential that tension be present on every page. If your heroine and her sidekick are standing still, it ought to be because they disagree.

Cliff-hangers are a tried and true, if clumsy, way to propel a reader from scene to scene or chapter to chapter. Chapter-closing cliff-hangers are a fixture of the Nancy Drew mystery stories, for instance, and they have been around for more than sixty years. John Grisham employs cliff-hangers. So does Sandra Brown. Cliff-hangers may be clunky, but can all these authors be wrong about them? Clearly not.

Cliff-hangers have degrees of tension, escalating upward from unanswered questions to surprise developments to sudden danger. There are also subtle ways to create cliff-hangers. A sudden plunge in a protagonist's fortunes, a low moment, is a kind of cliff-hanger. It provokes the unspoken questions, "What will she do now?" and "How will she get out of this?"

False success at the end of a scene also suggests a coming disaster. Readers are wise to certain authorial tricks! A rise is likely to precipitate a fall. Indeed, ever rising success can produce just as much tension as ever sinking fortunes. Steven Millhauser's *Martin Dressler* works like that. So does another big business saga, Barbara Taylor Bradford's *A Woman of Substance*.

What if you have no idea about your novel's pacing? What if you are too close to it? Do not worry. You cannot go too far wrong if your focal character is strong, your central conflict is clear and established early, and the main plotline always strides forward and is rarely more than a scene or two away. Work with solid plot fundamentals in this way and your story probably will maintain its drive of its own accord.

Voice

"I am looking for authors with a distinctive voice." I hear that from editors over lunch almost as often as I hear, "I am looking for big, well-written thrillers." (Aren't we all!)

What the heck is "voice"? By this, do editors mean "style"? I do not think so. By voice, I think they mean not only a unique way of putting words together, but a unique sensibility, a distinctive way of looking at the world, an outlook that enriches an author's oeuvre. They want to read an author who is like no other. An original. A standout. A voice.

How can you develop your voice? To some extent it happens all by itself. Stories come from the subconscience. What drives you to write, to some extent, are your own unresolved inner conflicts. Have you noticed your favorite authors have character types that recur? Plot turns that feel familiar? Descriptive details that you would swear you have read before (a yellow bowl, a slant of light, an inch of cigarette ash)? That is the subconscience at work.

You can facilitate voice by giving yourself the freedom to say things in your own unique way. You do not talk exactly like anyone else, right? Why should you write like everyone else?

Science fiction writer Neal Stephenson has a unique voice. His cyber-sensibility comes through in his very choice of words. At the beginning of his 1992 novel *Snow Crash*, Stephenson introduces his pizza-delivery hero and, in this passage, his car:

> The Deliverator's car has enough potential energy packed into its batteries to fire a pound of bacon into the Asteroid Belt. Unlike a bimbo box or a Burb beater, the Deliverator's car unloads that power through gaping, gleaming, polished sphincters. When the Deliverator puts the hammer down, shit happens. You want to talk contact patches? Your car's tires have tiny contact patches, talk to the asphalt in four places the size of your tongue. The Deliverator's car has big sticky tires with contact patches the size of a fat lady's thighs. The Deliverator is in touch with the road, starts like a bad day, stops on a peseta.

Another distinctive voice in science fiction belongs to my client Nalo Hopkinson, a Jamaican Canadian who not only envisions the future, but who envisions the future of people of color in Creole-spiced prose that is as flavorful as gumbo. Her 1998 debut novel, *Brown Girl in the Ring*, won her the John W. Campbell Award for Best New Writer, a stunning collection of reviews, and is in its fourth printing. In her 2000 novel *Midnight Robber*, Hopkinson pushes her voice even further. Its opening paragraphs introduce a storyteller narrator and the novel's heroine, the Midnight Robber:

> Oho. Like it starting, oui? Don't be frightened, sweetness; is for the best. I go be with you the whole time. Trust me and let me distract you a little bit with one anasi story:
> It had a woman, you see, a strong, hard-back woman with skin like cocoa-tea. She two foot-them tough from hiking through the diable bush, the devil bush on the prison planet of New Half-Way Tree. When she walk, she

foot strike the hard earth *bup!* like breadfruit dropping to the ground. She two arms hard with muscle from all the years of hacking paths through the diable bush on New Half-Way Tree. Even she hair itself rough and wiry; long black knotty locks springing from she scalp and corkscrewing all the way down she back. She name Tan-Tan, and New Half-Way Tree she planet.

That said, it is worth noting that the voice of many bestselling authors is as neutral as a national news anchor's accent. Some say it takes blandness of style to break out; or rather, to rub so few people the wrong way that millions can read the author without any discomfort. My own feeling is that voice is a natural attribute. You no more control it than you can control the color of your eyes—nor would you want to. Plenty of breakout authors have a distinctive voice.

To set your voice free, set your words free. Set your characters free. Most important, set your heart free. It is from the unknowable shadows of your subconscious that your stories will find their drive and from which they will draw their meaning. No one can loan you that or teach you that. Your voice is your self in the story.

Endings

Have you ever been disappointed by the ending of a novel? Funny, so have I. Why do endings disappoint? Often it is because they are rushed; that is, because the author has written it in a hurry due to fatigue or due to a looming deadline, perhaps both. Climaxes are both inner and outer, both plot specific and emotionally charged. The payoff needs to fully plumb the depths in both ways if it is to satisfy.

That said, milking an ending with an endless series of confrontations, plot turnabouts, emotional peaks and so on is not a good idea, either. When narrative momentum is at its height, that is not the time to slam on the brakes. The cure for this ailment is to construct the plot so that its conflicts, inner and outer, all converge at the same time and place. If possible, orchestrate your climax so that it comes to a head in one single visual instant. It will have more power.

Another problem with endings is they tend to be predictable. You can see them coming. The outcome is not seriously in doubt. I notice this fault particularly in genre novels, such as category romances and mysteries, haven't you?

A great storyteller leaves us in suspense right up to the final moments. Success is never sure; in fact, failure seems the far more likely result. The secret to unpredictable endings, I think, is to allow yourself—or, rather, to allow your protagonist—the possibility of failure. Hey, that is life is it not? There is no guarantee you or I will win. Why should fiction be safer than reality?

The resolution phase of the novel needs to tie up loose ends and, like the final chord in a symphony, provide a moment of rest and relaxation of tension. Resolutions also need to do that in as little space as possible, for one obvious reason: at this point, the reader is anxious to reach . . .

The end.

BREAKOUT Checklist: Multiple Viewpoints, Subplots, Pace, Voice, Endings

✓ Multiple points of view and subplots enrich a novel.

✓ Connect subplots quickly.

✓ Subplots must affect overall story outcome.

✓ Keep subplots to a minimum.

✓ Use character lists and plot chronologies to find nodes of conjunction.

✓ Interweave character relationships.

✓ Build range by drawing from different aspects of your milieu and having characters cross plotlines.

✓ Keep main plot scenes frequent; keep subplot scenes necessary to your purpose.

✓ Backstory belongs later.

✓ Pace your story by building to high moments, turning points and deaths.

✓ Mark turning points with character changes.

✓ Narrative drive resides in the main plot.

✓ Cliff-hangers, though sometimes clumsy, can keep things moving.

✓ Voice is more than style; it is infusing your self in your story.

✓ Good endings plumb the depths, inner and outer.

✓ Keep the outcome in doubt by making failure look likely.

CHAPTER NINE

Advanced Plot Structures

The novel is an ever evolving art form. When popular story patterns become frozen and rigid, their popularity withers. That happened with supernatural horror and shoot-'em-up westerns in the 1980s, and is happening to Regency romances today. Private eye novels became so stale that they nearly vanished from the mystery field in the 1990s. Family sagas, popular in the 1980s, completely disappeared in the 1990s.

More vigorous literatures like the crime novel, the contemporary romance, the thriller and science fiction change and grow over the years. They reflect their times. They grow in popularity. Their plot structures are simple and durable, and they can flex to accommodate new subjects and themes. Mainstream and literary fiction also evolve. We expect them to.

How have certain story patterns found expression—indeed, greater popularity than ever—in our times? In what incarnations do we find today's sagas, thrillers, speculative fiction, biographical novels, historicals, romances and episodic novels? There are trends in all these forms and reasons that some such novels have broken out. How can you be sure that your story will feel fresh?

I am particularly interested in some old and durable story types that have found new life, hence my focus on sagas, historicals and such. Mysteries, science fiction, fantasy and romances are among today's most popular forms of fiction, but there already are many fine books on writing in those categories . . .

many of those available from the publisher of this volume.

While I sell plenty of novels in those genres and have plenty of thoughts to share about them, others already are doing a good job covering that ground. In this chapter I would like to concentrate instead on a few less often examined plot forms; also on areas of romance fiction and science fiction, in particular, that have provoked much envy, anguish and misunderstanding in their respective communities.

Authors too easily imagine it is a plot formula or a publisher's push that makes a certain type of novel break out. I know better. It is something in the fiction itself.

That "something" is what I want to get at. How can an episodic novel, the most antique of novel forms, be the basis for a contemporary breakout? Why do some novels with slightly futuristic settings sell in huge quantities while similar, only slightly speculative novels by distinguished science fiction authors languish on bookstore shelves? I think I have some answers.

Families, Groups, Generations

High school and college reunions are both terrifying and compelling. They afford an opportunity both to look back and to measure how far we have come—or not. They bring together old friends, stir up old rivalries, remind us of lost loves, past mistakes, faded triumphs and the joy of being young, fresh and starting out. Bittersweet they can be, but they can also leave us with a satisfying sense that in spite of everything, we have not only gotten by, we have grown.

Is it any wonder that group and generational novels continue to be so popular? The grandmother of such stories is Mary McCarthy's *The Group*. A recent offspring is Rebecca Wells's *The Divine Secrets of the Ya-Ya Sisterhood*. Their subjects, Vassar graduates of the class of 1933 in *The Group* and four lifelong friends from the South in *Divine Secrets*, could not be more different. Yet these novels have techniques in common.

Start with structure: One of the ways to manage a large story, as we saw in chapter eight, is to limit subplots to a small number. In theory a generational novel, with its many equally weighted story lines, would seem to be the ultimate watery cocktail of fiction. Such novels should not work. They ought to feel thin and uninvolving. Their characters should be shallow, and hence only weakly sympathetic.

McCarthy's and Wells's characters are anything but thin, uninvolving and shallow. Both authors are gifted at character delineation, strength and sympathy. Both also establish a single protagonist about whom we care more than any other: the group itself. In their novels, the group takes on a life and a significance of its own. Its survival is the high stake that makes the outcome of the story matter. The value that underlies these stories, then, is friendship. Their message is that lifelong friends make life full, joyous and worth living.

Notice the élan with which Wells establishes the bond between the four Ya-Ya Sisters when we first meet them in chapter two of her novel:

> Necie and Caro had already arrived at Teensy's house when Vivi pulled up. Teensy's maid, Shirley, had pulled together some sandwiches and two thermoses of Bloody Marys. Climbing into Teensy's red convertible Saab, they took the same positions they had been taking in Teensy's convertibles since 1941: Teensy behind the wheel; Vivi, shotgun; Necie just behind the driver; and Caro in the backseat behind Vivi. Unlike in the old days, Caro did not kick her feet up on the seat back in front of her. Not because she was worried about propriety, but because she was traveling these days with a portable oxygen tank. She didn't need to use it all the time, but it had to be near, just in case.
>
> Teensy turned the air conditioner to high, and the Ya-Yas took turns reading Sidda's letter. When they had all finished, Teensy put down the top and Vivi slipped

the Barbara Steisand CD into the CD player. Each of the women put on a hat, scarf, and sunglasses. Then they blasted off in the direction of Spring Creek.

Structurally, McCarthy's and Wells's novels differ in one respect. While both are about friendship and change, *The Group* keeps all its action in the present, while *Divine Secrets* flashes back in time. Wells thus comes up against a problem common to all novelists with important backstories or past plotlines: How do you make the past matter urgently in the present?

Wells solves this problem with a strong framing device. *Divine Secrets* begins when a rift opens between one of the Ya-Ya Sisters, Vivi, and her daughter, Siddalee, who in the present day is a theater director. In a newspaper interview, Sidda describes a childhood episode in which a drunken Vivi beat her with a leather belt. The publicity generates great box office, but Vivi cuts her off. Sidda is distraught. Her attempts at reconciliation fail. Faced with a directing job (a musical version of Clare Boothe Luce's *The Women*) that she cannot handle, as well as an upcoming marriage for which she is not ready, Sidda decides to cocoon.

She postpones her wedding (her fiancé, Connor, is warmly understanding) and retreats to a cabin on Lake Quinault on the Olympic Peninsula. Sidda also sends a letter asking for the scrapbooks and memories of the Ya-Ya Sisterhood to help her prepare for her upcoming theater production. The Ya-Ya Sisters talk it over and decide to help, both to help Sidda understand close female bonding and to repair the broken mother-daughter relationship. Wells thus makes the novel's middle, a backward look at the divine secrets of the Ya-Ya Sisterhood, important and necessary.

Any good group novel will have some similar dynamic, as will family novels. Once family is established as the most important thing, there is a better chance that the threat to the family will have urgency.

Thrillers

Everyone loves a thriller. Everyone also wants to write one, it seems. The largest number of submissions I receive fall into this category. By far the largest number of submissions that I decline also fall into this category. Of all forms of popular fiction, thrillers are the easiest to enjoy, the simplest to understand and the hardest to write.

Why is that? First of all because a breakout thriller simultaneously accomplishes two mutually exclusive effects: (1) its plot events are utterly believable and (2) its plot events are utterly incredible. Thrillers can be inspired by real-world dangers. (Talk to any techno-thriller writer. They will tell you.) However, the fact is that the events in most thrillers are highly unlikely ever to happen. But while reading them, we are convinced they could. Breakout thriller writers master the detailing that creates high plausibility.

Next, breakout thriller writers universally have mastered the art of high stakes, escalating stakes and tension on every page. Does reading a James Patterson or Dean Koontz novel leave you feeling relaxed? No. It makes you—or me, anyway—feel tense. And we love it.

The issue of high stakes is especially important. What sort of stakes can keep millions of readers on the edge of their seats? *Will the master spy known as The Needle escape wartime England and bring the secret of D-Day back to Germany?* Ken Follett's 1978 novel *Eye of the Needle* sold millions of copies. The stakes are high and easily understood by anyone.

Given that the stakes in a thriller must be able to alarm just about anybody, you would think that killer viruses, nuclear terrorism, evil corporations, government conspiracies and the apocalypse would be the subject of just about every breakout thriller. Not so. Few thrillers on those subjects have equaled the successes of Michael Crichton's *The Andromeda Strain* (1969), John Grisham's *The Pelican Brief* (1992), Dean Koontz's *Dark Rivers of the Heart* (1994) or Stephen King's *The Stand* (1978).

One reason is that it is difficult to make such dangers appear not only credible but also immediate, urgent and unstoppable. Few authors have the expertise (or paranoia) to do that. When successful, the threat generally is brought to a personal and local level so the stakes are understandable and the scope of the action can be managed.

As for the apocalypse and after, novelists interested in tearing the world apart or imagining how it might look afterward can benefit from studying the science fiction novels *A Canticle for Leibowitz* (1960) by Walter M. Miller, Jr.; David Brin's *The Postman* (1985); and Octavia E. Butler's *Parable of the Sower* (1999). Richard Matheson's 1954 novel *I Am Legend* is a postplague classic. Postnuclear holocaust novels do not get much better than Russell Hoban's *Riddley Walker* (1980), although my personal favorite of this type is Nevil Shute's haunting story of nuclear war survivors *On the Beach* (1957). Once again, all of these novels shrink global-scale threats down to a size that is local and personal.

On the spiritual warfare front, the current craze for apocalyptic novels began in 1986 with Frank E. Peretti's *This Present Darkness*, and continues today most prominently with Tim F. LaHaye and Jerry B. Jenkins's *Left Behind* series. The handling of the theological basis for this series is especially effective. LaHaye and Jenkins employ a mentor-teacher called Tsion Ben-Judah, a useful character who continues from book to book. The seventh in the series, *The Indwelling* (2000), required a first printing of two million copies. Obviously, this team has found a way to make the apocalypse feel real.

Easiest of all to make convincing are military foes, geological disasters, bad medicine, serial killers and courtroom injustice. These threats are better understood, more widely documented and are more commonly experience by the public. You or I could fall victim to any one of them. In contrast, we are not terribly likely to be hurt by drug cartels, Middle Eastern terrorists or militia-type isolationists. As sources of potential disaster, they do not inspire visceral fear.

Of course, legal, serial killer and medical thrillers, which more easily inspire visceral fear, are therefore easier to write, and as a result, there is tough competition. Authors tackling these subjects will find themselves up against established market leaders like Robin Cook, John Grisham, John Sandford, James Patterson and Patricia Cornwell, to name a few.

One subcategory of thriller that crosses my desk quite often in manuscript is the paranoid conspiracy thriller. Close behind it in popularity is the type of thriller in which some ancient totem of power comes to light and, having fallen into evil hands, threatens to bring about cataclysmic doom. No doubt you can see the credibility problems inherent in these thriller forms. How often have real conspiracies wreaked real destruction? And archaeological artifacts with vast magical power . . .? Please. The worst that most genuine relics do is get your hands dusty.

Possibly even more difficult to pull off is the treasure hunt. Here the obvious problem is with stakes. If the enormous diamond, gold cache or whatever is not won or recovered . . . well, so what? There are fortunes elsewhere. Still, it is possible to make a dynamite thriller out of such stuff.

Clive Cussler's *Raise the Titanic* (1976) is a top example. Another is Wilbur Smith's 1995 novel, *The Seventh Scroll*, a classic archaeological adventure tale in which the location of a lavish pharaoh's tomb has been a secret for four millennia thanks to the design of its cunning chief engineer, Taita (introduced in Smith's earlier best-seller *River God*). When the location of the tomb comes to light after a pair of archaeologists begins to translate the seventh of a set of clue-filled scrolls, a deadly race begins.

How do Cussler and Smith make the outcomes of these stories matter? By making them matter deeply to the novels' protagonists, that is, by raising the personal stakes to a high degree. It is also important to make the outcome matter to the villains. Grisham's *The Partner*, analyzed earlier, derives much of its tension from the villains' hopes of recovering their stolen $90 million and crushing our hero, the thief.

Financial thrillers are another subcategory that ought not to work. Global financial meltdown just does not have a visceral fright factor. What's a bad day on Wall Street, even a *really, really* bad one? We will recover. Christopher Reich has found ways to craft high-caliber thrillers in the financial milieu. In his 1998 best-seller *Numbered Account*, a young banker, Nick Neumann, gives up a hard won and highly prized training position at Morgan Stanley, as well as his lively Boston Brahmin fiancée, to take a position at United Swiss Bank in Zurich. This is the bank at which Nick's father worked and, Nick believes, the numbered accounts of which hold the secret of his father's murder. Considering all he has given up to uncover the truth, Nick's personal stakes are very high right from the start.

Reich lovingly details the culture of privacy at the bank and the lengths to which it will go to protect its clients' identities. But there are public pressures to disclose information. Soon, the bank is forced to track the activity of likely criminal clients, among them a Turkish "pasha." The bank is also the object of a hostile takeover bid. Quickly, Nick is sucked into the middle of these conflicts. His loyalty is tested. In order to stay in place, maintain tradition, please his boss, and remain close to the information that he seeks, he must make a moral choice about whether or not to conceal the pasha's massive currency transfers.

He does, and his moral compromise for what to him seems a greater good raises the novel's stakes even further. All this is in the first one hundred pages. By now, Reich has so thoroughly detailed the milieu and so relentlessly raised his hero's personal stakes that he is free to add layers and complications for hundreds of pages. The public stakes grow a bit preposterous, but because Reich has solidly grounded them in strong personal stakes, he easily carries us through.

Reich would seem to be breaking the rule that thrillers must careen toward a fearful disaster. The meltdown of a Swiss bank is hardly the stuff of world panic. The high personal stakes of Reich's hero keep us reading.

My point is this: The more remote, abstract or exotic the threat is in a thriller, the more the novel must embrace high credibility and soaring personal stakes. For courtroom, serial killer and medical thrillers credibility is also important, but high personal stakes alone probably are not enough for a breakout. The closer you get to home, the more public stakes become important.

Crossover Fiction

Crossover fiction, in which two or more genres are blended, is a topic that provokes animated discussion, especially in science fiction and fantasy circles. Science fiction and fantasy authors feel that they live in a ghetto. There is fine writing in the field, but they believe that it gets scant respect. (They are right.) As a result, many science fiction writers long for acceptance in the mainstream.

Irritating to this group are breakout successes by authors with no history in, or loyalty to, science fiction or fantasy, yet who nevertheless win high praise, and sometimes high advances, by borrowing settings or story premises from science fiction. By far the most heated envy is provoked by Margaret Atwood's *The Handmaid's Tale* (1986). It is set in the future, and, slipstream writers feel, not a very believable one at that. Its themes are feminist, but that has been handled with greater depth and complexity by science fiction authors like Sherri Tepper.

Each new crossover success that borrows elements from science fiction—such as *The Sparrow* (1996), *Into the Forest* (1996), *Lives of the Monster Dogs* (1997), *The Club Dumas* (1998)—seems to produce new paroxysms of grief among science fiction writers. How can usurpers like Mary Doria Russell, Jean Hegland, Kirsten Bakis and Arturo Pérez-Reverte walk away with critical accolades while outstanding science fiction writers like Patricia Anthony, Jonathan Carroll, Bradley Denton and Sean Stewart, all of whom write fiction that is minimally speculative in the first place, are virtually ignored?

Frustrated, some folks in the science fiction field have tried to pin nonthreatening labels on such authors' work, labels like "slipstream," "borderline," or "literary science fiction." The hope is by implying that their work has only slightly speculative elements, that work will become more acceptable to the mainstream.

It does not work. It cannot. What determines whether one wins a following among general readers and literary critics is not labels, it is in the writing or, more precisely, in the nature of the reading experience that the author creates.

Mary Doria Russell's *The Sparrow* is a case in point. This novel begins in Rome in the future. Intelligent life has been discovered on another planet and an expedition of Jesuit priests and others has been sent by the Catholic Church. Only one priest, Father Emilio Sandoz, has returned. He is mentally and spiritually shattered. He has been physically mutilated.

What happened? That unanswered question drives the story, and in the process of Sandoz's counseling by an American priest, John Candotti, we learn the answer. In brief, the planet was an Eden in which the humans upset the balance. The humans' enriched gardens raised the population level bringing reprisal, infanticide, cannibalism of the unwanted babies and death.

The role of religion in the story is strong. It is a tale of misguided missionary zeal. While the alien setting gives the novel an exotic flavor, in fact by changing only a few details, the story might have been set in the African jungle or in some Shangri-la. *The Sparrow* is not about aliens or science. It is about the Church, faith, mission and cultural misunderstanding.

Slipstream writers protest that their work, too, is not about science but about people. They deliberately use few speculative elements, often only one. So why is their work ignored? There is another aspect to *The Sparrow* that is worth understanding: The characters are highly sympathetic. Although Sandoz is catatonic at the opening, Candotti serves as a bridging point of view until the backstory begins. Sandoz is somewhat controversial as expedition leader, but for the most part, he is a warm man trying to do good. Although it ends in tragedy, the mission's spirit is hopeful and positive.

Contrast that with the tone and plots of some of the slipstream writers. I have loved Jonathan Carroll's dark comedy since I read his debut novel, *The Land of Laughs*, as a young editorial assistant. His work lives on a dark edge, though, as do the lyrical novels of Patricia Anthony. Anthony's 1997 novel *God's Fires* concerns a Portuguese priest who tries to protect three angels (aliens) from the Inquisition. It is powerfully written, yet a tragic tone underlies the novel. Father Pesoa's mission is hopeless from the first.

Also dark is the work of Bradley Denton. His 1993 novel *Blackburn* concerns a serial killer with a "moral" code: He kills those who deserve to die. His 1997 novel *Lunatics* is an oddball fantasy concerning a man who tries to summon his lover (a dark goddess) down from the moon. Denton's work is mesmerizing and critically praised, but its gut emotional appeal is difficult to discern despite its dark beauty.

Crossover novels that break out usually feature sympathetic characters. The monster dogs in Bakis's novel, *Lives of the Monster Dogs*, are highly sympathetic. So are Eva and Nell, the sisters who learn survival together in a post-apocalyptic forest in Hegland's *Into the Forest*.

In Atwood's *The Handmaid's Tale*, handmaid Offred is not only sympathetic, her forced servitude and childbearing strike a powerful chord in contemporary readers. Atwood's premise has gut appeal. Grumpy science fiction writers resent Atwood's theft of a future setting, but they are missing the point. What made *The Handmaid's Tale* successful was its breakout qualities. The fact is, Atwood wrote a widely accessible novel. Much so-called slipstream fiction is less welcoming.

Susie Moloney's 1997 crossover best-seller *A Dry Spell* displays many of the breakout techniques that have made Stephen King's novels popular. The story concerns the town of Goodlands, North

Dakota, which has suffered a four-year-long dry spell that is ruining farms and lives, including that of mortgage officer Karen Grange, whose unhappy job it is to foreclose on the failing farms. Grange brings to town a mysterious, earthy stranger, Tom Keatley, a rain-maker who can "pull" rain from the sky. But there is something about Goodlands that he cannot fathom, a curse extracting a price for . . . what?

Moloney's novel has one magical element in the rainmaker Tom Keatley, but that magic is downplayed so far that Keatley becomes utterly human. However, that is not why *A Dry Spell* found a wide audience. That was due to Moloney's attention to the elements of breakout-scale storytelling. For example, the story's public stakes are reinforced at many points, as in this passage from Karen Grange's point of view:

> Karen opened her eyes. She smelled something— suddenly, strong. Smoke. Fire. She couldn't see any-thing from the kitchen window: she strained her neck and looked to either side. But she could smell it, carried in on the sudden breeze.
>
> Fire in a dry spell would be devastating. There had been so many fires lately. That poor man, Sticky, from the Badlands, had died not long ago. It was so dry.

Town history and inhabitants are detailed to a high degree. Little disasters compound the misery in Goodlands, deepening the public stakes. Karen's personal stakes reach a new level after Tom postulates that the town is paying penance. Karen, a loan officer who suffers from chronic debt (note her conflicting sides), imagines that the fault might be hers: "Her sin was covetousness and she was paying for it." That admission, deep in the novel (p. 200), is a good cue for Karen's backstory, and that is where Moloney places it.

Step by step, from many points of view and with tension on every page, Moloney brings her novel to a thunderous (literally) climax. Once the rain has come, Moloney includes a striking passage that marks the change in the town:

> Goodlands was in a state of celebration. Forever, when someone asked, "Where were you when it rained?" memories would turn to a clear, static moment as firmly and closely remembered as yesterday.

Moloney's spot on *The New York Times* best-seller list shows that crossover novels break out for the same reasons that other novels break out. Readers love speculative elements, but even more they love a layered, high-stakes story about sympathetic characters who have problems with which anyone can identify. Perhaps that is why mainstream writers more often break out with speculative elements than dark-toned, hard-edged speculative novelists score in the mainstream.

Whole Life

From time to time, I am pitched novels which portray a man or woman's whole life, from cradle to grave. Such manuscripts rarely work, principally because not every moment, nor even every year, of anyone's life has sufficient conflict, drama or color to keep me glued to every page.

Is there a secret to biographical novels? No single technique can ensure a breakout success, obviously, but I have noticed one factor that is common to novels as different as John Irving's *The World According to Garp* (1978), Barbara Taylor Bradford's *A Woman of Substance* (1979), Winston Groom's *Forrest Gump* (1986), Steven Millhauser's *Martin Dressler* (1996), Loren D. Estleman's *Billy Gashade* (1997), Jane Urquhart's *The Underpainter* (1997) and Alice McDermott's *Charming Billy* (1998). Since among these novels are winners of the Pulitzer Prize (*Martin Dressler*), the Governor General's Literary Award (*The Underpainter*) and the National Book Award (*Charming Billy*), not to mention several international best-sellers, it is a factor to which we might like to pay special attention.

The technique, simply, is this: From the very first moments of these novels, the subject's life assumes a grand scale and high significance. You do not have to read far to see this technique at work. Take a look at these openings:

> Emma Harte leaned forward and looked out of the window. The private Lear jet, property of the Sitex Oil Corporation of America, had been climbing steadily up through a vaporous haze of cumulus clouds and was now streaking through a sky so penetratingly blue its shimmering clarity hurt the eyes.
> —Barbara Taylor Bradfor, A Woman of Substance

> Let me say this: Bein a idiot is no box of chocolates. People laugh, lose patience, treat you shabby. Now they says folks sposed to be kind to the afflicted, but let me tell you—it ain't always that way. Even so, I got no complaints, cause I reckon I done live a pretty interesting life, so to speak.
> —Winston Groom, Forrest Gump

> There once lived a man named Martin Dressler, a shopkeeper's son, who rose from modest beginnings to a height of dreamlike good fortune.
> —Steven Millhauser, Martin Dressler

> My birth name doesn't matter, although that wasn't always the case. If you've patience enough to page through the New York Social Register—and in my time there were many who built entire careers on doing no more than that—you're sure to come across someone or other who bore it clear back to Peter Minuet.

No, my birth name doesn't matter, and I won't tell it now, even though my enemies are dead.
—Loren D. Estleman, *Billy Gashade*

Billy had drunk himself to death. He had, at some point, ripped apart, plowed through, as alcoholics tend to do, the great, deep, tightly woven fabric of affection that was some part of the emotional life, the life of love, of everyone in the room.
Everyone loved him.
—Alice McDermott, *Charming Billy*

Perhaps the greatest example of this technique can be found in John Irving's *The World According to Garp*. Irving's account of Garp's conception by his renegade, independent, sexually liberated mother, Jenny Fields, occupies the first thirty-one pages—*thirty-one pages!*—of the novel. Throughout this World War II backstory of brain-damaged ball turret gunner Technical Sergeant Garp, and his nurse Jenny's decision to have him father her out-of-wedlock child, Irving quotes passages from books that Jenny and her son will later write:

"My father," Garp wrote, "was a Goner. From my mother's point of view, that must have made him very attractive. No strings attached."

The tone of these fictitious excerpts establishes early the larger-than-life qualities of Garp and his amazing mother.

Biographical novelists must go on from their openings to construct a novel's breakout scale, setting, larger-than-life characters, layered plots, deep themes and so on, but when the subject is a single life, there is no point in doing so if we do not grasp from the very first that this life is special.

Historicals

Say "historical fiction" and most people think of sweeping sagas, novels that follow an individual's journey across the vast sprawling canvas of his times. Tolstoy's *War and Peace* is perhaps the greatest historical epic, but many of the top authors of the twentieth century worked on a panoramic scale. Margaret Mitchell, Mary Renault and Frank Yerby are a few. In our own times, John Jakes, James A. Michener and Edward Rutherfurd have carried on the tradition of the grand epic. Their work defines historical fiction.

Or does it? It is hard to find a true historical epic on the shelves these days. Readers increasingly have turned to other forms of fiction for their historical kicks. Among today's popular subcategories are historical romances and historical mysteries. These could be rationalized as twists on genre formulas, but in truth they are part of a larger trend.

In literary fiction and in the mainstream, historical novels that break out today have a tighter focus, a narrower range. In fact, a survey of recent breakout historical titles would suggest that the subject of such novels is historical objects: *Corelli's Mandolin*, *The Dress Lodger*, *A Conspiracy of Paper*, *The Fan-Maker's Inquisition*, *Girl with a Pearl Earning*, *The Binding Chair* and so on. Needless to say, consumers do not buy novels to read about objects. They want to read about people. But what kind of people, in what kind of story?

Let us take a closer look.

Corelli's Mandolin (1994) by Louis de Bernieres is set on the Greek Island of Cephalonia during World War II, where a brilliant and beautiful young doctor's daughter, Pelagia, is engaged to a fisherman, Mandras. Along comes the Italian occupation and with it a cultured mandolin-playing officer of the Italian garrison, Captain Corelli. Mandras joins the Greek partisans, while Pelagia begins a passionate affair with Corelli that leaves her torn between the two sides.

Corelli's Mandolin takes detours into history and mythology, and dramatizes the lives of Cephalonia's colorful inhabitants; however, it is the romantic tension that provides the story with its forward narrative drive. De Bernieres's novel is an historical and a literary tour de force, but underneath, structurally speaking, it is a romance.

Sheri Holman's *The Dress Lodger* (2000) is set in Sunderland, England, in 1831, where fifteen-year-old Gustine works as a potter's apprentice by day and a prostitute by night. (The fancy dress she rents from her loathsome landlord in order to attract a higher class of clientele gives the novel its title.) Also in Sunderland is physician Henry Chiver, who specializes in the diseases of the heart but whose research is hampered by a dearth of cadavers to dissect and his past association with the grave robbers Burke and Hare.

The Dress Lodger has many plot layers. A cholera epidemic strikes Sunderland, and Henry's progressive fiancée Audrey Place wars against its causes: poverty and filth. Meanwhile, in order to keep tabs on Gustine, her procurer Whilky Robinson has her followed by a mute woman known only as Eye. As the plague worsens, the public fears that doctors are sacrificing them in order to advance their researches. Worse, Henry's anatomy students are clamoring for the chance to practice surgery on real bodies. Tensions run high.

The most desirable dissection subject in town, if he were dead, would be Gustine's baby son, who was born with his heart beating *outside* his chest. To protect him, Gustine strikes a deadly bargain with Henry: The life of her son spared in exchange for fresh bodies. Shades of *Sweeny Todd!*

There is a looming disaster in *The Dress Lodger* that Gustine must prevent: Henry increasingly covets her son, the medical marvel. Can Gustine protect his life? Eventually, she turns to her watchdog Eye for help and the stakes, both public and personal, grow to a fever (sorry) pitch. In essence, then, for all its plot layers *The Dress Lodger* is a thriller.

David Liss's *A Conspiracy of Paper* (2000) is another historical that, structurally, feels familiar. It is based on the first stock market crash, The South Sea Bubble of 1720. In it, Benjamin Weaver investigates the death of his estranged father, a notorious "stockjobber." The case brings Benjamin into contact with organized crime, relatives who reject him for abandoning his Jewish faith and a cabal of evil financiers. Also layered in are a struggle between the Bank of England and the South Sea Company, and the controversy over the then new phenomenon of stock speculation.

Slowly, Benjamin transforms himself from a debtor hunter to a new kind of detective . . . and therein lies the structural secret of *A Conspiracy of Paper*. For all its character transformation, plot layers and historical color, *A Conspiracy of Paper* fundamentally is a mystery novel, just as surely as Caleb Carr's *The Alienist* (1994) is a serial killer novel.

If you think about it, then, the historical novel today is not mainly an epic. Its setting may be some era of history, but in the essentials of its plot, it is something else: a romance, a mystery, a thriller. To be sure, the authors of the new historicals are writing on a breakout level, but there is nothing secret about their underlying story structures.

Of course, the sweeping tale of one man's journey across his times is still possible. Anita Diamant's recent breakout *The Red Tent*, which spins the story of a minor Old Testament woman, Dinah, is a fine example. I also love the many wonderful series that depict the ongoing adventures of military heroes such as Patrick O'Brian's and Alexander Kent's nautical novels, and George MacDonald Fraser's utterly unique *Flashman* series. Civil War epics will also be with us for quite some time, I suspect.

Thank goodness! There are few pleasures so fine in fiction as getting lost in a good historical.

Out-of-Category Romance

Assuming that you are a woman, have you ever wanted to do the following:

✓ Provide an alibi to a murderer?

✓ Photograph the massacre of a Croatian orphanage?

✓ Examine the body of a woman who was sexually mutilated, then murdered by having knives pounded into the soles of her feet, then burned?

✓ Get a tattoo and hire a male prostitute?

✓ Stand in the sunroof of a man's moving car, strip topless, let your clothes fly away in the wind, then demand that the man pull over and "do" you by the side of the road?

These things are not on your fantasy list? Hmm. You had better think about them. These are all things thought about or actually done by heroines of some recent, highly popular "out-of-category" romances.

Yes, romances. OK, some of the earlier examples are from novels that are classified as "women's suspense." But there is still a lot of romantic content in these books. Their readerships do not include many men. They are aimed at the women's market. And yeah, OK, I have taken some of the above out of context, but I did so in order to make a point: This is not Harlequin or Silhouette. This is not the business of following tip sheets, adhering to word counts or fine-tuning "sensual" language. This is the business of out-of-category romance writing, the construction of big-scale novels in which the women and men are larger-than-life, the stakes are high, the stories are layered, and the sexual heat is a few degrees less than the surface of the sun.

Many category romance writers dream of breaking out. They would like to rub shoulders with Nora Roberts, Jayne Ann Krentz, Susan Elizabeth Phillips, Jennifer Crusie, Tami Hoag, Iris Johansen, Heather Graham, Elizabeth Lowell and other writers of that caliber. Most, though, are locked into story patterns that are too small. They imagine that breaking category barriers means writing longer and adding more points of view.

Writing out-of-category romance involves much more than that. It requires embracing breakout fiction technique and a level of effort far beyond that required for long contemporaries or even historical romances. It means writing scenes without the hero and heroine in them. It demands strong character delineation. It means dialogue that at times is laugh-out-loud funny or catch-your-breath rude. It means adding murder, kidnapping, death and destruction, and troubling to detail their consequences. It means writing sex scenes so hot they make even this seen-it-all ex-romance writer wonder if he should take a cold shower.

The application of breakout fiction techniques to romance fiction could easily occupy an entire volume of its own. For space reasons, I will look at one representative out-of-category romance: Jennifer Crusie's 1998 breakout *Tell Me Lies*. Crusie has captured the irreverent humor and sexy mind-set mixed with murder first made popular by Susan Isaacs.

Tell Me Lies concerns a woman in a small burg called Frog Pond whose life is thrown into turmoil when her bad-boy high-school sweetheart returns to town. This premise could describe any number of category romances, but Crusie takes it further. What keeps Maddie Faraday and C.L. Sturgis apart? For one thing, Maddie is married to someone else. Not just married for convenience, but seriously married with an eight-year-old daughter named Emily. Of course, her husband is no prize. While cleaning out his Cadillac, she finds under the front seat a pair of women's black lace crotchless underwear. And they do not belong to Maddie.

Already we have left Kansas. Crusie immediately pitches her characters on a larger-than-life level. Maddie brings the crotchless panties into her kitchen, and when her daughter unexpectedly comes in, she thrusts them into a mac-and-cheese pan soaking in the sink. Emily notices:

"What was that?" Em stared at her, her brown eyes huge behind her glasses.

Maddie stared back stupidly for a moment. "What?"

"That thing." Em came closer, sliding her hip along the yellow counter as she moved, bouncing over the cabinet handles. "That black thing."

"Oh." Maddie blinked at the pants floating in the pan and shoved them under the water again. "It's a scrub thing."

A little later, Maddie confides in her friend Treva. Treva is no sweetly supportive mirror. Her reaction to Brent Faraday's cheating is blunt: "Just divorce the son of a bitch. I never liked him anyway." Later, Maddie drives around looking for Brent's car at bars and the town's one motel. Then she realizes he would probably be at the Point, the local make-out overlook. Maddie has decided on divorce but wants proof before she screws up her daughter's life. She climbs up through the steep woods and, sure enough, Brent is there, screwing a blonde in the backseat of his car . . . or so Maddie surmises. She cannot get near. A local security guard is already there, peeking through the window.

This kind of comic action distinguishes Crusie's novel from the crowd. Meanwhile, she is building a fire under Maddie and bad-boy C.L., who is now an accountant. An *accountant?* Crusie chooses that profession for her hero not only to give him conflicting sides, but to enhance her theme of accountability. Brent gives Maddie a backhanded fist across the eye for taking his lockbox, and C.L. resolves that Brent will pay for what he has done. And Brent does. Two hundred pages into the novel, he is shot. Crusie uses high moments and death.

Tell Me Lies has a number of interconnected plot layers. Maddie's mother provides the small-town mind-set. Treva is a quarter-owner of the real estate development company that Brent also owns. Brent keeps a locked box which proves to contain old love letters, including two from a girlfriend who was pregnant, as well as two tickets to Rio, and passports for himself and daughter Emily. Before he can fly away, he is shot, and Maddie becomes the chief suspect in his murder. Crusie does not spare little Em in this development. Her coping-with-death scenes are vivid, and later she runs away because the adults are not telling her the whole truth. Later still, it emerges that Brent was skimming money from the business. Treva knew about it; in addition, years before she was Brent's pregnant girlfriend but never told Maddie.

There is more, but you get the idea: Crusie weaves together her character's backstories and plotlines. Meanwhile, she also delivers some scorching sex. C.L. does not overwhelm demure Maddie with his masculinity, category fashion. If anything, C.L. is not fast enough for Maddie: "I want you now. Make love to me *now*." Following an explicit backseat scene, C.L. says, "I've had good sex before, but this was nirvana. Was it the car? I'll buy one. I swear."

During a second sex scene, Maddie is again impatient:

> The problem was not C.L. Any man who could do to her what he's done to her in the back of a car was obviously capable of even greater heights in a bed. The problem was his approach. This respectful, slow-motion stuff had to go because she wanted him inside her *now*.
>
> However, telling him was not a good idea. From sixteen years of marriage to Brent, she knew that critiquing a guy's performance *in medias res* only led to grief. So grabbing C.L. by the ears, and screaming, "Will you please just fuck me?" was not going to work, even if she could bring herself to talk dirty.

I do not mean to suggest that using the word "fuck" is all that is required for out-of-category sex. It is more than that. It is an attitude, a willingness to get hot and wet and rock the world. Sexual heat does not derive from a vocabulary. It flows from the mind—sometimes a dirty mind. Romance authors who want to break out need to throw their fantasies into high gear.

The end of *Tell Me Lies* ties up all the plot threads. Maddie deduces who murdered Brent, and C.L. decides to stay in his pokey hometown. The fun of the novel, though, lies in the middle. It is the sexual heat between Maddie and C.L., as well as Maddie's larger-than-life outlook that brings the story to breakout level. The plot layers help. So do the many distinctive characters and their interwoven destinies.

All in all, Crusie builds an expansive-feeling story with lots to say about lost love, lies and their cost. And about chocolate. Did I mention the chocolate? How she uses it I will leave, like the possibilities of out-of-category romance, to your imagination.

Linked Short Stories

Unquestionably, the factor that keeps readers turning the pages of a novel is plot. It must be. What else can explain how certain best-sellers have reached the top of the lists in spite of flat characters, plain prose and tried-and-true themes? Plot, and only plot, is all they have to offer.

How, then, is it possible for a work of fiction to break out when it altogether abandons plot? That is exactly what has happened with successful breakouts like Amy Tan's *The Joy Luck Club* (1992), Whitney Otto's *How to Make an American Quilt* (1991) and a host of recent Bridget Jones read-alikes. These are volumes of linked short stories. Why do they work?

Obviously, something must compensate for the missing plot. Larger-than-life characters with strong conflicts or inner drives are one essential element. Highly dramatic individual stories is another. It is not enough merely to have connecting characters or a common theme. The other story elements must have a dazzling impact.

One helpful structural element is a framing device, a group, event or motif that surrounds the separate stories and makes them necessary. The mah-jongg club in *The Joy Luck Club* is one example. The quilting circle in *How to Make an American Quilt* is another. However, the telling of the stories in Whitney Otto's collection is made most urgent by the need of its central character, twenty-six-year-old Finn Bennett-Dodd, to get her drifting life on course. Otto's prologue lays out Finn's dilemma and her need:

> I enrolled in graduate school. Then I lost interest. I cared and then I didn't care. I wanted to know as much about the small, odd details that I discovered here and there when looking into the past as I did about Lenin's secret train or England's Victorian imperialism or a flawless neo-Marxist critique of capitalism.

* * *

> Then Sam asked me to marry him.
> It seemed to me a good idea.
> Yet it somehow led me back to my educational concern, which was how to mesh halves into a whole, only in this case it was how to make a successful link of unmarried to married, man to woman, the merging of the roads before us.

* * *

> The other good idea was spending the summer with my grandmother Hy Dodd and her sister Glady Joe Cleary. Their relationship with me is different from that with the other grandchildren; we share secrets. And I probably talk to them a little more than my cousins or their own children do. I think they have a lot to say and I am more than willing to hear it. All of it.

* * *

> We are all drawn to beauty. I think it is a beacon for us; makes us want to listen.
> Well, I am ready to listen.

Otto's six-page prologue is one of the most perfect expressions of inner conflict in contemporary fiction. *How to Make an American Quilt* was a best-seller and a movie. Its stories are sharp and moving, and have much to do with my favorite character quality, forgiveness. What ties it together is not plot, but a powerful framework provided by a young woman's yearning.

Another excellent frame can be found in Alan Lightman's delicate, lyrical and meditative short novel *Einstein's Dreams* (1994), in which a young patent clerk ponders his strange dreams about time just prior to the publication of his first paper on relativity. Pulitzer Prize-winner Robert Olen Butler's wildly inventive novel *Mr. Spaceman* (2000), concerns a zoot-suited alien, Desi, whose mission is to reveal himself to humanity at the turn of the millennium. Fearful, Desi prepares by surveying some of the haunting and revealing human memories that he has harvested. Butler's superb book reads as both a novel and a story collection.

The connecting element in Susan Vreeland's story collection *Girl in Hyacinth Blue* (1999) is a painting by Vermeer. Vreeland's stories progress backward in time from the present, to Amsterdam during the Nazi occupation to, eventually, the creation of the picture itself, a portrait of Vermeer's daughter Magdalena. Although very different, the stories work together gradually to illuminate the meaning of the painting.

The splash of Helen Fielding's *Bridget Jones's Diary* (1996) has set off a tidal wave of novels and story collections about single, smart, underemployed, neurotic young women searching for the right job and the right man. It is almost impossible to keep track of them all: *In the Drink* (1999) by Kate Christensen, *The Cigarette Girl* (1999) by Carol Wolper, *Love: A User's Guide* (1997) by Clare Naylor, *The Trials of Tiffany Trott* (1999) by Isabel Wolff, *Use Me* (2000) by Elissa Schappell, *My Date With Satan* (1999) by Stacey Richter . . . I am only scratching the surface, here.

Sex, plentiful sex, is obviously one of the appeals of these books, but in the best collections, there is more at work. On the surface, Melissa Bank's *The Girls' Guide to Hunting and Fishing* (1999) is another set of linked stories about a single, smart, underemployed, neurotic young woman searching for . . . well, you know. But Bank's protagonist Jane Rosenal is a vivid young woman whose firecracker witticisms and self-deprecating humor make her unusually sympathetic. Her need for love is as strong as her uncertainty about how to win it. She also has the larger-than-life ability to blurt out the obvious just at the moment when no one else wants to hear it, such as at a delicate moment in a strip poker game.

The emotional appeal of Bank's stories is backed up by their equally emotional resolutions. Characters recur and are revealed to have unsuspected sides. Finally, Jane meets Mr. Right:

> We keep talking of books, and when I tell him that *Anna Karenina* is my favorite, it seems to have the effect "I'm not wearing any underwear" has on other men.

Jane blows it, though, by playing too hard to get. Mr. Right falls in love with someone else. Up until the final page or two, it seems that Jane will not win the love of her life after all. Banks puts the ending in real doubt. Does all end happily? I did not know until the final pages. (It does.)

As you can see, even where a plot is absent, a sympathetic single protagonist and a powerful central conflict can nevertheless unite short stories with breakout force.

Inventing Your Own Advanced Plot Structure

Getting lost in a great novel is one of life's pleasures. Hours slip away. Another world comes alive. Fates are enacted for good or ill. If a novel is really absorbing, I project myself into the story and imagine alternate outcomes, trying to make everything that is going wrong work out right. Do you do that too, or did I just embarrass myself?

Most readers say what carries them along is a good story. But what does that mean? Most novelists would acknowledge, I think, that a "good" story is one that is unpredictable. It is tough to build surprises and hold readers in thrall when following a strict formula. Great mystery writers can do it, needless to say, but for most authors, the way to surprise readers, and themselves, is to embark on a plot that is expandable, possibly long and certainly complex. That leaves a story room to go in unexpected directions, take detours, add layers, surprise us.

Advanced breakout plotting demands an adventurous spirit regarding structure. Breakout novelists are willing to experiment, reverse direction, throw out large chunks of manuscript, add length . . . in short, do whatever it takes to wrestle the many interwoven elements of a large-scale novel into shape.

The point of view in a scene might shift. An inner conflict discovered late the first draft might result in a subplot being added in the second. A soundly constructed premise, as we have seen, is so rich in inherent conflict that there is probably little chance that it can all be resolved in a simple, short, elegantly symmetrical package. Breakout novels sprawl. If not long, they generally are lavish in other ways: depth of character, setting detail, theme and so on.

It can be a scary prospect, this business of writing large. In midmanuscript a breakout novelist can feel lost, overwhelmed by possible scenes and the challenge of tying up every thread. A detailed outline can help, if you have one, but in the expanding universe of breakout novels, it is common for outlines to break down. Late in the game, many breakout novelists realize they have not looked at their outline for months. Instead, they are pushing forward on instinct, using some inner sense of direction to keep them driving toward the high moments and, eventually, the final line.

Is there a way to manage the sprawl? Are there rules of the road, maps of the terrain or cheat books to help you master the game? We are, for the most part, foregoing the comfort of formulas. However, the compasses that can keep you pointed toward true north are the techniques described throughout this book.

Go ahead. Create your own advanced plot structure. Invent a new twist on a familiar genre, revive an old story form or conjure a plot that is uniquely your own. As you do, attend to the qualities that make breakout fiction work. They cut across genre lines. They will keep whatever you do bubbling at breakout level.

BREAKOUT Checklist: Advanced Plot Structures

✓ Dynamic story forms evolve; stagnant genres wither.

✓ The protagonist in a group novel is the group itself.

✓ Regardless of type, thrillers make unlikely disasters seem terrifyingly real.

✓ "Crossover" science fiction is not primarily about science and when successful does not feature dark protagonists.

✓ Breakout biographical novels portray, from their opening lines, lives that are clearly significant.

✓ Today's historical novels usually are not sweeping sagas but are rather some other plot form—mystery, thriller, romance, etc.—set in another time.

✓ To break "out of category," a romance novel must be built on a breakout scale.

✓ When linked short story collections break out, they may be episodic in structure, but nevertheless they feature powerful central conflicts and/or framing devices that unify the stories.

✓ Great stories go in unpredictable directions.

✓ Breakout novels tend to sprawl.

✓ Inventing your own advanced plot structure demands experimentation, an understanding of the principles of breakout novel writing and a clear vision of your novel's purpose.

CHAPTER TEN

Theme

Have you ever been trapped at a party talking with someone who has nothing to say? It's awful, isn't it? You sip your drink, look around surreptitiously, mentally work up excuses for slipping away, check to see if your bladder feels full. Experienced party goers know how to disengage smoothly.

So do readers. When they run across a novel that has nothing to say, they snap it closed and slap it down—or perhaps hurl it across the room. It is not worth their time, which seems odd when you think about it: Most people are opinionated. They have pretty much made up their mind about things. They may listen to other people's ideas but mostly are looking for evidence and arguments that support their own views.

Why, then, do opinionated people bother with novels, which sometimes have challenging things to say? First, a basic fact: Novels are moral. In fact, all stories convey society's underlying values, whether they are danced around a campfire or packaged in sleek black trade paperbacks. Stories are the glue that holds together our fragile human enterprise. Novels are included. For the most part, they validate our values. And no matter what your values, there are novels to affirm them.

Fact two: Readers tend to seek out the novels that accord with their beliefs. Techno-thriller readers are largely military; science fiction readership is heavy with scientists; romance readers are largely women; the fantasy audience includes many computer programmers. The number of fiction readers who deliberately seek to have their morals tested and minds changed are few.

Readers want to have their values validated, true, but usually not in simplistic, moralizing ways. They may not want to be converted, but they do want to be stretched. They want to feel that at the end of the book their views were right but that they were arrived at after a struggle. A skillful breakout novelist can even spin a tale so persuasive that at the end, the reader feels the underlying point was one with which they always have agreed, even though they may have never before considered it.

Just as readers are compelled by the inner tensions of a character or the outer tensions of a plot, they are engrossed by the deeper tensions that arise when the author is working out his point. When critics discuss theme, they most often employ the formula of "man vs. nature," "reason vs. emotion" . . . really, any "A" vs. "B" that represents a genuine dichotomy. When conflicting ideals, values or morals are set against each other in a novel, it grips our imaginations because we ache to resolve that higher conflict.

If a powerful problem is a novel's spine, then a powerful theme is its animating spirit. How can you infuse your breakout novel with such a theme? It starts with having something to say.

Having Something to Say

I do not believe you have no opinions. It is simply not possible that you have never observed a fact of human nature or uncovered a social irony. You no doubt also have some thoughts on the meaning of the universe itself. You are an aware, observant and discerning person. You are a novelist.

What you may not have done is allow yourself to become deeply impassioned about something you believe to be true. That is natural. It is not easy to vigorously express one's views, especially in our Postmodern, politically correct era. We fear offending others. We respect other's views. We listen and defer. We weigh pros and cons and sit quietly through countless meetings.

We admire those who respect others, but I believe there are those whom we admire even more: people who take a stand. Do you remember Tienamen Square? Chinese students rallied for democratic reforms, and the world was moved. What stirred us most deeply, though, was the image of the nameless man who lay down in the path of a rolling tank. Do you remember him? Of course you do. He was a true hero. He had great courage and deep convictions. That same spirit has made Howard Roark in Ayn Rand's *The Fountainhead* one of the great characters in modern fiction. In every new generation he inspires devotion.

A breakout novelist needs courage, too: the courage to say something passionately. A breakout novelist believes that what she has to say is not just *worth* saying, but it is something that *must* be said. It is a truth that the world needs to hear, an insight without which we would find ourselves diminished.

In chapter four I mentioned Anne Perry's Victorian era mystery *Slaves of Obsession*. Its story takes agent of inquiry William Monk and his wife Hester from London to America during the early days of the Civil War. Indeed, their pursuit of a fanatical Unionist fugitive and the impressionable sixteen-year-old British girl who has fled with him brings Monk and Hester all the way to the battle of Bull Run.

Given its setting, you might think Perry's message would be a condemnation of slavery, the selling of arms or war. Reviewers have praised Perry's battle scenes, calling them "relentless in their intensity, unflinching in their truth-telling detail" (*The New York Times*) and comparing them to Thackery's unflinching portrait of Waterloo (*Kirkus Reviews*). Perry has things to say about war, but she also has something to say about a more particular human failing. The fugitive, Breeland, is highly devoted to the Union cause; less so to the young runaway who loves him, Merrit. After their capture and return to London, Breeland's lack of care is noticed by the lawyer hired to defend them, Henry Rathbone, following his first interview with Breeland in his cell:

What made him clench his hands as he strode along the footpath, holding his shoulders tight, was that not once had Breeland asked if Merrit [who is also jailed] were alright, if she were frightened, suffering, unwell, or in need of anything that could possibly be done for her.

Later Merrit, too, realizes this lack in her fiancé:

Merrit lowered her eyes. "I don't understand him," she said under her breath. "He didn't ever really love me, did he? Not as I loved him! . . . He believes the cause is great enough to justify any means of serving it. I . . . I don't think I can share that belief. I know I can't feel it. Maybe my idealism isn't strong enough . . ."

In response, Hester speaks for the author:

"To see the mass and lose the individual is not nobility. You are confusing emotional cowardice with honour." She was even more certain as she found the words. "To do what you believe is right, even when it hurts, to follow your duty when the cost in friendship is high, or even the cost in love, is a greater vision, of course. But to retreat from personal involvement, from gentleness and the giving of yourself, and choose instead the heroics of a general cause, no matter how fine, is a kind of cowardice."

Soon after, Merrit breaks off her engagement to Breeland:

"Love is more than admiration, Lyman," Merrit said with tremendous difficulty, gasping to control her breath. "Love is caring for someone when they are wrong, as well as when they are right, protecting their weakness, guarding them until they find strength again. Love is sharing the little things, as well as the big ones."

This particular point is not as obvious as a simple condemnation of war, but it is more striking thanks to the conviction with which Perry makes it . . . or, rather, has Hester make it. Perry also has learned another secret of conveying passionate opinions: They are always stronger in the mouths of characters than in the prose of the author. They also are more effective when characters have a reason to express them; better still when they express them through concrete actions.

Throughout her thirty novels, Perry's passion is unmistakable. She is driven to write by a keen appreciation of the pain of injustice. Without that, I have no doubt her Victorian mystery stories would still be popular; however, they might not be as memorable. She lets her characters speak for her, too, so although her people may seem moralistic, Perry herself is never didactic. For Perry, story comes first.

I have noticed Perry's sort of inner fire in other breakout novelists. It comes out in panels at writers conferences and at the hotel bar at the end of the day. Strong novelists have strong opinions. More to the point, they are not at all afraid to express them. Scratch the surface of a best-selling author and very likely you will not find a marshmallow underneath. You will find a fiery, impassioned advocate.

What do you care about? What gets your blood boiling? What makes you roar with laughter? What human suffering have you seen that makes you wince in sympathetic pain? That is the stuff of breakout novels. Stories lacking fire cannot fire readers.

Cleave to your convictions. Cherish them. Let them stoke your story with an energy that will drive it like the giant pistons of a steam locomotive. Let yourself care because that is to live with passion—and it is passionate stories that your readers crave.

Step-by-Step Theme Building

One problem with talking about theme is that any discussion necessarily makes "theme" sound like something extra that is added to a story at the end, like cheese baked on top of a casserole in its final twenty minutes in the oven. If authentic, theme is not something apart from story but something intrinsic to it. It is not embedded, but rather emerges.

Some theorists state with respect to theme that either you have it or you don't. I am not of that school. I feel it is beneficial to work in advance on the moral forces moving underneath your story, but I do feel that such work generally involves strengthening what the people in the story believe rather than what you, the author, may feel. And even that may not save your novel from sounding preachy at times!

To avoid a preachy tone, it may be helpful for the breakout novelist not to grapple with theme on a global scale, but rather first to examine individual scenes for ways in which they each can be made sharper and more impassioned. Ask: What is driving your focal character through this scene?

In other words, examine a scene with the assumption that the convictions of the subject of the scene (usually, but not always, the point-of-view character) are weak. Now, you may not feel that about any given scene in your current novel, but work with me for a moment. It is all too easy for an author to project into his novel more than is actually there.

Pick at random a scene from your current novel. Any scene. What is happening? A point-of-view character, in all likelihood your protagonist, is experiencing something: a problem, perhaps; at any rate, something that adds a layer to, or complicates, that character's main course of action. Right? Good. Now, ask yourself this question: Why is this character here? I do not mean the plot reasons. I mean the inner reasons, her motivations. List them. Yes, really.

OK, got a short list? You will probably find that at the top of your list are the character's immediate needs: her physical and emotional requirements. Further down the list probably are the character's secondary needs: information, support, avoidance, comfort, curiosity and so on. Finally, down at the bottom of the list are the higher motivations, the ones that are not immediately relevant and that would sound a bit silly to include in your scene: the search for truth, a thirst for justice, a need to hope, a longing for love.

Next, reverse the list. That's right: Write it out again, starting with the reasons at the bottom of your original list. Now rewrite your scene with your character motivated first by the reasons at the top of your new list, last by your original reasons. The scene feels a little different, does it not? I will bet that your character is acting a bit differently, too. Motivating your characters according to higher values will do that. It adds passion to action.

Enhancing motivation is what you will need to do if you want to give your protagonist the inner fire that, developed step-by-step through your manuscript, results in a powerful theme. Work on it. Naturally, it is important to avoid overplaying high motives or making them too obvious. Understatement and restraint are the watchwords. However, when high motives are made believable and integral to a given character, it is like sending a ten thousand volt electric current through your novel. It will light it up like a beacon in the dark.

Symbols

Another way in which to enhance your theme is through your use of symbols. Symbols—which generally are physical objects but may also be phrases, gestures, animals or just about anything—pack a powerful lot of meaning into a small package.

For purposes of the breakout novel, probably the most effective pattern to follow is that of a single symbol that recurs. Deployment of multiple symbols is possible too, of course, but what kind of power would J.R.R. Tolkien's *The Lord of the Rings* have had if Frodo's quest had centered not only a ring, but also on a sword, a comb and a sack of flour?

Some novelists feel that symbols are stagy and obvious, but in my observation, they are frequently present in a novel whether the author intended them to be or not. Evoking symbols is often a matter of making use of what is already there. If a symbol would otherwise naturally occur in a story, use it. It will not feel stagy. In fact, many readers may not consciously notice it.

In Anton Myrer's great novel of the World War II generation at Harvard, *The Last Convertible* (1978), Myrer needs to give his group of high-spirited men, who call themselves the Fabulous Fusiliers, a means of transportation. And so together they purchase a green convertible. After the war, the convertible is kept on blocks in a garage by George Virden, the group's stalwart center. The car comes to symbolize all the love, longing, hopes and suffering the group has undergone. The moment when George passes the keys to the convertible to his future son-in-law, and thus symbolically to the next generation, is a surefire tearjerker.

Myrer finds his symbol right in the story, and so can you.

Becoming Passionate

Are you having trouble getting a grip on what exactly it is that you are trying to say in your current novel? There is help for that problem.

One technique is to censor yourself. Try this mental exercise: Imagine government agents bursting into your writing room, smashing your computer, grinding your backup disks under their heels, burning your hard copy and hauling you off to prison.

Now imagine that you are subjected to a monkey trial in which you are not allowed to defend yourself. You are sentenced to hang. In the week before your execution, the compassionate warden of the prison lends you a typewriter and paper . . . *but only ten sheets.* You have time and paper to type out only one scene from your novel . . . *which one is it that you begin to type?*

Take this mental exercise a further step: To torment you, a sadistic guard seizes your scene, rips it to pieces and laughs as she walks away with the scraps. All that is left is one blank half sheet that fluttered to the floor. Now you have room only for one paragraph from your novel. You roll the soiled scrap of paper around the platen of your typewriter and tap out . . . *what?*

Go to your word processor right now—yes, this minute—and type out the paragraph from your novel that you would have written in prison on the last day of your life. What does it say?

Are you surprised at what you typed? Most people who try this exercise are. What this means is that what most passionately matters to you in your story has been hidden, both from you and very likely from your eventual readers. To write a breakout novel, you need to bring it forward. It has got to matter to you or, more to the point, to your protagonist.

And it should. It is your legacy to our literature and to us. It is your message. Classic novels have messages. So do the breakout novels of today. If you do not believe me, look through the novels on your own shelves. Novelists are taking stands all over the place. They have a great deal to say, just like you.

Right and Wrong in the Novel

One problem that can keep a novel from breaking out is a failure to draw a clear line between good and bad. Most readers are moral people. They turn to fiction—really, to any form of story-telling—for affirmation of the values we hold in common. They long to know that what they believe is right. Contemporary life offers few opportunities to take a strong moral stand, but fiction deals heavily with such moments.

Now, I am not arguing for a revival of the moral fable or the novel of social conscience so popular in the nineteenth century: 1850s *The Scarlet Letter* by Nathaniel Hawthorne and 1885s *The Rise of Silas Lapham* by William Dean Howells spring to mind, as to some extent do the novels of psychological realism of Edith Wharton and Henry James. Even early twentieth century novels of social realism by Upton Sinclair, Theodore Dreiser, Jack London, Sinclair Lewis and John Steinbeck (especially *Of Mice and Men* [1937] or *The Grapes of Wrath* [1939]) strike most readers today as heavy-handed morality tales.

Certainly contemporary novels can have a sharp moral tone—especially social satires like Joseph Heller's *Catch-22*

(1961) or Tom Wolfe's *The Bonfire of the Vanities* (1987)—but in general as readers we prefer that our fiction make its point in a restrained rather than an overt fashion. That means, as we have seen, keeping the message out of the mouth of the author and instead conveying it through the actions of a novel's characters.

If you think about it, what many breakout authors are doing is boxing their characters into a situation with inescapable moral choices and dilemmas. Facing a moral choice is perhaps one of the most powerful conflicts any novel can present. Does the protagonist of your current novel face such a choice? If not, take a look at your climactic moment. Is it a moment of outward change? A plot turning point?

It is probably also an inward turning point. The time when things are darkest and most dire is also the time when a character's fortitude and inner convictions are most sorely tested. Even if the choice is as simple as whether to give up or go forward against high odds, there is even so a moral dimension to the decision. What would make that decision more difficult?

As a mental exercise, pile on some of those added difficulties. List them. Even the easy option of giving up can be deepened. For example, what if giving up on reaching a goal would not just be easy but would be rewarded? Worse, what if saving the day means sacrificing something of one's self? Worse still, what if that part of one's self up for offering has been hard won and is of high importance? Already the simple choice of "give up" vs. "go forward" has new dimensions.

It is not such a difficult matter, then, to build an escalation of these dimensions into your story. Go back to your outline, or simply list the scenes in your latest draft. Find one, two or three points at which the factors that complicate the heroine's climactic choice can be planted.

What I am arguing for here is a story that follows both inner and outer tracks. In discussing the construction of complex characters (chapter five), I mention that what makes a character intriguing is conflicting sides. A corollary principle is that a character's beliefs also follow a path of development. They have their own plot. Weaving an inner struggle into the fabric of the outer events of the narrative magnifies a novel's final impact, particularly if the inner and the outer conflicts can reach a simultaneous climax. Adding a moral dimension will make it that much stronger.

Many novelists are rightly wary of moral content. It is too easy to turn preachy. It is essential, then, that the moral outlook of one's protagonist be embedded in her actions. Likewise, the inverse of her outlook may be best embedded in the actions of her antagonist—even if your heroine's greatest enemy is herself. Self-doubting or self-destructive protagonists are hard to like, naturally, but on the other hand, a protagonist without any flaws or blind spots will feel bland.

One of the most highly moral science fiction writers working today is Orson Scott Card. While his convictions are clear, in his best work they emerge from the action of the story rather than from his characters' mouths. In his Nebula and Hugo Award-winning 1985 novel *Ender's Game*, young Andrew "Ender" Wiggin is taken from his family and put into a military training school where he is conditioned with highly stressful virtual warfare simulations. At the climax of the novel, following a thousand-to-one odds battle in which the enemy's home planet is destroyed, Ender learns that what had seemed to be a computer game is not a simulation at all.

Ender, a child genius, has been fighting an actual alien invasion. The fighter pilots he wasted in order to win really died. The ten billion aliens he wiped out "were as alive and wise as any man." At the end of the novel, he departs on a colony ship in order to learn about the enemy he has destroyed. Card's novel has volumes to say about children, computer games and the human culture of violence, but nowhere in the novel are these themes stated overtly. Instead, Card allows his story itself to send the message.

Whatever the point you wish to make, it will be more effective if it lives as a conviction that drives the heroine forward rather than an overtly expressed opinion that stops the story dead. However, there is one possible exception to that rule. When properly applied, it can add a stirring high point to a breakout novel.

The Protagonist's Declaration of Purpose

As I said, a commitment to a high principle is most effectively tested at a dramatic high point—or, I suppose, low point. If a heroine's conviction can be passionately and lyrically conveyed at such a time, in a way that is both natural to the situation and understated in its poetry, that passage can become a powerful defining statement, the protagonist's declaration of purpose.

Another way to get at it is this: What keeps your protagonist going? When does she most need to recognize the source of her inner drive? That moment is the moment for her to declare her purpose.

In *Shōgun*, the love between John Blackthorne and Mariko is strictly forbidden but powerful. Nevertheless, Mariko is inescapably Japanese. When late in the novel her duty requires that she commit seppuku, ritual suicide, rather than risk disgrace, she prepares to do so. Blackthorne asks why. Mariko then declares her most fundamental convictions:

> "My life's never been my own, Anjin-san. It's always belonged to my liege Lord, and, after him, to my Master. That's our law."
>
> "It's a bad law."
>
> "Yes. And no." She looked up from the mats. "Are we going to quarrel about things that may not be changed?"
>
> "No. Please excuse me."
>
> "I love thee," she said in Latin.
>
> "Yes. I know that now. And I love thee. But death is thy aim, Mariko-san."

"Thou are wrong, my darling. The life of my Master
is my aim . . ."

It is not only the strength and nobility of Mariko's convictions that make them memorable, but also Clavell's timing in
expressing them.

What Makes a Theme Universal?

If an author has effectively constructed a moral conflict, first
planting its seeds and then bringing it to a simultaneous climax
with the outer events of the plot, the overall effect will be a
message that probably will be well and long remembered.

Notice the word "probably" in that last sentence. Some messages are memorable. Others are not. Why? I believe the answer
to that question goes to the essence of what makes a theme
universal.

A message, moral or point that is widely believed is in one
sense universal, but that does not guarantee it will have impact.
Half-hour family sitcoms on TV often have a familiar moral, but
usually it is forgotten by the time the final credits roll. Why? The
sitcom message is often simplistic and weakly dramatized. The
very same point can have a devastating effect in a breakout novel.
That is because the novelist builds a problem or dilemma over
the long span of her narrative, deepening it in a sequence of
highly dramatic episodes of a type that are difficult to enact in
twenty-two minutes.

What matters more than whether a point is widely accepted,
then, is whether it is developed in depth. Needless to say, thematic impact does not automatically come with length. It must
be crafted. The author of a breakout novel must make the choice
to make her characters choose; must fire them, and then sustain
them, with deeply held convictions.

But which convictions? Easy, often expressed, commonly
held ones? Sometimes. "Love matters above all" is pretty much
the universal theme of romance fiction. Much of the time, it

does not have a high impact, though. Few category romances leave me with that satisfying feeling of *Yessss!* at the final moment of resolution, the "kiss," between heroine and hero. The theme is the same as in the great romance novels, but somehow in most category romances, it arrives with all the *whomp* of a feather hitting a carpet.

A great romance novel makes love matter more than anything else in the world. It does that with the depth of development discussed above but also, perhaps, by arriving at the expected message from an unexpected direction. That is one reason the periodic appearance of unusual elements in romance fiction—say, time travel or paranormal plot strands—generally sells well for a little while. The familiar values of the genre are refreshed by a new context. (Of course, successful reinventions of the formula soon become fads and grow stale with overuse, but that is a different story.)

One solution to building powerful themes, then, is to apply the principle of originality discussed in chapter two. In other words, travel to a familiar moral destination but by an unfamiliar route.

What about the truly original theme, though? Is it possible for readers to accept a point that is unfamiliar, perhaps even unpopular? Certainly it is. Few novelists want to say exactly what has been said before. Most would like to be visionary. That is fine, and indeed it is one of the purposes of literature; as opposed to genre fiction, the thematic purpose of which is to validate familiar beliefs. But there are ways to make an unpopular point compelling, and there are ways to make it repellant. A novelist hoping to break out will, naturally enough, shoot for the former effect.

From time to time I find in my slush pile manuscripts that deal in moral absolutes. Usually their authors have an axe to grind: idiotic public policy, hypocritical politicians, uncaring health care, an unjust justice system or the like. For all their evident passion, these novels do not greatly persuade me. Moral absolutes do not play well in fiction. Fiction is about people, and people are fallible. Also, these manuscripts tend to preach what most of us already believe. Why listen to that? As I have said, even when the message is familiar, the medium needs to be new.

If you want to be morally daring in your breakout novel, it would be wise to construct your case subtly, building it by indirection; for instance, by catching your readers up in a compelling character first before taking that character on a moral detour. Contemporary literary fiction is crowded with characters who are transvestite, addicted, odd, outcast or in any number of ways different. When these novels break out, the author has succeeded in making readers feel that their outcast characters are *just like us*, which is a sort of moral victory all by itself, don't you think?

It is even possible to construct a contemporary antihero. Mystery novelist Donald E. Westlake scored a major critical and sales success with his 1997 novel *The Ax*. In it, paper company executive Burke Devore, out of work for two years and desperate, decides to raise his chances for a new job by eliminating his strongest competition; i.e., by murdering them one by one. Devore's justification for his actions comes late in the novel. This masterful passage is a ringing, if satiric, endorsement of contemporary American values that shows the depth of Devore's madness, or perhaps his sanity:

> Every era, and every nation, has its own characteristic morality, its own code of ethics, depending on what the people think is important. There have been times and places when honor was considered the most sacred of qualities, and times and places that gave every concern to grace. The Age of Reason promoted reason to be the highest of values, and some peoples—the Italians, the Irish—have always felt that feeling, emotion, sentiment was the most important. In the early days of America, the work ethic was our greatest expression of morality, and then for a while property values were valued above everything else,

but there's been another more recent change. Today, our moral code is based on the idea that the end justifies the means.

There was a time when that was considered improper, the end justifying the means, but that time is over. We not only believe it, we say it. Our government leaders always defend their actions on the basis of their goals. And every single CEO who has commented in public on the blizzard of downsizings sweeping America has explained himself with some variant on the same idea: The end justifies the means.

The end of what I'm doing, the purpose, the goal, is good, clearly good. I want to take care of my family; I want to be a productive part of society; I want to put my skills to use; I want to work and pay my own way and not be a burden to the taxpayers. The means to that end has been difficult, but I've kept my eye on the goal, the purpose. The end justifies the means. Like the CEO's, I have nothing to feel sorry for.

You know, I almost agree with him! Westlake makes a fresh comment upon our values by having Devore say what we expect him to say, but calmly and rationally do the opposite of what we want. Devore is wrong—but Westlake is original.

Discovering Theme

So, do you now have a better idea of what your current novel is about? Do you have a plan for revising it to make its themes stronger?

If you do, great. If not, do not worry. Writing is, if nothing else, an act of discovery. I did not know everything I wanted to say in this chapter until I started writing it. As it unfolded, though, I realized that reading several decades worth of raw manuscripts has indeed taught me a few things about why some novels move me and live in memory for years, while others are forgotten almost as soon as I stuff them into an SASE.

One of those things is that an indifferent author cannot ex-cite me. An author who is fired up, however—or, rather, who fires up his characters as his proxies—stands a much better chance of crafting a story that will hold me spellbound.

Having something to say means having something for one's characters to say. Think of some main characters of some of the last century's best-selling novels and series: Travis McGee, Howard Roark, Scarlett O'Hara, George Smiley and so on. They are not diffident, deferential people. They are principled, opin-ionated and passionate. They do not sit on the sidelines. They act. Their inner fire fires us—as well as the sales of their author's books. Their beliefs inspire, their opinions linger in our mind and mingle with our own.

Even mousy Mrs. deWinter in Daphne du Maurier's *Rebecca*, who is so timid that she does not even have her own name, is not a wholly passive heroine. Take a fresh look at *Rebecca*. Notice how much Mrs. deWinter braves out of love for her husband. Don't you wish you had a spouse so devoted? (You have? Con-gratulations. So do I.) OK, then put him or her in your next novel, or at any rate a character infused with those values that you treasure so deeply in your spouse, or whoever it is in your own life story who has inspired you.

Now put that character to the test. Ah. Feels good, doesn't it? Now you have the stuff of greatness at work in your fiction. You are on the road to building a breakout theme.

BREAKOUT Checklist: Theme

✓ Novels are moral.

✓ Conflicting ideals or values create tension.

✓ Become impassioned about your story.

✓ Express convictions through characters.

✓ Use the reverse motive exercise to deepen your characters' convictions.

✓ Develop symbols from what is at hand.

✓ Strengthen your own passion with the oppression exercise.

✓ Map the moral development (or decline) of your protagonist.

✓ Universal themes usually are familiar, but in the breakout novel, they are portrayed in depth.

✓ If you must go out on a moral limb, anchor your readers in a sympathetic character.

✓ Don't push theme; let it flow.

✓ Put your characters to the test.

CHAPTER ELEVEN

Breaking Out

You have done it. Your breakout novel is complete. Your critique group raves; you have taken a leap in your writing, they say. You think so, too. This one was more work, a lot more. You are proud. You are also nervous. Will the folks in New York publishing recognize what you have accomplished?

Are you even sure yourself?

Whether or not you have written your breakout novel is a major question. Riding on the answer is years of work, lots of hope, perhaps the only shot you feel that you will ever have at the top of your publisher's list. You probably believe that this is *it*: the make-or-break book. If this doesn't work, you certainly are not going to go to this much trouble ever again!

So, who or what decides whether this is indeed your breakout novel? Your agent? Your editor? His editorial board? An auction? Catalog position? The media in twenty cities? The sales force? The bookstore chains? I have some good news and some bad news, and they are the same: The jury that will decide whether or not you have written your breakout is the public.

That is bad news because publication is a year or more away; plus, there are so many other factors that influence a book's success in the retail marketplace: cover, promo, season, timing, competition. *Heck, my novel could wind up coming out the same month as the next Harry Potter! I could get buried!*

Yes, you could. Almost makes you want to crawl back to the

midlist, doesn't it? Except, of course, the midlist is no longer a safe haven. Besides, there *is* stuff to look forward to over the next year: people's reactions, possibly more money, the thrill of taking your shot, of rolling the dice.

The good news is that if you have indeed written your break-out novel, chances are some people along the road to publication are going to think so, too. Big things are going to happen. You have in store some exciting moments. Let us take a look at the road to publication and beyond, and see what are some of the key events, issues, warning signs and signals that will tell you if you are on a breakout track.

Agent and Editor

Probably the first person who will see your manuscript is your agent, if you have one. If you do not, you probably will want to get one. How to go about it? There are many volumes on the subject of agents, query letters, contracts and the rest of the game. From the receiving end, let me share a bit of experience with you based on my twenty years as a fiction agent.

Far worse than having no agent is having the wrong agent. Well over half my clients are ex-clients of some other agency. What went wrong? There are as many answers as there are clients, but some common themes are lack of communication, lack of editorial feedback, indifference, poor follow-through, lack of expertise with a given market and so on. Some of the ex-agents are part-timers, not in New York or, occasionally when I meet them, just not on the same planet.

How did those authors wind up with those agents? One factor is haste. Getting an agent is a profound personal validation for a writer, and at a certain point—generally when success is close enough to taste, yet still somehow elusive—the writer simply cannot stand to wait any longer. He signs up with the first agent who says "yes." A couple of years later, the mistake becomes evident. A divorce is needed, but of course divorce is a messy business and dating again is a scary prospect. Some writers put it off too long.

Do you need a new agent? If you do, you will probably know. Calls go unreturned. Marketing reports are scanty. In many ways, your agent does not seem involved with you. I am not talking about being taken for granted; that happens, and it usually can be cured with an honest phone call. No, I am talking about plain indifference, which can be just as hurtful as lack of experience.

To be fair, that indifference may be plain weariness. If you are impossibly demanding, sweating every detail, living or dying depending on the tone of your agent's voice in your last phone call, then your agent may have cause to be tired of you. Conversely, if you are indifferent to your career, writing weakly or all over the place, and frankly are not making money, then your agent may also be justified in his attitude.

True lack of experience is another matter. With your breakout novel in hand, you may be wondering if your agent is up to the job. Does he have the contacts, the savvy and the clout to get you a major deal and keep you on course throughout the publication process? One sign is how helpful your agent is *before* you are done writing: Is he giving you early feedback, is he cheering you on? Once the manuscript is done, is there quality evaluation and detailed planning for the sale?

You cannot measure those things if your attitude is, "Oh, I just let my agent handle that." You have to be involved. You will want to have some idea of what you need in terms of publisher, deal, format and so forth. If your agent is not on the same page, fine. Listen. If his ideas make sense, you might want to go with them. If they do not, talk about it. If your agent is excited, then at least he is on your side.

For one reason or another, you may find that the first publishing person with whom you connect is an editor. You may have interested one at a writers conference. If so, you probably have started a correspondence, and may even have received revision suggestions and more than one reading. If so, congratulations!

There is nothing wrong with this route into publishing.

However, once it becomes clear that the editor would like to buy your book, it is time to get an agent. If an offer has been made, do not say yes or no; instead, ask if you may take the time to find an agent. Most editors will gladly consent. They are professionals. They know that a good agent can be an asset to everyone. As to timing, do not worry. Your agent search will not take long with an offer on the table.

How do you find an agent? Ask several sources for referrals. Check the guidebooks. (The publisher of this volume produces a good one, which is updated annually.) Be sure that the agents to whom you are talking know your field. That is as easy as asking about their other clients and recent sales. Also be sure that what they have to say about your novel is specific, insightful and sensitive. The same goes for their outlook on the market and your upcoming deal.

With luck, you will have a choice of several good agents. Who will be right for you may come down to chemistry, but I recommend you consider agents who are members of the Association of Authors' Representatives, Inc.; AAR, for short. The membership requirements and Canon of Ethics of this national trade organization are the only standards for experience and fair dealing in the otherwise unregulated business of literary agency. I am a member. Many good agents are.

Whether or not you have an offer on the table, what is the best way to approach your prospects? Oh boy, do I have some advice for you!

The Pitch

Query letter, fax, phone call, e-mail? The guidebooks will tell you what each agent prefers. Generally speaking, skip fax and e-mail. The first feels arrogant, I don't know why but it does, and the second is too casual. If you have an offer from a publisher in hand, a phone call is appropriate, if a little nerve-wracking.

With no offer in hand, a query letter with SASE (that is, a

self-addressed stamped envelope with sufficient postage to return to you the agent's reply and/or your material) is a businesslike way to make your first approach.

Do not be intimidated by the legendary volume of agents' query mail, the so-called "slush pile." (My office receives several hundred letters a week.) A well-written letter and a solid premise always stand out. When the good ones come in, my staff knows to get them on my desk right away. Hot prospects usually have written to my competition, as well, and experience has taught me that the first agent to phone the prospective client is quite often the one who wins out.

Now, the pitch: Why are novelists so bad at selling their own stories? Never mind, I know why. This is the crucial moment, though, when it pays to practice the art of the pitch. A good query letter has four components: introduction, summary, credentials, closing. The first and last should be, and usually are, short. It is the middle two that give people problems.

First, the summary: How to sum up your long, layered break-out novel in 100–200 words? It is a challenge, but there are guidelines. First, remember the purpose of your query letter is not to tell the whole plot or to convince me you are the hottest new writer since last week. Rather, the purpose of your query is simply to get me to read your manuscript. With that in mind, a summary gets easier.

There are only three things you need to get me, or anybody, hooked on a story: setting, protagonist, problem. Deliver those briefly and with punch, and you have a basic pitch. Conveying some of your story's layers is a tougher challenge. My advice is to be brief and to focus on the elements that lend your story plausibility (its real-world inspiration, *briefly* stated, can help), inherent conflict, originality and gut emotional appeal. No-no's to avoid are adjectives, superlatives and anything more than a word or two on your theme.

Also, skip all that junk about the size of the audience for your novel. Your ambition, years of effort, professional attitude, willingness to promote, etc., are also unnecessary. You are ahead of yourself. What matters at this stage is your story.

Publishing credentials, though, can be helpful to include. Prior novel publications always make me sit up and take notice, although self-publication has the opposite effect—unless it resulted in an Edgar Award nomination, or similar. Short story sales to recognized magazines are also good. Journalistic experience, professional articles, ad writing and the like are nice but do not imply skill as a novelist.

What if you have never been published? What if this is your first piece of writing? No doubt about it, you may have a tough time persuading any top agent that your book is worth a look. The novel is a vastly complicated art form that takes years to master. For that reason, I am happier to hear that the offered manuscript is the author's third or fourth. That said, the right first novel pitched well, can be a big winner.

There are other things that get my attention, too. An M.F.A. in writing or study with a reputable teacher are pluses. So are referrals from published novelists. The best recommendation of all, needless to say, is a novel that sounds dynamite. Work on your pitch. Mention your models. If your premise is good, your approach professional and your skill evident, it is entirely possible to interest even a top New York agent.

Outlines

If your query letter scores, you will be asked for part or all of your manuscript. You may also be asked for an outline. Here is another area of angst and confusion. What is an outline? How long is it? One page? Twenty-five? Is it the same as a synopsis, or what?

Here are the basics: Regarding length, an outline can be any number of pages, and different agents and editors prefer different sizes. Ask. Why not have ready a one-page summary as well as a more detailed outline? Can't hurt. With longer formats, five to twenty-five single or double-spaced pages is plenty. Really long outlines of fifty pages or more are cumbersome. When we say "outline," we really mean "synopsis." Skip chapter headings, unless requested, and forget about Roman numerals and all that. What you want is to give your prospect the feeling of reading the actual novel.

The best outlines relate the whole story in miniature, and include scraps of setting detail, characterization and dialogue, which nicely highlight the story's turning points. Outlines are most effective when they are in the present tense and third person, regardless of the tense and person of the novel.

In outlines, standard manuscript formatting (double-spaced text, generous margins, single-sided pages) is clean and easy to read. Use it.

With your novel written, your pitch made, your agent selected, a marketing plan and deal goals decided upon, you are ready to embark on your breakout journey. Waiting is harder than writing, but once the sale is accomplished the excitement begins. What are you looking for now? What is your role? What are the pitfalls? How do you measure success?

Breakout Publishing, Breakout Living

Prior to publication, a number of things happen. One of them is revision. Another is copyediting. It is well to treat these tasks as professionally as possible. If there are problems, talk with your editor. If that does not help, ask your agent to step in. That is one of the things he is there to do.

The earliest promotional activity is lining up advance blurbs. Here is where your contacts and connections can pay off, though be aware that the name of the blurbing author on your cover sends a signal to consumers. A Kinky Friedman quote means something different than an Anne Perry quote. Think semiotics.

Speaking of that, the format of your book (hardcover, trade paperback or mass-market paperback) is important. It is a decision that in general belongs to your publisher, but it is one that you will want to discuss with your agent in advance of the sale. Hardcover gets reviews and is the format of choice for breaking out. However, hardcovers are expensive. Your publisher may decide to launch your novel in a lower-priced trade paperback edition. For certain novels, especially hip literary fiction and first novels, that can be a very smart move.

Thrillers, mainstream and literary novels rarely break out in mass-market paperback, although that is the format in which they may backlist and in which they probably will sell the most units. Possible exceptions to this rule are romance novels and science fiction. Consumers of these genres like paperbacks, or at any rate are used to them, and can send their sales sharply upward. Still, if for review reasons only, hardcover is the nearly universal breakout choice. It puts your novel into stores twice and tells bookstores that your publisher is taking your new novel seriously.

What about advances? Aren't they the surest indicator of a publisher's enthusiasm? Pay more equals work harder, and all that? Without a doubt, a high advance says that a publisher is excited. I do not turn them down, but I do caution my clients that high advances also carry high risk. You can get great reviews and sell lots of copies, but still lose money for your publisher. If you lose them too much, you will feel a chill in the air when you submit your option novel.

That might not be a worry—unless you have purchased a fat mortgage and racked up big credit card bills. Remember, while advances do not have to be paid back if unearned, they are nevertheless an estimate (sometimes generous) of eventual royalty earnings. It is wrong to assume that advances always will go up. Like the stock market they can fall sharply.

Be wise about advances and adjust your lifestyle in stages. Of course, it is difficult to budget when one's income arrives in infrequent, large lump sums. You would think that a six-figure advance would wipe out cash flow crunches, but I can tell you from experience that six-figure authors are just as desperate for acceptance checks as four-figure authors; often more so. One common mistake I see is authors budgeting their money to last for the time that it will take to write and deliver a novel. They fail to take into account the months that it may take for the editor to read it, send revision suggestions, for revisions themselves to be written, and then for the check finally to wend its way through the publisher's Dickensian accounting system.

Why is that a problem? Because it makes for hasty revisions, which makes for flawed novels, which makes for unhappy readers.

Authors also fail to anticipate life's emergencies: the car dying, Mom needing live-in assistance, the teenage son's court costs and so on. One emergency can shrink a six-figure advance pretty fast. Be smart. Do not go overboard if you get a breakout advance. Do not order your yacht until you have a couple of successful novels on the shelves.

But back to your publishing . . . as the publication date approaches, publicity plans are laid and printings are planned. How big a printing do you want? Contrary to what some authors think, big printings do not generate big sales. How could they? The public does not care how many copies come off the press. Thus, two-million-copy first printings are only safe for proven bestsellers. For the breakout novelist, printings will be based on advance orders and that is good. I would rather a novel go back to press a couple of times than leave half of a 200,000 printing in cartons.

Publicity is a religion that inspires awe in most novelists. A promo budget is the object of their quest, and a tour is the grail. But are these always desirable? The signings and media tour are still book publishing's primary promotion tools, but samplers, ARCs (advance reading copies), and other word-of-mouth tools can be as effective in building a breakout.

Newspaper reviews are welcome, but they appear in one paper, on only one day. For the most part, consumers only see them excerpted in the paperback edition. The most meaningful reviews are thus those that come far enough in advance to effect trade orders, like *Publishers Weekly* and *Kirkus Reviews*. That explains why agents, editors and publicists call excitedly to say,

"Did you see your *PW?*" when in fact *PW* is a trade magazine that the public does not read. *PW* gets copies into stores.

Should you do self-promotion? At breakout level, it should not be necessary. If your novel is flying off the shelves, your publisher will probably be doing its job. You may have ideas to contribute, especially if the subject of your novel has an angle that can be worked. For instance, when Jennifer Chiaverini's *The Quilter's Apprentice* came out, Simon & Schuster worked with her to reach her special audience. They sent her to the American Quilter's Society's annual show, an event attended by thirty thousand people. The author also has a Web site where you can view a quilt featured in the novel.

Web sites, in fact, are the new low-cost, high-impact piece of self-promotion that every novelist ought to consider. One thousand dollars will not take you very far on the road, but it will buy you an excellent Web site that will bring at least as many "hits" as a short signing tour, and last much longer. Also effective is publishing an e-mail address for fans in your books. Keeping up the correspondence can be a chore, but it is the most direct way to reach your core readers.

What if you are an ivory tower type? Must you go out to meet and greet? Truman Capote and Harold Robbins liked promotion better than writing, but not everyone is such a publicity hound. Anne Perry is sent by her publisher on twice-a-year twenty-city tours that last four weeks each. It has helped her to build a powerful audience, and she enjoys meeting her fans. However, she also writes in hotels and on airplanes to keep up her two-books-a-year output. It is a pace that would exhaust an author with less energy. Me it would kill.

Authors such as those with physical challenges, family commitments or, perhaps, an antisocial attitude can do just as well staying home. Thomas Pynchon has never, to my knowledge, been seen in public, but that did not prevent his 1999 novel *Mason & Dixon* from selling well. Of course, he is Thomas Pynchon, and there lies the ultimate truth about promotion: The best publicity of all is between the covers of your book.

Success, Sequels, Series and Beyond

How can you measure the progress of your breakout novel? What are the signs of success? Best-seller lists are the most closely watched indicator. Chain lists, regional lists, the *Publishers Weekly* list, *USA Today*'s list and so on will hit before *The New York Times*. Or you may not hit the lists at all.

It may not matter. Any sharp upward jump in sales, review attention, awards, etc., is good. Each trip back to press is also validation for author and publisher. If you have not badly over-sold yourself in your deal, your career will continue upward.

Well, it will continue upward if your writing also continues upward. I am amazed at how quickly the public figures out that a second novel or the fourth mystery in a series is not worth buying. I mean, *I* know. I read the manuscript. But the public is only browsing the first page or two in a store. . . . How do they figure it out? And so many of them all at once?

I do not know but they do, just as they also discover great new novels that even the publisher did not realize would break out. If word of mouth is a kind of magic, readers are wizards. You and I cross them at our peril. Once you have broken out, your job is not over. Delivering breakout-scale novels on a regular schedule is the one sure path to continued success.

Second novels in particular are a proving ground. So are the later books in a series; and by the way, it is not true that all breakout novels are stand-alones. Mystery series can break out with their first titles or deep into the series. Patrick O'Brian's nautical novels have been around for several decades, but they did not break out in the United States until recently.

If your novel breaks out, should you write a sequel? It seems natural, but sequels can disappoint. Irwin Shaw knocked us out with *Rich Man, Poor Man* in 1970, but then followed up with the weaker *Beggarman, Thief* (1977). Mary Doria Russell's 1996 novel *The Sparrow* dazzled, but its sequel *Children of God* (1998), while worthy, was unexciting. Sequels need careful thought, unless they are definitely part of a series. Readers like to revisit favorite characters, which is why series work, but in the world of breakout publishing, it is important that the breakout scale of the storytelling be maintained.

With a sequel, as with any novel, it is well to question why you are writing it. Do you have something new and urgent to say? Yes? Great. If not, work on it until you do. If the passion that drove you to write your breakout novel is missing from its follow-up, the wizards certainly will find you out.

There is, of course, pressure to follow up a successful novel quickly. That pressure can be crippling. In an interview with *Publishers Weekly* in 1997, Whitney Otto told of the difficulty she had writing after the success of *How to Make an American Quilt*. Her second novel, *Now You See Her*, showed the strain, although it is still a novel worth reading.

Is there any way to relieve the pressure? It is not easy. To hold off your eager editor, publisher and agent, you will have to stick to your guns and demand the time you need to make your next novel as great as your last. Most people in publishing understand there is a trade-off between speed and quality. Let them know you know that, too, and generally they will respect your integrity and leave you alone.

How about planning your career? Are there master plans that, like value investing in the financial realm, have stood the test of time? Should you stay loyal to your publisher, or does there come a point when you should be seduced by the highest bidder?

Sticking with one publisher has undeniable benefits. Long-term loyalty yields deep commitment on a publisher's part. Backlist stays together, which is a powerful tool for building both earnings and word of mouth. A publisher with long-term commitment will not only keep backlist in print but will refresh its look from time to time with new cover designs. Authors like

Danielle Steel and Tom Clancy have prospered mightily by staying in place. It is the plan that I prefer to follow.

Unfortunately, it is not always possible to do so. Rifts develop. Sometimes an author feels the strength of his growing
mastery of craft before his publisher sees it in sales. At times like
that, the friction between author and publisher can cause the
relationship to burst into flames. At times like that, I may have
no choice but to engineer a move; and indeed, a new publishing
relationship can bring fresh ideas and new energy to an author's
career. Knowing when to make the move is an art, though, one
that must be practiced for the right reasons. Be sure your need
is extreme.

A wrong reason to make a move is envy of other authors'
superior advances, covers, promotional treatment or whatever.
Each author is unique. No career is like any other, and that
includes the pace at which it develops. It is difficult not to feel
envy, let alone act upon it, but envy is worth resisting. Not for
nothing is it one of the seven deadly sins.

As to master plans, in my book *The Career Novelist* (Heinemann, 1996), I laid out the one plan that I have found over the
years that yields results: Delight your readers with your own brand
of story, then continue to delight them in a similar way (only
better) on a regular basis. That is the way to build an audience.
It is the only way to become a brand name author.

Five years later, I hold to that advice and offer it to those
who would write the breakout novel. As a breakout novelist
moving forward, you will prosper that way, writing novels of ever
expanding scale.

BREAKOUT Checklist: Breaking Out

✓ Whether your novel is your breakout will be decided by the public.

✓ Get the right agent.

✓ Have some idea of what you need.

✓ The essence of a pitch is setting, protagonist, problem. Add layers sparingly.

✓ Compare your novel not to classics or best-sellers but to other breakout novels.

✓ Outlines are the novel in miniature.

✓ Hardcover is the preferred format for breaking out.

✓ Big advances are great, but they carry big risks.

✓ Going back to press is better than big printings that do not leave the warehouse.

✓ The best publicity is between the covers of your book.

✓ Any upward jump is success.

✓ Sequels can disappoint; write them with passion.

✓ If possible stick with one publisher.

✓ The best career plan is simple: Please readers on a regular basis.

INDEX